This is the first book to explore the full range and import of Lacan's theory of poetry and its relationship to his understanding of the subject and historicity. Gilbert Chaitin provides a lucid and accessible study of this famously complex thinker. He shows how Lacan moves beyond the traditionally hostile polarities of mythos and logos, poetics and philosophy, to conceive of the subject as a complex interplay between symbolic systems, desire and history. Lacan incorporates the function of historical contingency into the formation of subjectivity, a combination which in turn illuminates the role literature plays in the creation of selfhood. Lacan's metaphor of the subject, Chaitin argues, drew not only on Saussure, Jakobson, Freud, Heidegger and Hegel, but on hitherto unacknowledged influences such as Bertrand Russell and I. A. Richards. Chaitin explores the ambiguities, contradictions and singularities of Lacan's immensely influential work to provide a definitive account of Lacan's theoretical development across the entire career.

Rhetoric and culture in Lacan

Literature, Culture, Theory

❖❖❖

General editors

RICHARD MACKSEY, *The Johns Hopkins University*

and MICHAEL SPRINKER, *State University of New York at Stony Brook*

The Cambridge *Literature, Culture, Theory* series is dedicated to theoretical studies in the human sciences that have literature and culture as their object of enquiry. Acknowledging the contemporary expansion of cultural studies and the redefinitions of literature that this has entailed, the series includes not only original works of literary theory but also monographs and essay collections on topics and seminal figures from the long history of theoretical speculation on the arts and human communication generally. The concept of theory embraced in the series is broad, including not only the classical disciplines of poetics and rhetoric, but also those of aesthetics, linguistics, psychoanalysis, semiotics, and other cognate sciences that have inflected the systematic study of literature during the past half century.

Rhetoric and culture
in Lacan

GILBERT D. CHAITIN

CAMBRIDGE
UNIVERSITY PRESS

Published by the Press Syndicate of the University of Cambridge
The Pitt Building, Trumpington Street, Cambridge CB2 1RP
40 West 20th Street, New York, NY 10011–4211, USA
10 Stamford Road, Oakleigh, Melbourne 3166, Australia

© Cambridge University Press 1996

First published 1996

Printed in Great Britain at the University Press, Cambridge

A catalogue record for this book is available from the British Library

Library of Congress cataloguing in publication data

Chaitin, Gilbert D.
Rhetoric and culture in Lacan / Gilbert D. Chaitin.
p.   cm. – (Literature, culture, theory; 18)
Includes bibliographical references.
ISBN 0 521 49728 0 (hardback) ISBN 0 521 49765 5 (paperback)
1. Lacan, Jacques, 1901– Contributions to criticism.
2. Historical criticism (Literature)   3. Poetry – History and
criticism.   4. Psychoanalysis and literature.   II. Title.
II. Series.
PN98.H57C43 1996
801'.95'092 – dc20   95–20578   CIP

ISBN 0 521 49728 0 hardback
ISBN 0 521 49765 5 paperback

For Joy and Sharon

Contents

Acknowledgements

I wish to express my gratitude to all those who, through their comments and encouragement, have helped this book come into existence, especially: Samuel Weber, Herbert Marks, Richard Macksey, Kevin Taylor, members of the Indiana University Theory Group, and my graduate students in French and Comparative Literature at Indiana University. I also want to thank the following presses for granting permission to reprint passages from Lacan's works:

Les Editions du Seuil, for *Ecrits*
Le Séminaire I: Les Ecrits techniques de Freud
Le Séminaire II: Le moi dans la théorie de Freud
Le Séminaire III: Les Psychoses
Le Séminaire VII: L'Ethique de la psychanalyse
Le Séminaire VIII: Le Transfert
Le Séminaire XI: Les quatre concepts fondamentaux de la psychanalyse
Le Séminaire XVII: L'Envers de la psychanalyse
Le Séminaire XX: Encore
'Proposition du 9 Octobre 1967 (Première Version)', in *Analytica* 8 (1978)
'L'Etourdit', in *Scilicet* 4 (1973)
Ornicar? 24
Le résumé du *Séminaire IV: La Relation d'objet*, in *Bulletin de Psychologie* 10–11 (1956–7)
Le résumé du *Séminaire VI; Le Désir et son interprétation*, in *Bulletin de Psychologie* 13 (1959-60)

W. W. Norton and Company, for *Ecrits, A Selection*
The Seminar of Jacques Lacan. Book I: Freud's Papers on Technique
The Seminar of Jacques Lacan. Book II: The Ego in Freud's Theory and in the Technique of Psychoanalysis

Acknowledgements

The Seminar of Jacques Lacan. Book III: The Psychoses
The Seminar of Jacques Lacan. Book VII: The Ethics of Psychoanalysis
The Four Fundamental Concepts of Psycho-Analysis

Routledge, for
The Seminar of Jacques Lacan. Book III: The Psychoses
The Seminar of Jacques Lacan. Book VII: The Ethics of Psychoanalysis

Tavistock, for
Ecrits, A Selection

and Random House/Hogarth Press, for
The Four Fundamental Concepts of Psycho-Analysis

1

❖❖

Introduction

❖❖

'Le psychanalyste est un rhéteur, pour continuer d'équivoquer je dirai qu'il *rhétifie*, ce qui implique qu'il rectifie. L'analyste est un rhéteur, c'est-à-dire que *rectus*, mot latin, équivoque avec la rhétification. On essaie de dire la vérité mais ce n'est pas facile parce qu'il y a de grands obstacles à ce qu'on la dise – ne serait-ce qu'on se trompe dans le choix de mots. La vérité a affaire avec le réel et le réel est doublé si on peut dire par le symbolique.'   Lacan, 'Une pratique de bavardage'

Most psychoanalysts explain poetry by means of psychoanalysis; for many years, Lacan explained psychoanalysis by means of poetry. 'The symptom is a metaphor.' 'Desire is a metonymy.' 'The primary processes of condensation and displacement are equivalent to the rhetorical tropes of metaphor and metonymy.' 'The subject is a poetic creation.' 'Love is a metaphor.' 'Transfer-ential repetition is a poetic process.' 'Psychoanalytic interpreta-tion is metaphoric.' 'The only thing you need to find in psychoanalysis is the trope of tropes called destiny.' 'Destiny is a figure, a figure of fate, as well as a rhetorical figure.' If it is obvious that such statements must appear totally alien to the positivist or idealist perspectives of standard analysts, it is equally clear that they will seem rather opaque to the student of literature, whether educated in traditional rhetoric or in structur-alist or poststructuralist poetics. In fact, the theory of poetry which subtends these assertions is not to be found in any text-book, nor can it be attributed to any single well-known figure or school of thought. It is a theory that Lacan himself developed over the period stretching from the late forties to the early sixties.

As such, it has a legitimate claim upon all those who are interested in literature; yet, although many provocative studies of Lacan's rhetoric have been published in the last fifteen years, none has explored the full range and import of that theory. For the most part, these enquiries assume that the ancient quarrel

1

between mythos and logos is irreconcilable, so that psycho-analysis simply cannot be both poetic and scientific at the same time. One passage in the 1957 article, 'The Agency of the Letter in the Unconscious, or Reason since Freud', a lengthy excursus on the word 'tree', has served as an exemplary case of the allegedly deceptive intrusion of poetry into theory for several commentators. As an illustration of the problems presented by Lacan's characteristic style, and therefore of the doctrine he is expounding, that text serves to frame my presentation of the larger debate in American criticism over the meaning and value of Lacan's rhetoric. This controversy has been shaped chiefly by the theorems of deconstruction: metonymy represents the un-limited play of differance, whereas metaphor stands for the fixing of meaning. As a corollary, metonymy is supposed to be the liberating function of the literary, while metaphor is the servile aspect of poetry, rhetoric in the service of truth. Those who value truth either decry Lacan for his supposed flight into irrationality, or praise him for going beyond mere 'deconstruc-tive poeticism'. Those who see truth as a mask of the will to power criticize him for privileging metaphor over metonymy, or they acclaim his articulation of rhetoric as the rejection of referentiality, or they even find that his teaching issues a blanket condemnation of metaphor and the patriarchal constraints which it promotes.

His best-informed readers on this topic, such as Rose, Weber and Grigg, recognize that for Lacan the two tropes and their concomitant values are inextricably intertwined. Nevertheless, their analyses are limited by what is found in the main texts they bring to bear on the question of Lacan's rhetoric, his 'Agency', Jakobson's 'Two Aspects of Language and Two Types of Aphasic Disturbances' and Saussure's *Course in General Linguistics*. While it is true, as Grigg maintains, that Lacan first attributed special importance to the combination of metaphor and metonymy after reading the Jakobson article,[1] it is also true, as Grigg and many commentators have acknowl-edged, that the divergences between Lacan's rhetoric and that of Jakobson are almost as great as their similarities. Although

---

[1] Grigg, 'Metaphor and Metonymy', p. 67.

the linguist's paper certainly helped Lacan crystallize his conception of the relations between meaning and non-meaning in language and in what Freud identified as the primary processes of unconscious thought, there is nothing in that essay, or in Saussure, to suggest why or how these linguistic functions should determine what Lacan calls the being of the subject. Yet that is precisely the crux of his explanation of psychoanalysis in terms of poetry.

Lacan gave the most coherent exposition of his theory in his seminars in the spring of 1956, the year before 'Agency'. It is there that he announces that metaphor is a matter of identification rather than similarity; it is there that he claims that metonymy is another name for the positional structure of language; and it is there that he links that structure to philosophical theories of predication which describe the copular function of the verb '*to be*' as the determination of the relation between the grammatical subject and its attributes. Careful reading of those seminars leads to the conclusion that, in accordance with the principle enunciated in the 'Seminar of the "Purloined Letter"', the apparently deceitful tree passage forms, when properly read, the expression of the truth Lacan is conveying.

Lacan may have devised this theory himself, but he certainly did not do so by himself. On the contrary, in accordance with his own theory of the creative function of metaphor, he constructed its fabric by weaving together many strands and reconnecting them in innovative ways, elaborating on trains of thought developed in the philosophical, linguistic and rhetorical theories he had studied in the decades preceding the heyday of structuralism. Well before Jakobson's piece on aphasia was published, and prior to re-reading Saussure in 1956, Lacan had already ascribed an important role to rhetorical figures in 'The Function and Field of Speech and Language in Psychoanalysis' (1953) as well as in *Freud's Papers on Technique* (1953–54).[2] Moreover, several of the fundamental notions he puts forth under the names of the tropes were present as early as 'Propos sur la causalité psychique' [Remarks on Psychical Causality],[3] which dates from 1946.

---

[2] In future references the title is abbreviated as *Papers*.
[3] All uncredited translations are my own.

From Hegel he had adopted the idea that the subject of thought is basically a lack, a nothing, a hole in the fabric of the real, and from Freud the notion of unconscious thought. Jakobson's version of the rhetorical functioning of language allowed him to combine the two with Heidegger's view of the creative force of symbolization to arrive at the theory that metaphor is capable, however fleetingly, of substituting something for the original nothingness of the subject. In developing this essentially catachretic theory of the 'Metaphor of the subject', Lacan drew not only on Saussure and Jakobson, Hegel, Heidegger and Freud, but also on the linguistic and rhetorical theories of writers he had consulted in the thirties and forties, Bertrand Russell and I. A. Richards, Ernst Cassirer and Suzanne Langer. Examination of the tradition of British and German constructivist thought, which built upon the romantic, symbolist and surrealist theories of the creative function of metaphor, makes it possible to isolate the diverse elements he recast in his rhetorical theory of the subject and thus to make that theory and its rational justification comprehensible.

The theory of the subject is at the same time a theory of culture for Lacan, since both arise through the process of symbolization. Raymond Williams, for instance, states that 'the making of a society is the finding of common meanings and directions'.[4] To this notion of ordinary culture Lacan adds the claim that the metaphoric process which creates meanings is actually two-fold: first the catachretic substitution of something – a signifier – for nothing; then the substitution of another signifier for the first. The completion of the symbolic procedure gives rise to the full signifier of the paternal metaphor, which frees the subject from enslavement to the enigma of the mother's desire and enables him to take his place in society. Symbolization has the creative power to confer identity on the members of a culture, providing modes of living that may be entirely distinct from those of other groups, but it does so only at a huge price, the cost of covering over the fundamental nothingness that forms its foundation. That first catachretic signifier is, and must be, meaningless, and it is this meaningless signifier that Lacan assimilates to the phallus.

If Lacanian psychoanalysis has as its primary goal the un-

---

[4] Williams, 'Culture is Ordinary', p. 6.

earthing of the meaningless signifier to which the subject is subjected,[5] Lacanian cultural study will not stop at analysing the cultural code, as in standard semiotics and structuralism, but will seek to uncover the utterly senseless object at the basis of the system. It is culture, not nature, that abhors a vacuum, above all that of its own pure contingency. Yet its very existence depends on its ability to convince its members of its substantiality; that is, to deny the non-being at its heart. That is the force of Lacan's notion of the *manque-à-être* [want-to-be], whether applied to individual subjects or to a culture. Precisely because it is impossible to prove the necessity of one's own cultural system, one must have recourse to the Other. As every inquisition, holy war and colonization has demonstrated, the best way to persuade oneself of that substance is to force others to acknowledge it. Conversely, the most potent weapon of colonization is the exposure of the senselessness of the subjugated nation's cultural symbols. More powerful than the will to power, which in fact derives from it, this thirst for being is at the root of the narcissistic identification which divides humanity into a perpetual conflict among segregated groups.[6]

There would appear to be only one type of alternative to the unbridled individualism and rampant ethnic strife provoked by narcissism – invocation of the Other as social bond, whether in the form of communal values opposed to egoism, or as cosmopolitanism versus nationalism. And indeed Lacan preached something of the sort in the fifties when he envisioned the paternal metaphor as the overcoming of the imaginary by the symbolic. His first theory of the letter forged a link between metaphor and transference, which served as a transition from the unconscious to the Other. Noting that Freud used the term 'transference' in two different ways, first to refer to the relation of the unconscious ideas at the heart of dreams to the day residues used to image them forth, and then to the intersubjective bond that acts as the driving force of psychoanalysis, Lacan argued that in both senses transference operates as an incomplete form of the double process of catachretic metaphor, in which a signifier takes as its signified another signifier which has been emptied of its signified. Lacan's letter is the resultant of this metaphoric composition of

---

[5] *Les quatre concepts fondamentaux de la psychanalyse*, p. 226.
[6] See 'Proposition du 9 octobre 1967', and *L'envers de la psychanalyse*.

the signifier with itself, whether it be the units of the various writing systems that human societies have evolved over the course of history, or the 'little letters' of formal mathematical notation essential to the development of modern science.

Unconscious formations, such as dreams or transferential phenomena, arise as interruptions of the normal flow of signification whenever a required signifier is missing. In his early teaching, Lacan maintained that the function of analysis was to complete the signifying process by supplying the analysand with signifiers that he or she hitherto lacked. Transference was necessary to the analytic process precisely because the missing signifier could only come from the Other, from the society that had called the subject into being in the first place by assigning her a place and a mission, a 'mandate' as Lacan called it. Analysis served to repair a malfunction in the process of universalization, of integrating the subject into society.

The danger of such a Hegelian view is that it would seem to preclude all forms of individuality. Symbolization may help us to overcome anxiety and to comprehend our lives, but it also leaves us open to social constraint and dictates.[7] Ultimately, it can lead to that form of madness which Lacan liked to describe as that of the king who thinks he's really a king; that is, a reification in which the subject becomes totally identified with the social role. On a broader level, universalization leads to speaking of all people as 'him' and 'man', excluding the specificity of women's experience. Under the benign guise of science, historical progress and human rights (in French still the rights of *man*), the universalization of the Enlightenment has served to justify and to motivate the conquest of 'primitive' peoples and the eradication of cultural differences that is tantamount to cultural murder.[8]

In the later fifties, Lacan became more sensitive to this menace, contending that metaphor is an open-ended process, a pact directed toward the future which enables the particularity of the subject to emerge in the singularity of the phallic letter. Starting from the seminar on ethics (1959–60), he emphasized the uniqueness of the individual path towards death which Freud isolated in his death drive. The death in question is, first of all, the fusion with the maternal object which was lost through the birth of the

---

[7] See Langer, *Philosophy in a New Key*.
[8] Cf. Lyotard, 'Universal History'.

subject into language. For Lacan, the loss of this object is not the result of paternal or societal prohibition, but the unavoidable result of the fact that human beings are obliged to express their needs in language. The trope of destiny, as in Freud's *Schicksals-neurose*, is the system of repetitive substitutions whereby the subject seeks to refind and supplement this lost object. Henceforth, metaphor can serve two opposing purposes. As the predicational joint attaching subject to attributes, it can either subordinate the former to the latter, in which case the universality inherent in all linguistic categories would dominate. The individual being of the subject is crushed by the universality of meaning. Or it can act to maintain the non-sense, and hence the unique unknowability, of the subject behind its attributes, that is, separated from any and all definable qualities. In the first case, as the trope of substitution, it advances the narcissistic aim of making oneself loved, pleasing the social authorities (the ego ideal) by replacing the good object lost through the imposition of language with the host of socially acceptable goods of consumer society. In the second, it strives to quench the thirst for being by giving shape to the subject of desire, substituting the role of lover for that of the beloved in the process Lacan calls the metaphor of love, and thereby maintaining, at least for a time, the sheer, ineffable, otherness of the Other, the pure uniqueness which must ever remain inexpressible in the universal terms of any language.

On one level, Lacanian metaphor shows that there is never any danger of eliminating communal values; even individualism is dependent on the community it disavows. Without the Other there can be no subject, no matter how narcissistic. And conversely, community is simply one guise of the universalism that always risks making the birth of the subject a still-birth. That is not to say, however, that Lacan considers all possible arrangements equal, for on another level his rhetoric demonstrates the need to preserve a place for contingency, whether it be that of the individual subject *vis-à-vis* her culture, or that of one culture in relation to another. Within the confines of analysis this means that, in order not to overpower the subject, interpretation must sustain a margin of ambiguity in tune with the homophonic equivocations within language by means of which the subject manifests itself. In the larger sphere, it implies that although a culture, like a literary text, exists to make sense of life, the heart of the one, as of the other, resides precisely in those points where they resist meaning. Even in his last seminars, in 1977, he still insisted that the last best hope against imprisonment in categorization is poetry.

From the mid-sixties on, however, Lacan tended to replace the language of rhetoric with that of set theory. The real was now determined as the impossible, namely that which is logically excluded from any set of signifiers that form a system. Such a signifying system, which makes belief and knowledge possible for its adherents, and which he now designates as s2, is the Other in that each of its members is defined solely by its difference from the others. The real is therefore that which necessarily de-completes the Other, showing up its lack of solidity, of foundation. He now assigns a quasi-algebraic designation, small *a*, to what was formerly designated as the love object in psychoanalytic terminology, and expands its meaning to include anything which serves to guarantee the being of the subject, such as the body of knowledge of a scientific discipline that reassures the scientist of her identity.[9] The a-object functions to cover the rent in the fabric of meaning opened by the real; it thus acts as a sign of the real. No longer the hole in the real created by the signifier, the subject is now the gap in the Other produced by the real. Still drawing on Kant and Cassirer as well as on modern formalist mathematics, Lacan now defined the signifying units or elements established by the phallic letter as the abstract unification imposed by grouping disparate objects together in a single set. The mark by which these objects are identified as units he now called the *trait unaire* (unitary trait), and denoted it as the set s1. The subject has become that unifying trait which is missing from the set of all its a-objects. The goal of repetition was now understood to be the subject's attempt to

---

[9] I have chosen to translate *objet petit a* as 'a-object' throughout this text, rather than keep it in French, as has become standard in many studies of Lacan. He preferred that the term be left untranslated so that it would retain the meaningless quality of algebraic terms, which gives them the aspect of foreign elements that disrupt the signifying system. But in my experience the effect has been mystification rather than non-sense; the practice has contributed to the aura of quackery or esoterism that too often surrounds his teachings in English-speaking countries, an impression which this book is designed to combat. 'A-object' retains a certain algebraic opacity while remaining visibly anchored in the English language, just as *objet petit a* betrays its roots in the most ordinary French.

find that trait, to discover its unity, as what is called in calculus the 'integral' of the set of its a-objects. He wants to find his uniqueness by reproducing the 'identically identical,' the pure particularity, of the original object of satisfaction, a patent impossibility since by its very nature every repetition must differ from previous instances of the 'same.'

In this scheme, the real takes over the role formerly held by the void in symbolization, and the a-object that of the catachretic metaphor which supplements that lack. This reorganization is, however, consistent with Lacan's earliest formulations concerning the real. With Cassirer, for example, he had long maintained that the gods are a direct revelation of the real, and that the function of myths is to frame that part of the real that remains inexplicable in terms of the logical consistency of the signifier, that is, of coherent philosophy or science. Like the biblical handwriting on the wall, the impasses of the real have always disclosed themselves in the form of writing. Experimental 'confirmations' of scientific hypotheses formulated in the 'little letters' of equations, like the apparent fulfilling of an omen or premonition, may act as such 'answers of the real'.[10] But whereas the letters of science, universalized through and through, leave no room for play in their reading, the writing of literary texts, like the letters of the unconscious, may be open to an infinity of readings. The gaps of the real become a kind of refuge within the universalization of knowledge for the particularity of the subject. From the gaps of the real emerges a text, like the strands of a web from a spider's belly. By exploiting the ambiguities inherent in languages, a literary text may trace the contours of those gaps and bring out the places of singularity in which the subject may live.

Lacan's real is therefore profoundly ambivalent: as that which escapes symbolization it is both the traumatic *par excellence*, the unassimilable kernel at the heart of human experience, and the contingent, the only haven for human subjectivity. The complete universalization of the signifier left entirely to itself, a kind of pure desire which forms the ideal of science, paradoxically allows the subject no defence against the real. It is the obverse, so to speak, of the absence of distance from oneself which obtains

[10] See Miller, 'Réponses du réel'.

9

when the symbolization necessary to the formation of desire is lacking. In the latter case, as Freud observed, the unsymbolized returns as hallucination or delusion in the real. It is not surprising, therefore, that so much of popular fiction, especially the movies (and definitely not 'cinema'), should deal with the horror of apparently psychotic themes and forms that seem to represent the unvarnished real, ghosts and ghostbusters, terminators and exterminators, aliens, murderous dolls and all the rest. In fact, this is not the pure, unsymbolized, real manifesting itself as hallucination, but rather the totally autonomous symbolic of modern science pushed to such an extreme that, instead of substituting for the real, it coincides with it. Nor is it surprising that the real struggle for supremacy in today's world should not be that of capitalism versus communism, but that between science and the nostalgia for the original revelation of the real, fundamentalism.

In such a context, it is all the more important to take into account the 'impure' desire of the analyst that aims to achieve absolute difference.[11] Desire is not something that is simply found; it must be created. But it can be created only on the basis of the sheer contingency of experience, whether that of an individual person or of a culture. As the attempt to refind the traumatic but individuating object of the first satisfaction, desire is always historical. It involves a retrospective reading of the past that rearranges that past, simultaneously giving it a new meaning and cordoning off within it a zone of senselessness, of sheer otherness, in short, of the real. In his later teaching, when Lacan presents this process in terms of the theory of infinite sets, he distinguishes two kinds of *jouissance*. The masculine type seeks its enjoyment in the relation to the phallus, understood as a limit to the potentially infinite rails of metonymic desire, a limit which assures identity within the symbolic order. The feminine aspect of the thirst for being he designates as the relation to the pure differentiality of sheer Otherness.

During the seventies and early eighties, Lacan was seen in English-speaking literary circles primarily as a proponent of deconstruction and phallocentrism, although precisely how he could manage to espouse both these apparently contradictory

---

[11] *Concepts*, p. 248.

tendencies was not always clear. His emphasis on writing was often assimilated to a deconstructive extension of the formalist notion of the transcendent value of the literary as opposed to mere practical, social or material concerns. Alternatively, and contradictorily, his attacks on the American psychoanalytic school of ego psychology gave rise to a strand of interpretation in which the social and historic import of his symbolic register was pitted against the illusory individualism of the imaginary. Feminist critics either attacked him for his phallocentrism and his undermining of the subject, or praised him for putting into question and into play the naturalist, biological definitions of sexual identity.

The last decade has witnessed a major revision in the evaluation of Lacan's significance for literary, ethical and cultural theory. Consideration of his latest teachings on the real and the subject as flaws in the Other has opened up fresh perspectives on the potential for resistance to domination in the critique of authoritarian regimes and colonial discourse as well as in feminist thought. His conception of the formation of various types of desire has given rise to a potent and original analysis of the power of culture. Most significant, perhaps, is the new light his analysis of the interaction of the universal and the particular has begun to shed on the question of maintaining a democratic social order which can safeguard universal human rights while protecting the difference of competing political and ethnic groups.

❖❖❖

2

Treeing Lacan, or the Meaning of Metaphor

❖❖❖

The chain of associations always has more than two links; and the traumatic scenes do not form a simple row, like a string of pearls, but ramify and are interconnected like genealogical trees.

(Freud, 'The Aetiology of Hysteria')

All of what I experienced with my patients, as a third [person] I find again here [in my self-analysis] – days when I drag myself about dejected because I have understood nothing of the dream, of the fantasy, of the mood of the day; and then again days when a flash of lightning illuminates the interrelations and lets me understand the past as a preparation for the present.

Freud to Fliess, 27 Oct. 1897

Lacan summons reason and the letter together in the title of his 9 May 1957 lecture at the Sorbonne, 'The Agency of the Letter in the Unconscious or Reason since Freud'. This joint convocation, made before the Philosophy Group of the Fédération des Etudiants ès Lettres, seems to imply that the epoch of Freud has effected some historical shift in the ancient relation of logic and language, philosophy and poetry, metaphysics and metaphor. Whether the connective word 'or' signifies a conjunction of the two terms, in the sense that western philosophy has always considered language to be the instrument, or even the essence, of reason, or a disjunction, along the lines of Plato's primordial quarrel between mythos and logos, the title does not specify. Although Lacan is quick to point out that speech is the key to the truth of psychoanalysis, and that 'nous désignons par lettre ce support matériel que le discours concret emprunte au langage' ['by "letter" [he] designate[s] the material support that concrete discourse borrows from language'],[1] his readers are far from reaching a consensus

---

[1] *Ecrits*, p. 495; *Ecrits, A Selection*, p. 147 (hereafter abbreviated as '*Ecrits* Eng.').

about the meaning of this definition, the validity of his claims, or the precise nature of the relation he describes.

Both friendly and hostile critics have struggled to pull Lacan entirely into the camp of science or into that of poetry, some maintaining that ultimately he calls rhetoric and poetry forth only in order to impress them the more surely into the service of truth, others praising his escape from the narrow confines of an oppressive reason or decrying his flight into irrationality. All are convinced, however, as was Plato, that the ultimate stakes of this debate about poetry are the fundamental tenets of ethics and politics. So deeply involved in the ancient quarrel between mythos and logos, almost all, moreover, either ignore or attempt to refute the historical dimension of Lacan's claims, whether it be the role of historicity within Lacanian psychoanalysis, or the assertion that the psychoanalytic movement 'constitu[e] une révolution insaisissable mais radicale' ['[has] founded an intangible but radical revolution'], altering 'la relation de l'homme au signifiant' ['the relation between man and the signifier'] and thereby changing 'le cours de son histoire en modifiant les amarres de son être' ['the whole course of history by modifying the moorings that anchor his being'].[2]

Now there is one passage in 'Agency' that concentrates the issues involved in this critical debate precisely because it enacts within Lacan's text the relation between truth, poetry and history that he is at pains throughout the lecture to describe.

Car décomposé dans le double spectre de ses voyelles et de ses consonnes, il appelle avec le robre et le platane les significations dont il se charge sous notre flore, de force et de majesté. Drainant tous les contextes symboliques où il est pris dans l'hébreu de la Bible, il dresse sur une butte sans frondaison l'ombre de la croix. Puis se réduit à l'Y majuscule du signe de la dichotomie qui, sans l'image historiant l'armorial, ne devrait rien à l'arbre, tout généalogique qu'il se dise. Arbre circulatoire, arbre de vie du cervelet, arbre de Saturne ou de Diane, cristaux précipités en un arbre conducteur de la foudre, est-ce votre figure qui trace notre destin dans l'écaille passée au feu de la tortue, ou votre éclair qui fait surgir d'une innombrable nuit cette lente mutation de l'être dans l'*Hen Panta* du langage:

> Non! dit l'Arbre, il dit: Non! dans l'étincellement
>   De sa tête superbe

[2] *Ecrits*, p. 527; *Ecrits* Eng., p. 174.

13

vers que nous tenons pour aussi légitimes à être entendus dans les harmoniques de l'arbre que leur revers:

> *Que la tempête traite universellement*
> *Comme elle fait une herbe.*

Car cette strophe moderne s'ordonne selon la même loi du parallélisme du signifiant, dont le concert régit la primitive geste slave et la poésie chinoise la plus raffinée.

Comme il se voit dans le commun mode de l'étant où sont choisis l'arbre et l'herbe, pour qu'y adviennent les signes de contradiction du: dire 'Non!' et du: traiter comme, et qu'à travers le contraste catégorique du particularisme de la *superbe* à *l'universellement* de sa réduction, s'achève dans la condensation de la tête et de la tempête l'indiscernable étincellement de l'instant éternel.

[For even broken down into the double spectre [spectrum] of its vowels and consonants, it can still call up with the robur [British oak] and the plane tree the significations it takes on, in the context of our flora, of strength and majesty. Drawing on all the symbolic contexts suggested in the Hebrew of the Bible, it erects on the barren hill the shadow of the cross. Then reduces to the capital Y, the sign of dichotomy which, except for the illustration used by heraldry, would owe nothing to the tree however genealogical we may think it. Circulatory tree, tree of life [arborvitae] of the cerebellum, tree of Saturn, tree of Diana, crystals formed in a tree struck by lightning, is it your figure that traces our destiny for us in the tortoise-shell cracked by the fire, or your lightning that caused the slow shift in the axis of being to surge up from an unnameable [innumerable] night into the *Hen Panta* [All things come from one] of language:

> *No! says the Tree, it says No! in the shower of sparks*
> *Of its superb head*

lines that require [can be heard in] the harmonics of the tree just as much as [in] their continuation:

> *Which the storm treats as universally*
> *As it does a blade of grass.*

For this modern verse [by Valéry] is ordered according to the same law of parallelism of the signifier that creates the harmony governing the primitive Slavic epic as [*sic*] the most refined Chinese poetry. As is seen in the fact that the tree and the blade of grass are chosen from the same mode of the existent in order for the signs of contradiction – saying 'No!' and 'treat as' – to affect them, and also so as to bring about, through the categorical contrast of the particularity of 'superb' with the universality that reduces it, in the condensation of the 'head' (*tête*) and

14

the 'storm' (*tempête*), the indiscernible shower of sparks of the eternal instant.[3]

For several readers, this text appears as a kind of digression from the main line of argument Lacan pursues in 'Agency', a significant example of the unwarranted intrusion by poetry into theoretical discourse. As such, it seems to invite particular attention as a characteristic sign of Lacan's turn of mind as well as of the doctrine he is expounding. From the positivist perspective, the tree passage appears to indicate Lacan's irrationality,[4] whereas read through the deconstructive lens,[5] it only confirms his allegiance to traditional metaphysics. For some, it illustrates the inability of scientific abstraction to free itself from the concreteness of the phenomenal world,[6] while for others it represents the escape of Lacan's rhetoric from the constraints of prosaic linearity.[7] Examination of the tree passage in light of these various claims can therefore make it possible to evaluate the nexus of poetry and science in Lacan's work.

For one set of critics, the lengthy excursus on the word 'tree' provokes a mixture of puzzlement and suspicion concerning both its function and its legitimacy. They take this passage to be an obviously 'poetical' deviation from the style of 'coherent arguments' which form the main thread of the essay, and therefore question its presence there.[8] This positivist critique arises within a text organized by a classic series of oppositions (see Plato, Hobbes and Frege, among others) which take poetry, metaphor, playfulness and whimsy to be the others of 'coherent arguments'. The system assigns to the former, inferior, terms a place within which they are granted validity, provided they make no attempt to escape from that confinement, to mix disciplines, to cross the boundary, to overstep the line. The validity to which poetry can presumably lay claim derives from its usefulness, its capacity to serve some other, higher, purpose: 'In order to show how words cross the bar [dividing the signifier from the signified] at these moments of punctuation, Lacan evoked the power that words

---

[3] *Ecrits*, p. 504; *Ecrits* Eng., pp. 154–5; my clarifications added in brackets.
[4] Benvenuto and Kennedy, *The Works of Jacques Lacan: An Introduction*.
[5] Nancy and Lacoue-Labarthe, *Le titre de la lettre*.
[6] MacCannell, *Figuring Lacan*.
[7] Gallop, *Reading Lacan*.
[8] Benvenuto and Kennedy, *Introduction*, p. 116.

have in poetry, using as an example the word tree – "arbre" in French, an anagram of "barre" (bar).[9] The presence of the deviant tree passage is excusable to the extent that it contributes to the overall, scientific, psychoanalytic purpose of the essay. Poetry is acceptable as long as it is used logically; it may even be necessary as the only means of understanding something like itself, that is, play, the inter-play of the signifier. But even this usage is questionable, for such playfulness always threatens to become an end in itself, beyond the bounds of answerability to the criterion of truthfulness which governs the logic of coherent arguments. At that point, beyond that line, playfulness threatens to become quackery. To the extent that it threatens the discourse of truth, poetry thus appears as an infringement of the standards of professional ethics, and as a menace to the status of psycho-analysis as a scientific discipline.

One of the assumptions underlying this criticism is that it is possible to distinguish various styles, to tell the poetic or the whimsical from the logical or argumentational. Thus the critics are convinced that Lacan is illustrating the power that words have in poetry, presumably as opposed to their function in prose. I call this an assumption here, for neither evidence nor arguments are adduced to substantiate the claim that the tree passage is in fact poetic. Within this system of interpretation, this text wears its poeticalness on its face, so to speak; any reader would presum-ably take this stretch of language to be 'a poetical interpretation or presentation'.

But is that the case? While it is true that Lacan cites one stanza from Valéry's poem, 'To the Plane Tree', and refers to Jakobson's theory of the law of the parallelism of the signifier in poetry, it is by no means apparent that the rest of the segment has anything whatsoever to do with poetry, evocative or not. On the contrary, several parts clearly deal with scientific terms and concepts and lose their aura of poetic mystery when read as such. Lacan writes, for instance, that the word 'tree' can be broken down into the double *spectrum* (unfortunately translated as 'specter') of its vowels and consonants, the way white light can be decomposed into its components by refraction through a prism. The choice of the robur and plane trees thus becomes quite comprehensible and

---

[9] Ibid., p. 114.

entirely coherent in an article about the letter: 'rbr' are the components of the consonantal spectrum in *arbre* as in *robre;* likewise 'ae' are the vowels of *arbre* and *platane.*

The circulatory tree refers of course to the branching shape of our veins and arteries, and the arborvitae to a similar form in the cerebellum. Even the apparently allegorical references to the ancient gods are simple chemical terms: the trees of Saturn and Diana are tree-shaped clusters of crystals formed from the salts of the metal lead (called Saturn by the alchemists) and of silver (Diana in alchemy). The mysterious 'crystals formed in a tree struck by lightning' are nothing more than 'crystals precipitated around a metal shaft that conducts electricity [*arbre conducteur de la foudre*] dipped in a solution'. There is a kind of poetry here, to be sure, but it is just Lacan's metaphorical use of *'foudre',* lightning, to mean electricity, and the French language's use of the term, *arbre,* to signify both a tree and a shaft.

It is true, however, that the links connecting one reference to the next seem arbitrary and incoherent, somewhat like the free associations of a person in psychoanalysis. Yet according to Freud, free associations are never really free, in the sense of constituting a purely arbitrary, random sequence; rather they are guided by a principle of coherence of which we remain ignorant.

Since, however confusing it might appear on a first reading, this text is not the simple record of free associations, Lacan has been careful to enunciate for us that principle of coherence. A few pages earlier he wrote: 'seules les corrélations du signifiant au signifiant y donnent l'étalon de toute recherche de signification, comme le marque la notion d'*emploi'* ['only the correlations between signifier and signifier provide the standard for all research into signification, as is indicated by the notion of "usage"'].[10] Just before introducing the excursus on the tree, Lacan reiterates his general claim that meaning can only be understood as a matter of the relations of signifier to signifier, provided one take into account usage:

Nulle chaîne signifiante en effet qui ne soutienne comme appendu à la ponctuation de chacune de ses unités tout ce qui s'articule de contextes attestés, à la verticale ... de ce point.

[There is in effect [indeed] no signifying chain that does not have, as if

---

[10] *Ecrits,* p. 502; *Ecrits* Eng., p. 153.

attached to the punctuation of each of its units, a whole articulation of relevant [attested] contexts suspended 'vertically' ... from that point.[11]

Now an attested context, like an attested form in linguistics, is presumably one which is 'actually in use or found in written records in contrast to one that is hypothesized or reconstructed',[12] that is, one justified through 'the notion of "usage"'. Where better to find cases of the actual use of 'tree' than in the dictionary? Moreover, two pages later Lacan obligingly specifies that he was using the Quillet dictionary. That work does indeed list most of Lacan's references under the entry on 'tree', and, for the most part, in the order he imitates: the Hebrew Bible, the cross, heraldry, the genealogical tree, circulatory tree, cerebellum, trees of Saturn and Diana. The principle of coherence of this sequence is therefore no more random or mysterious than the banality of a series of listings in a dictionary.

The dictionary is of course not the sole record of meanings that have been attached to the signifier 'tree' through history, and several of those Lacan adduces, especially in the latter part of his listing, are not found in the Quillet. But the inclusion of each item follows the same principle of historical usage, and when each case is seen in the light of an attested context, it loses its aura of mystery and mystification. Used to stand for the notion of branching, the tree was schematized in the letter Y as the sign of the diverging paths of vice and virtue in a tradition which traced its origin, perhaps mistakenly, to the Pythagoreans (see the new *Oxford English Dictionary* entry for Y). The zig-zag pattern of cracks that appears when a tortoise shell is heated over a fire (*passée au feu*) was read in the process of 'tortoise-shell divination' practised by the ancient Chinese. The petitioner would write on the shell the question he wanted to ask his ancestors or the gods, and the seer, who was also a scribe, would then read the cracks as the response to the question.[13] In fact, the correlation between patterns of ramified marks, the question of one's destiny, and writing is enshrined in the Chinese word *wen*.[14]

Why should Lacan attribute lightning to the tree in the clause, 'your lightning that causes the slow shift in the axis of being ...'?

---

[11] *Ecrits*, p. 503; *Ecrits* Eng., p. 154; my translations in brackets.
[12] *Random House Dictionary of the English Language*, 2nd edn unab.
[13] Février, *Histoire de l'écriture*, pp. 71–2.
[14] Gernet, 'La Chine: aspects et fonctions psychologiques de l'écriture', p. 33.

Because French has the expression *éclair arborescent*, or *éclair ramifié* (arborescent or ramified lightning), which corresponds to the English 'forked lightning'. The connection between forked lightning and the disclosure of being in the Hen Panta ('One is All') of language is asserted in the fragments of Heraclitus.[15] The relation thus evoked between philosophy and poetry now serves Lacan as a fluid transition, finally, to Valéry's poem and thence to the linguistic theory of poetics.

As befits the theme, in this section Lacan's language does indeed become more dense and evocative, especially since a knowledgeable reader will hear these verses as a reprise of the 'plane tree' mentioned with the robur as symbols of the strength and majesty accruing upon the reorganization of the letters that form the 'spectrum' of the word *arbre*.

Most commentators, following Alain, take the plane tree's outburst in the first two lines of the final stanza (the one cited by Lacan) as the expression of its refusal to be drawn into the metaphorical process of poetry, a rejection of the poet's loving caress thematized in the previous stanza. The tree thus allegedly insists on its status as a pure existent, a real object outside the bonds and snares of language. Lacan stresses that it is just as legitimate to hear these first two lines in the harmonics, or overtones, of the tree, as to perceive the last two lines of the stanza there, even though the two contradict each other. Both sets of verses can be heard in the harmonics of the tree because of the law of parallelism that his friend, the linguist Roman Jakobson, considered to be the essence of poetic language: 'Rhyme is only a particular, condensed case of a much more general, we may even say the fundamental, problem of poetry, namely *parallelism*.'[16] Jakobson alludes to Slavic and Chinese poetry in 'Linguistics and Poetics', and no doubt had discussed these matters with Lacan. In an article written well after 'Agency', the linguist returns to this problem, delving into the history of the notion of poetic parallelism and its use as an explanatory principle in the study of the Bible, Chinese poetry and Russian folklore, from Robert Lowth in 1778 to Gerard Manley Hopkins and beyond. Jakobson finds that the notion of parallelism is encoded into one of the very names of poetry:

[15] See Heidegger, *Early Greek Thinking*, p. 72.
[16] Jakobson, 'Linguistics and Poetics', p. 39.

We have learned the suggestive etymology of the terms PROSE and VERSE – the former, *oratio prosa* < *prorsa* < *proversa* 'speech turned straightforward', and the latter, *versus* 'return'. Hence we must consistently draw all inferences from the obvious fact that on every level of language the essence of poetic artifice consists in recurrent returns.[17]

This discovery no doubt accounts for Lacan's unusual usage of the word *'revers'* (= reverse, reversal) to designate the second half of the stanza. The second word is thus a re-verse, a reverberation of the first, a return of the same phonemes, or letters, precipitated into a longer word in which the repetitive and the aversive senses of the prefix 're' are locked in a never-ending battle, just as storm and logic treat the plane tree and the blade of grass in both opposite and similar, parallel, ways. Both come from the same natural, vegetable world ('the same mode of the existent'), yet the storm causes both of them to rustle in the wind and thus to 'speak', to say 'No!'. By their syntax these lines are structured according to the second principle of parallelism explained by J. F. Davis, one of the students of Chinese poetry Jakobson cites: 'the correspondence of sense, whether it consists in equivalency or opposition, is almost always attended by correspondence of construction'.[18] Both the 'head' and the 'blade of grass' are objects of the verb 'treat', 'do' being a simple repetition of 'treat'; but this syntactic correspondence opens the way for the ironic opposition in sense, the 'signs of contradiction' of which Lacan speaks.

For by making the tree and grass speak, the storm also contradicts their vegetable mode of existence. By treating both in the same manner, the wind denies the uniqueness of the tree; it obliterates the difference in quality between the tree and the grass. *'Superbe'* means 'proud' or 'haughty' as well as 'splendid'; in saying 'No!' the tree is pointing proudly to its uniqueness, but shaking its head 'no' in the storm and thus causing its leaves to glitter (*'étincellement'*) moves it from the singular to the universal. On one level it shares the same status *vis-à-vis* the wind as all of (vegetable) nature; on the other, by using language it participates in a structure that does not admit pure individuals. It enters into the Hegelian dialectic of 'sense-certainty' in which the intuitive conviction of the uniqueness of the 'this, here, now' dissolves into the generality of those words we call 'shifters' or 'indexicals',

[17] Jakobson, 'Grammatical Parallelism and Its Russian Facet', p. 98.
[18] Ibid., p. 101.

which apply to any and every object, place, moment. 'The pointing out of the Now is thus itself the movement which expresses what the Now is in truth, viz. a result, or a plurality of Nows all taken together; and the pointing-out is the experience of learning that Now is a *universal*'.[19] What would seem to be the most particular thing, the now, turns out to be a universal, since it applies to a whole series of situations; indeed, in a sense, to all situations, for everything has been or will be a now to someone.

Hegel concludes the section on sense-certainty by stressing the inherent universality of language and its consequent inability to express the unique:

[Some philosophers] speak of the existence of *external* objects, which can be more precisely defined as *actual*, absolutely *singular*, wholly *personal*, *individual* things, each of them absolutely unlike anything else; this existence, they say, has absolute certainty and truth. They *mean* 'this' bit of paper on which I am writing – or rather have written – 'this'; but what they mean is not what they say. [To *say* 'this' bit of paper] is impossible, because the sensuous This that is meant *cannot be reached* by language which belongs to consciousness, i.e. to that which is inherently universal ... If we describe it ... as 'this bit of paper', then each and every bit of paper is 'this bit of paper', and I have only uttered the universal all the time.[20]

In language, then, all bits of paper are 'indiscernible', all trees are indistinguishable, as are all nows. The last stanza of Valéry's 'Plane Tree' is thus doubly ironic: not only does the storm equate the tree and the grass, treating them 'universally'; but also, by expressing its refusal in language, the tree participates in the very universalizing tendency of consciousness its 'No!' was meant to reject.

It is this same universalizing tendency of language which makes possible the metaphorization of the tree, its use in a series of equations earlier in the poem as athlete, musical instrument, martyr, flame, bow, procreating body.[21] The heroism of the tree, its resistance to the violence of the storm and the sexual caress of the poet, can assert itself only by taking on the movement it strives to overcome. In Hegelian terms, the tree can reach 'particularity' only when its 'singularity' passes through the moment of 'universality'. The completion of this process is

[19] Hegel, *Phenomenology of Spirit*, p. 64.   [20] Ibid., p. 66.
[21] Lawler, *Lecture de Valéry*, p. 50.

marked in the poem by the inclusion, the 'condensation' as Lacan calls it, of the head – *tête* – in the storm – *t(emp)ête* – in which the head both loses and continues to assert its identity.

Given the passionate nature of the poet's advances to the plane tree:

> Oh as a lover, rival to the dryads,
> Let the poet alone
> Caress your polished body as he would the Horse's
> Self-vaunting thigh! ... [22]

and the dominant role of desire in psychoanalysis, it might not be amiss to hear in Lacan's concluding mention of 'the eternal instant', along with the eternal present of the now that condenses within itself all previous, contradictory, stages of history, an overtone of Faust saying to the moment, 'Abide, you are so beautiful.' Indeed, Hegel alludes to that context in discussing the loss and recapture of identity in the dialectic of desire.[23]

The major themes connecting metaphor to being – universality and particularity, negativity, destiny and lightning – come to fruition in the law of poetry in terms of which Lacan analyses Valéry's poem. In later pages of 'Agency' Lacan underlines this conjunction by referring repeatedly to poetry with various forms of the signifier *étincellement*. Crossing the bar of signification is thus something like the spark of lightning that jumps across the gap in an electric arc.[24]

If this passage 'vividly reveals the difficulty of assessing Lacan's work',[25] that difficulty does not arise, in the first instance, from its poetry, playfulness, or deception. The problematic qualities of this text are of a different order. They arise, above all, from the necessity of recognizing the many allusions that form the attested contexts for the use of the signifier 'tree', a job occasion-

---

[22] Valéry, *Poems*, p. 121.

[23] See Hegel, *Phenomenology*, Section v, on 'The Certainty and Truth of Reason', especially sections B and C. The Goethe text itself refers, of course, to Rousseau's definition of desire as presence in his 'Fifth Walk'. For a discussion of Hegel's eternal present, see Koyré, 'La terminologie hégélienne', pp. 220–1.

[24] The metaphor of the flash of lightning has been used at least since Longinus to describe the sudden surge of power produced by language, especially by figurative language. This metaphor of metaphor was especially prevalent among those in the tradition that stretches from German idealism (e.g. Schelling, *Zur Philosophie der Kunst*), via romanticism and symbolism, to surrealism (Breton, *Manifeste du surréalisme*).

[25] Benvenuto and Kennedy, *Introduction*, p. 115.

ally complicated for the English-speaking reader by difficulties in translation. All readers, however, must confront the additional task of identifying the function and purpose of this passage within the larger context of the article of which it is a part. It is the conviction that any text that is not immediately comprehensible must form a deviation from the norm of the truthful, the rational, or the everyday, which gives this passage the appearance of a digression, if not that of an attempt at obfuscation or deception.

Yet that impression is not wholly misleading, for in a sense the tree passage certainly does illustrate the poetic power of words; but for Lacan that power is not restricted to divergences from the rational or prosaic use of language. On the contrary, as Grigg has convincingly argued, however extraordinary individual acts of poetry may be, that force is inscribed in the structures of language itself.[26] If it is difficult to assess Lacan's work from the positivist perspective, it is because, as the tree passage illustrates, for Lacan the boundary between poetry and prose is not the clear-cut border such a perspective supposes. In fact, as we shall see, it is metaphor that has created so-called everyday language, as well as the truth of science.

If to the positivists the tree passage appears to violate the proper separation of the frivolous from the scientific, for the deconstructionists, on the contrary, it represents an unwelcome reassertion of the primacy of truth over the play of language. While the former considered it to betray insubordination to the canons of professional and institutional ethics, for the latter it manifests acquiescence to the repressive forces of language and society.

They agree that the tree text is the 'crucial episode' which marks 'the intervention of the poetic in the theoretic',[27] but they do not simply define the poetic as just any deviation from the prose of coherent argument. Noting that in 'Agency' Lacan refers only to poets of the period from Victor Hugo to surrealism, they characterize his conception and practice of poetry as a poetics of the Word (*le verbe*); that is, of the evocative 'power' or even 'magic' of words. They place Lacan in that posterity of symbolism whose principal literature textbooks describe as *'the alchemy of the*

---

[26] Grigg, 'Metaphor and Metonymy', p. 73.
[27] Nancy and Lacoue-Labarthe, *Titre*, p. 77.

word or evocatory witchcraft', and which they summarize as 'a poetics of metaphor'.[28]

It is thus metaphor which, according to the deconstructive argument, provides the link between the symbolist and structuralist notions of poetry. In the latter conception, rhetoric is an extension of the basic properties of language. Metaphor is aligned with what Saussure called the associative, Jakobson the paradigmatic, axis of language, that is, the set of linguistic elements capable of performing similar functions – sounds, words, grammatical forms – from which one must choose in order to construct an utterance. To this 'axis of similarities' is opposed the syntagmatic axis, the positional relationships among the elements of an utterance which depend on the property of linearity (in time or space) fundamental to speech or writing. Jakobson assimilated this 'axis of combinations' to metonymy.[29]

Just before introducing the excursus on the tree, Lacan claims that 'si [la linéarité] est nécessaire en effet, [elle] n'est pas suffisante' ['if this linearity [of language] is necessary in fact, it is not sufficient']. There is more to language than linearity, and this more – which is both necessary and sufficient – is precisely poetry: 'Mais il suffit d'écouter la poésie ... pour que s'y fasse entendre une polyphonie et que tout discours s'avère s'aligner sur plusieurs portées d'une partition' ['But one has only to listen to poetry ... for a polyphony to be heard, for it to become clear that all discourse is aligned along the several staves of a score'],[30] those staves being the very attested contexts Lacan describes as hanging vertically from each point of an utterance, or signifying

---

[28] Ibid., pp. 59–60, 77. Here is a typical passage, not from a textbook, but from a work on the symbolist theatre: 'Il s'agit donc pour le poète – et c'est là sa fonction, – d'élever constamment son esprit vers les sphères les plus élevées, hors des limites desquelles il ne saurait respirer. Et ... de restituer le monde véritable, mystérieusement voilé, en passant d'un univers quotidien à l'accession, à la possession d'un Cosmos ordonné sous le signe de l'Idée pure. – Mais comment s'effectuera ce transfert? – Par une sorte d'alchimie verbale. Car le *mot*, ici, est un *talisman*; le tabernacle d'où s'échappe le frisson mystérieux de l'esprit et, par là même il est la base d'un langage initiatique ... C'est pourquoi le théâtre symboliste, – théâtre d'idées, – revêt le plus souvent la forme d'une poésie incantatoire.' G. Marie, *Le théâtre symboliste*, p. 61.

[29] Saussure, *Course in General Linguistics*, pp. 122–7; Jakobson, 'Two Aspects of Language', pp. 58–62. See Weber, *Return to Freud*, chapter 4, for an excellent discussion of Lacan's relation to Saussure and Jakobson. See my 'Metonymy/metaphor' for a brief synopsis of the relation of these two master tropes to literary theory in structuralist and poststructuralist thought.

[30] *Ecrits*, p. 503; *Ecrits* Eng., p. 154.

chain. It would seem then that Lacan privileges vertical depth at the expense of horizontal linearity, a vertical depth, moreover, which is constituted by semantic and lexical connections; in short, poetry, the 'essence' of language, is a matter of relations of meaning.[31]

Now in 'White Mythology' Derrida ascribes the search for metaphorical depth to a 'symbolist' conception of language and poetry, in that symbolism, as Jakobson maintains in 'Two Aspects', concerned itself primarily with exploiting the resources of the axis of similarities.[32] Derrida claims that the symbolists sought to find hidden resemblances between the metaphysical and the physical meanings of words that have been 'worn away' through use and the passage of time, thus showing that 'what is symbolized maintain[s] a tie of natural affinity with the symbol'.[33] And such a conception is precisely one of poetry as essentially metaphoric, for

Metaphor has always been defined as the trope of resemblance ... the link of the signifier to the signified has ... [remained] a link of natural necessity, of analogical participation, of resemblance ... To take an interest in metaphor ... is to take an interest in semantic 'depth', in the magnetic attraction of the similar, rather than in positional combinations, which we may call 'metonymic' in the sense of Jakobson ...[34]

To characterize the tree passage in 'Agency' as belonging to the posterity of symbolism is thus to contend that Lacan's notion of poetry consists in privileging hidden semantic resemblances at the expense of those positional combinations in language alternatively known as metonymic, syntagmatic, syntactic, or linear.

The symbolist devaluation of the metonymic is not a simple omission, but a magical denegation; the alchemy of the verb, the witchcraft of poetry, is not so much the conjuring up of a departed spirit as it is an exorcism, the attempt to 'conjure linearity away'.[35] Or rather, it is necessary to conjure the one away in order to be able to call the other up, in accordance with the oldest tradition of western metaphysics. As Derrida explains, since Aristotle metaphor has been correlated to the '*semantic order* ... which ... claims . . [to be] intelligible by itself, outside

---

[31] Nancy and Lacoue-Labarthe, *Titre*, p. 58.
[32] Jakobson, 'Two Aspects of Language', pp. 77–8.
[33] Derrida, 'White Mythology', pp. 212, 215.   [34] Ibid., p. 215.
[35] Nancy and Lacoue-Labarthe, *Titre*, p. 58.

any syntactic relation, [and which] can be nominalized'.[36] The syntactic must be exorcized because it threatens to undermine the possibility of a purely autonomous meaning which, in that it exists independently, outside of the language that expresses it, is capable of being designated in a pure, single act of naming. And this univocal naming of the world – the possibility of a systematic correspondence, or similarity, between denoting and reality – has always been considered to be reason itself.

Now poetry as Lacan defines it would appear to consist precisely in such an autonomous act of nominalization. 'But one has only to listen to poetry .... for a polyphony to be heard (*se fasse entendre*)'; Lacan seems to be claiming that poetry is language that requires no analysis, explanation, commentary. All one need do is listen to it in order to hear ... the truth. Lacan's 'whole exercise' of the tree functions according to the incantational procedures of symbolist poetry in France[37] – one might think of the later Mallarmé, or of Duras's scenario for the film, *Hiroshima mon amour*. There is a certain magical connotation to intoning a text without commentary, as though it were beyond the reach of rational discourse, an incantation that would make truth appear from behind her veil, like a spirit evoked in a magical ritual which liberates it from its shackles in the underworld – the snares of the syntactic.

Why, though, would Lacan wish to suppress linearity, since he expressly rejects the possibility of a one-to-one correspondence of words to things that such extra-linguistic meaning would require?[38] Because, he argues, despite the 'glissement incessant du signifié sous le signifiant' ['incessant sliding of the signified under the signifier'], 'toute notre expérience va là-contre' ['all our experience runs counter to this linearity [incessant sliding]'].[39] For Saussure as for Derrida, linearity constitutes the principle of language as a system of differences 'without positive terms'; that is, without any free-standing units of meaning.[40] In its broadest implications, the problem of linearity is the problem of pure difference, and any 'solution' to this problem is bound to remain

---

[36] Derrida, 'White Mythology', p. 233.
[37] Nancy and Lacoue-Labarthe, *Titre*, p. 58.
[38] *Les écrits techniques de Freud*, pp. 271–3; *Les psychoses*, p. 43; *Papers* 247–9.
[39] *Ecrits*, 502, 503; *Ecrits* Eng., p. 154.
[40] Saussure, *Course*, p. 120; Derrida, *Grammatology*, p. 38; see also Nancy and Lacoue-Labarthe, *Titre*, p. 57; Weber, *Return to Freud*, pp. 25–32.

suspect from the perspective of deconstruction, for it must succeed in curtailing the endless movement of meaning introduced by metonymic differentiality. If there are indeed no such fixed 'meanings' in the referential sense of the term, how then, asks Lacan, can we ever determine the sense of an utterance? What accounts for what he calls the 'effect of meaning'? Saussure responds that positive terms are formed by the linking of individual signifiers to specific signifieds,[41] but Lacan rejects this solution as inadequate.[42] He proposes instead that which is both necessary and sufficient, namely metaphor.

Poetry would thus constitute the solution to the problem raised by linearity. Metaphor is the adequate response to metonymy. What appeared at first as a magical incantation beyond reason paradoxically turns out to be the very manifestation of that same reason. In other words, like the symbolists he supposedly emulates, Lacan conceives of poetry as the recuperation of truth, but, as it were, on a higher level. Metaphor can serve as the link between symbolism and structuralism insofar as it 'rémunère le défaut des langues' [compensates for the defect of languages], the defect Mallarmé refers to in this famous phrase being precisely the lack of correspondence between the sounds of words and their meanings.[43] Poetry establishes a new level of similarity between word and world, between naming and the things named, thus facilitating what Derrida calls the *re*-appropriation of truth in 'the vocation of a pure nomination':

the reappropriation of a full language without ... differential syntax, or in any case without a properly *unnameable* articulation that is irreducible to the semantic *relève* or to dialectical interiorization.[44]

The argument, however, is not that Lacan's brand of reappropriation is a simple return to the Adamic process of directly naming objects as they emerge fresh from creation. On the contrary, his act of pure naming names the impossibility of direct nominalization. The 'proper', or literal, that founds and institutes Lacan's rhetoric of the unconscious is not a simple presence but that 'nucleus of our being' (*Kern unseres Wesens*) which always

---

[41] Saussure, *Course*, pp. 120–1. [42] *Psychoses*, pp. 296–7.
[43] Mallarmé, 'Crise du Vers', in *Œuvres complètes*, p. 364.
[44] Derrida, 'White Mythology', p. 270. See also Nancy and Lacoue-Labarthe, *Titre*, p. 148.

remains inaccessible.[45] In the 'Seminar on "The Purloined Letter"', Lacan refers to Heidegger's notion of *a-letheia* (non-forgetting, un-concealment) to explain that, even while remaining inaccessible, truth makes its presence known in the act of speaking:

> Aussi bien quand nous nous ouvrons à entendre la façon dont Martin Heidegger nous découvre dans le mot *aletheia* le jeu de la vérité, ne faisons-nous que retrouver un secret où celle-ci a toujours initié ses amants, et d'où ils tiennent que c'est à ce qu'elle se cache, qu'elle s'offre à eux *le plus vraiment*.

> As well, when we are open to hearing the way in which Martin Heidegger discloses to us in the word *aletheia* the play of truth, we rediscover a secret to which truth has always initiated her lovers, and through which they learn that it is in hiding that she offers herself to them *most truly*.[46]

It is this 'presence beyond language' of the act of uttering which frees metaphor from the differentiality of the linear.[47] By putting a label on the truth that no system can effect univocal, referential naming, and that, as a result, the only truth we can have is that of language, it thus purports to do what Derrida imputes to metaphoric reappropriation – eliminate any unnameable metonymic (syntactic) articulation. But if speech is truth – see the prosopopeia in 'The Freudian Thing': 'I, Truth, speak ...'[48] – then similarity dominates Lacan's theory of metaphor after all, just as it does those of all his predecessors. Only in his case it is the resemblance of reason – logos – speech – to itself: there is a perfect correspondence between the utterance, the naming of truth, and the 'content' of the statement, or assertion, the true nature of truth as the process of unconcealment. The latter thus becomes manifest in a kind of 'primary language' uncontaminated by the difference that would be introduced by syntactic relations.[49]

From the perspective of deconstruction, the question of 'reason since Freud', that is, the question of whether Lacan's rhetoric

---

[45] *Ecrits* Eng., p. 166; see Nancy and Lacoue-Labarthe, *Titre*, p. 129.
[46] *Ecrits*, p. 21; 'Seminar on "The Purloined Letter"', p. 37.
[47] Nancy and Lacoue-Labarthe, *Titre*, p. 148.
[48] *Ecrits* Eng., p. 121. This translation misleadingly reads, 'I, truth, will speak.'
[49] Nancy and Lacoue-Labarthe, *Titre*, pp. 139–40, 148.

makes psychoanalysis an adherent or opponent of the Enlightenment, depends on two major issues: the claim that his notion of
metaphor is based on similarity; and the allegation of a radical
opposition between the two master tropes, which enables him to
assert the priority of metaphor over metonymy. Taken together
they constitute the charge that his theory reinforces the imprisoning effect of traditional fixed meaning instead of supporting
the liberation associated with the movement of difference. Now
the majority of literary scholars who have sought to defend
Lacan's rhetoric against these charges, especially those in
America, have nevertheless taken the deconstructive analysis of
these issues as their starting-point. As a result, although reason,
liberty and happiness are the ultimate stakes in the war over
psychoanalysis, the crucial battles have pitted the one trope
against the other.

Thus the authors of *Titre*, while conceding that metaphor 'must
borrow the turns and detours' of metonymy in order to produce
itself, assert that for Lacan 'metaphor dominates, founds and
precedes metonymy'.[50] Instead of 'disrupting the opposition'
between metaphor and metonymy, Lacan supposedly effects a
clear separation between them. Weber, on the other hand, argues
that:

The fact that the 'vertical' dimension of language is, in [Lacan's] account,
'suspended' from 'the punctuation of each of its units', indicates that the
'paradigmatic' or 'metaphorical' axis is construed in terms of syntax
rather than semantics.[51]

Like those with whom he takes issue, Weber does not question
the superiority of syntax over semantics; but for him it is clear
that in Lacan's rhetoric, the 'metonymic movement of signification' overrides, or rather undermines, the metaphysical concepts
generally associated with metaphor.[52] Whereas *Titre* had to
maintain that metaphor must be strictly quarantined from the
contagion of metonymy in order to uphold the charge that in
Lacan literal, proper, meaning can be reappropriated, Weber
retorts that metonymy has always infested metaphor from the
start. In this sense, he reaches the conclusion diametrically
opposed to that of *Titre*: for him metonymy precedes and
dominates metaphor.

[50] Ibid., pp. 78, 143.   [51] Weber, *Return to Freud*, p. 54.   [52] Ibid., p. 63.

Not so Zizek, who agrees with the proponents of deconstruction that Lacan insists 'on the primacy of metaphor over metonymy, his thesis [is] that metonymical sliding must always be supported by a metaphorical cut ...'[53] No doubt that is because for him it is self-contradictory to assert that there is no fixed meaning; the assertion that there is no fixed meaning can only be made from a place where meaning is fixed. Without the 'metaphorical cut' which produces a certain void, or absence, there would be no incessant sliding of meaning. In a sense one might say that in Zizek's version Lacan claims that metaphor does not fix meaning but its lack. The priority of metaphor entails neither enslavement to the meanings fixed by culture nor freedom from the latter, but the paradoxical Lacanian 'forced choice' which undermines this neat distinction.[54] The apparent contradictions between Weber and Zizek can be explained in part by the fact that the former limits his study to the Lacan of *Ecrits*, that is, of 1966 and before, while the latter relies mostly on the later Lacan. Yet they also raise genuine issues in understanding the specifics and the purport of his theory, which we will have to confront in subsequent chapters.

In 'Turning the Screw of Interpretation' Felman gives a reading of Lacanian metaphor which appears to be the polar opposite of those we have considered. Far from fixing meaning or its lack, metaphor, here equated to rhetoric, constitutes 'the very textuality of the text'; 'the rhetorical function [consists in] the movement and energy of displacement through a chain of signifiers'.[55] As such, it is precisely that movement from signifier to signifier whose inertia combats any tendency toward mastery, toward the domination of meaning over textuality. In her analysis of *The Turn of the Screw*, Felman contends that the phallic metaphors of helm, mast and screw embody this rhetorical motion. She uses this concept of metaphor as a criticism of those 'Freudian' readings of the James story which seek to enlist phallic symbols in the endeavour to find the one true meaning of the tale. That is, they want to ride along the detour of metaphor only until it takes them back to their original destination. To this conception of interpretation as the simple return from the purely verbal figure to the solid ground of the literal, 'the circular reappropriation of

---

[53] Zizek, *The Sublime Object of Ideology*, p. 154. [54] Ibid., pp. 157–61, 165.
[55] Felman, 'Turning the Screw of Interpretation', pp. 117, 137.

literal, proper meaning', she opposes the idea of metaphor as textual movement itself. Like the Lacanian phallus, to which she refers a few pages earlier, the screw becomes the metaphor of metaphoricity itself; it enacts, and thus stands for, the very rhetorical motion of the text of which it is a part. The truth of this metaphor is therefore that there is no truth, no substantive essence or being as source and justification of the metaphor. Metaphor is nothing other than the turn of the trope which undermines all literality.

But this troping on the etymological significance of tropicality does nothing to disorient the traditional geography of rhetoric. Whether it be a substance or a function, the signified of the metaphor is still simply represented by the shape or function of its signifier. The connection between signifier and signified remains one of correspondence, of similarity: metaphors of the turning motion of objects stand for the turning of textuality. In Felman's theory, metaphor cannot be based on resemblance, for it stands in the place of an absence, the non-existent literal. But in the practice of her text, as in *Titre*, metaphor, understood as rhetoricity in general, resembles itself. Self-referentiality simply replaces referentiality.

By contrasting metaphor (rhetoric) only to the extra-linguistic other of literal meaning, Felman espouses the global opposition of poetry to logic we have encountered already in the positivist interpretation of Lacan. She thus gives up the possibility of describing the interaction of the various modes of intra-linguistic functioning Lacan in fact distinguishes. Although she uses the term 'displacement' extensively to designate the rhetorical movement from signifier to signifier which thwarts all attempts to immobilize the text, she never specifies the relation between metaphor and metonymy.

In *Reading Lacan*, Gallop strives to analyse the relationship of metaphor to metonymy but, unlike adherents of pure deconstruction, she refuses to reduce it to one of polar opposition. In chapter 5, 'Metaphor and Metonymy', she distinguishes between two types of rhetorical interpretation:

Whereas a metaphoric interpretation would consist in supplying another signifier which the signifier in the text stands for (a means b; the tie represents a phallus), a metonymic interpretation supplies a whole context of associations. Perhaps this metonymic interpretation might be called feminine reading.[56]

She quickly abandons the radical bipolarity of this scheme, however, acknowledging that such thinking derives from the phallic phase, in which the 'binary opposition between phallus and lack [predominates] ... The adult sexual model sees the masculine dependency on the feminine', in that metonymy is what makes metaphor possible. Moreover, her reading of 'The Signification of the Phallus' convinces her that the latent, metonymic, term (−s) in Lacan's algorithms from 'Agency' is the (maternal) phallus, a finding which suggests 'that metonymy is more truly phallic than metaphor'.[57]

By this path she reaches the conclusion that 'any polar opposition between metaphor and metonymy ... is trapped in the imaginary order, subject to the play of identification and rivalry'.[58] Privileging the horizontal bar of metonymic linearity in Lacan's formulae is just as wrong as granting precedence to the vertical bar of metaphor, for either move is linear in the sense of being unidimensional. Lacan's rejection of linearity is encoded in the two strokes of metaphor's plus sign, which indicate that the trope must be read in two dimensions at once. Gallop thus finds herself in agreement with Rose, who contends that 'Lacan's statements on language need to be taken in two directions – towards the fixing of meaning itself ... and away from that very fixing to the point of its constant slippage'.[59]

Like Felman, then, Gallop ultimately does advocate metaphor; but while Felman takes metaphor to be the force that opposes the fixing of meaning, Gallop considers that it encompasses both the anchoring and the loosening of meaning. By stressing the two-dimensionality of metaphor, she attempts to reconcile Lacan's claims of its primary ethical and political significance as a liberating function with those passages in his texts that appear to give it the opposite role of fixing meaning. The precise relation between the two tropes nevertheless remains unspecified in Gallop's presentation. Although she refers to Jakobson's equation of the figures to the two axes of language, she does not explain

[56] Gallop, *Reading Lacan*, p. 129.
[57] Ibid., pp. 129, 130.   [58] Ibid., p. 132.
[59] Rose, 'Introduction', in Mitchell and Rose, eds., *Feminine Sexuality*, p. 43; cited in Gallop, *Reading Lacan*, p. 124.

why Lacan claims that metonymy should be the necessary precondition of metaphor. In what way is the slippage of meaning necessary to its fixing? How is such fixing a liberation? What is the connection between meaning and the difference between the sexes? If metaphor is the origin of social law, why does it require metonymy to 'get around the obstacles of social censorship' and thereby to 'produce itself'?[60]

Many of these difficulties can be traced to the fact that Gallop, along with Lacan's other supporters and detractors, shares the conviction that the principle of metaphoric substitution is *similarity*: '. . . a metaphoric reading in that, by use of **similarity** (Jakobson's metaphoric relation), it replaces one term by another'.[61] In order to establish the similarity of two terms, whatever the preliminary role of negation may be, one must be able to examine their meanings simultaneously, to make them both present. This possibility presupposes, in turn, either that they exist outside language, or that they can be mustered in a univocal, self-identical, language. But if either of these possibilities obtain, then meaning must indeed be fixed, entirely determinate, or at least determinable. If the principle of metaphor is in fact similarity, then no amount of twists and turns will prevent it from supporting determinism rather than freedom. Alternatively, if metaphor is somehow dependent on the metonymic substitution of something for nothing, as Gallop comes close to suggesting in her discussion of desire in Chapter 6, 'Reading the

---

[60] Gallop, *Reading Lacan*, p. 129, referring to *Ecrits* Eng., p. 158. In subsequent chapters, Gallop does address these questions, but her answers remain problematic. She explains the relation between feminine metonymy and masculine metaphor, for instance, by making the excellent point that for Lacan the phallic signifier signifies nothing because the object of desire that would be its signified is undefinable (ibid., pp. 139–40, 151). A crucial step in this equation is supplied by Lacan's discussion of the '*La barrée*' in *Encore*, that is, the erasure of the definite article in the French expression for women in general, '*La femme*'. Lacan emphasizes that this erased article is the phallus as the signifier that 'bars' meaning. From that assertion Gallop infers that since '*La femme*' means women in general, Lacan must be speaking of femininity. Hence she concludes that he is making the phallus both feminine and masculine, both transgressing and enforcing the Law at the same time (ibid., pp. 138–40). Nevertheless, a careful reading of the key passage from *Encore* (pp. 74–5), which we will undertake in chapter 6, shows that Lacan's point is quite different, that he is distinguishing two different bars and two different functions, only one of which is associated with metaphoric substitution. He reiterates this argument in *Sinthome, Ornicar?* pp. 9, 39.

[61] Gallop, *Reading Lacan*, p. 131.

Phallus', then it cannot function according to the principle of similarity, for how can something resemble nothing?

Wishing to reconceive Lacan's notion of the figure 'along the lines that deconstruction, *à la* de Man and Derrida, has taught us', MacCannell rejects the ambiguity Gallop finds in metaphor.[62] Although, like Zizek, MacCannell draws heavily from Lacan's later teachings and emphasizes the relation of the literary to desire and culture in his thought, because of the perspective chosen her interpretation univocally denounces metaphor and celebrates metonymy. The former trope is the instrument of 'the phallic truth', a power that exercises a tyrannical hegemony over the members of society by holding out the 'fiction of unity', the 'creation of "oneness"'. 'The metaphoric mode dominates culture, repressing the metonymic mode', which is combinatory, associative. She does not accuse Lacan of being a 'partisan' of phallic power, however; on the contrary, she maintains that 'the phallic truth is precisely that against which Lacan re-writes every line'. For Lacan, the meaning of speech is 'the desire for mutual recognition', which she glosses as 'the inter-human recognition of mutuality'. It is this function as social tie which metonymy, 'the combinatory mode in which self might be "with" the other', is capable of exercising, and which metaphoric civilization represses. She claims that a 'pre-civil' desire can be imagined, not outside or before language, but inside it in the form of the linguistic figure which dominates the unconscious that resists culture – metonymy. The latter is thus, paradoxically, a social tie that is opposed to culture.[63]

Lacan's teaching charts the cultural battlefield in which the two linguistic figures struggle for control of the unconscious. Metaphor's strategy in this battle is to dangle before society the lure of a unity constantly promised but never delivered, in order to induce its members to sacrifice their desire for mutual connectedness and to submit to the modes of alienated desire that will

---

[62] MacCannell, *Figuring Lacan*, p. 14.

[63] Ibid., pp. 21, 40, 91, 158. I prefer to translate Lacan's *parole* by 'speech' rather than 'word', precisely because 'speech' generally entails the dimension of the Other, of the relation to an addressee. Of course, the creative connotation of 'word' in the theological tradition is thus lost, but this loss is perhaps compensated by the circumstance that although Lacan drew upon this tradition, he did so for resolutely anti-theological purposes.

perpetuate the phallic, metaphoric, order. Under the guise of uniting people into a cultural whole, metaphor actually works to split them apart, to separate them from each other, producing 'absolute division and separation'. Instead of fostering true community, metaphor fathers the Other, that personified Symbolic Order whose 'drive is the prevention of natural necessary (and sexually satisfying) combinations'.[64]

The key that unlocks this reading is MacCannell's conception of the role played in metaphor by negativity. '[Metaphor] is, ironically, a form which, based on negation and opposition, ideologically parades in the positive character of identity and unity'. As the trope of selection and substitution according to Jakobson's definition, metaphor implies choice, classification into categories. Now this preferential inclusion of one thing depends on the exclusion of something else; 'this, not that'. Moreover, the transition between selection and substitution can be achieved only 'on the basis of a prior negation: "not like that"'; for in order to conceive *similarity* one must first draw the distinctions necessary to isolate the things compared from other things. 'This principle of distinction and division ... supports comparison – our familiar literary version of metaphor'.[65]

To recapitulate the logic of MacCannell's argument: metaphor is the trope of substitution; substitution is made on the basis of similarity; similarity can be established only by means of distinctions; distinctions involve choice; choice requires opposition, exclusions; and exclusion is a process of negation. As with the critics previously discussed, the keystone of Lacan's metaphorical structure is once again similarity, understood here as the principle of substitutability. Under this building, however, she has uncovered the necessary foundation of negativity.[66]

But from this account it is not at all clear why negation should be the exclusive property of metaphor. She argues that the plus and minus signs in Lacan's algorithms for the tropes – in which metonymy is noted by a '$(-)s$', and metaphor by a '$(+)s$' – :

[64] Ibid., pp. 14, 77, 103. [65] Ibid., pp. 95, 96, 97.
[66] In *Titre* Nancy and Lacoue-Labarthe discover a similar negativity as the foundation of Lacanian metaphor, the lack of reference which allegedly founds the autonomy of the signifier. MacCannell, *Figuring Lacan*, differs from them in the aspect of the Lacanian concept of castration she chooses to emphasize – the mother–child relation she sees as the prototype of pre-civil desire, or metonymic community.

[sum] up the process his discourse never ceased to be about: the ideological substitution of a faith in the additional surplus value that is derived from the act of deletion, subtraction. We submit to castration because we believe it gives us added, indeed, infinite, value.[67]

Yet the very algorithms MacCannell reproduces from 'Agency':

$$f(S \ldots S')S \cong S(-)s \text{ [metonymy]}$$
$$\frac{f(S')\,S}{(S)} \cong S(+)s \text{ [metaphor]}^{68}$$

clearly distribute the role of negation in rhetoric – the minus sign – to metonymy. Indeed, when Weber stresses that metonymy has always already infiltrated Lacanian metaphor, he means to assert thereby that the latter does *not* operate solely on the basis of that Hegelian 'determinate negation' which defines traditional philosophical concepts.[69] As a symbolic function in the Lacanian sense, metaphor relies on the purely *differential* character of the signifier: 'Dans l'ordre symbolique, tout élément vaut comme opposé à un autre' ['In the symbolic order every element has value through being opposed to another'].[70] And it is precisely this Otherness, derived from the *in*determinate negativity of metonymy, which makes the full presence of the concept ever irrealizable.[71]

MacCannell, however, wants to keep the good work of metonymy entirely separate from metaphor. She is therefore obliged to deal with the apparent contradiction to her reading represented by Lacan's algorithms by claiming that this is a false, perverted form of metonymy: '[Metaphor] drives the subject by means of an alienated form of desire that Lacan calls the "rails of metonymy". But it is a desire that only mimics the combinatory, linking modality of metonymy.'[72] Nowhere, however, does she produce a Lacanian text in which this distinction between a true and a false metonymy is drawn. In fact there are none, for, although Lacan did distinguish several forms of 'inter-human' connections, which he calls 'social bond', 'relation', 'love', 'desire' and 'drive', depending on the case and the specific stage of his thought, and while in his later teaching he did suggest that psychoanalysis might lead to a new type of social bond, he did not link the latter to a special form of metonymy. The confusion seems to arise from

[67] MacCannell, *Figuring Lacan*, p. 166.
[68] *Ecrits*, p. 515; *Ecrits* Eng., p. 164.
[69] Weber, *Return to Freud*, pp. 9–10.
[70] *Psychoses*, p. 17; *Psychoses* Eng., p. 9.
[71] Weber, *Return to Freud*, pp. 25–32.
[72] MacCannell, *Figuring Lacan*, p. 97.

her desire to make metonymy into a positive factor, against all the evidence of Lacan's texts, which always assign to that trope a negative sign, of loss or of lack. Unable to reconcile the positive function of metonymy as the principle of combination with its negative sense as lack, she is forced to invent a second metonymy whose negativity derives from its subservience to the metaphoric process. This desire prevents her from acknowledging that for Lacan the desire to combine arises only from the experience of loss.[73]

The desire to keep metonymy free of any negativity also raises problems in MacCannell's treatment of metaphor. In order to avoid the trap of imagining metonymy as a mere utopian nostalgia for an impossible pre-linguistic state, she must maintain that it can exist within language. The combinatory, or associative, mode of linguistic functioning must therefore be completely separate from the substitutive function (since the latter involves negativity). Replaceability cannot be the property of language in general, but must be restricted to the one noxious, illusory, dimension of metaphor, which is then equated to the principle of substitutability in general. Yet, although Lacan does assimilate metaphor to substitution fairly consistently, it does not follow that he excludes metonymy from that process. In fact, he specifically states that 'la métonymie ... concerne la substitution à quelque chose qu'il s'agit de nommer' ['metonymy ... involves substitution for something that has to be named'].[74] And in one seminar, *La relation d'objet*, he describes metonymic substitution as 'supplementation' [*un élément suppléant*]. Regardless of the name, the essential point is that the rhetorical process that interests Lacan involves substituting one thing for the *lack* of another, and in many texts the factor which introduces that lack, that negativity, is metonymy.[75]

In fact, at the time of 'Agency' Lacan's aim was not to discredit the metaphoric process but to endorse it, and the negativity of

---

[73] MacCannell, ibid., does recognize that the metaphoric process leads to the 'combinatory', but she rejects this form of pseudo-combination as cultural, and thus false, metonymy, because based on negation. The main point at issue is the relation of metaphor and metonymy to the superior form of human connection which Lacan recommends at the end of several of his seminars, e.g. vols. I, VII, IX and XX, and which he generally calls 'love'.

[74] *Psychoses*, p. 250; *Psychoses* Eng., pp. 220–1.

[75] *La relation d'objet*, p. 400. It is true, however, that in *Sinthome* he uses the term to indicate both types of substitution together. This alternation in the usage of

metonymy served a positive function in the production of meaning. Moreover, the status Lacan attributed to metaphoric 'significance' in relation to 'meaning' as the recognition of the Other, varied from one period of his career to another. From the start, he conceived of speech in analysis as divided between two slopes, one of which was indeed oriented toward the Other, but the second of which was directed toward the particular truth of the speaker.[76] By the time of the 'Proposition du 9 octobre 1967', as we shall see in our discussion of transference, he defined the goal of psychoanalysis – training analysis at least – as the institution of a desire 'most radically opposed' to the need for recognition. Consequently, as Weber maintains, the attributes of the two tropes cannot be neatly and categorically divided into bad and good in accordance with MacCannell's schema: metaphor = similarity, negativity, substitution, division, the noumenon; (true) metonymy = association, positivity, combination, phenomena.

While it will prove necessary later on to complete MacCannell's presentation by reconsidering the intricacies of Lacan's more complex formulations and the changes in his teaching over time, her discussion of negation enlarges our understanding of the tree passage as a demonstration of Lacanian metaphor. Her insight into the involvement of negation in the formation of the symbolic abstractions that make comparison possible – the definition of a 'this' opposed to all other 'that's' – allows her to bring out a hitherto unexplored aspect of the tree excursus, its illustration of the inherent limits of the metaphorical – that is, the symbolic or conceptual – process.

The metaphorical cancellation of the tree by all the figurative trees of human cultural memory ... demonstrates the failure of the concept to appear without the concourse of the imaginary.[77]

Guided by her reading of Lacan's remarks on Kantian ethics and Cartesian certitude, she concludes that symbolic negation is unable to overcome its ties to the phenomenal world (the 'imaginary' in this context). Despite its promise of a meaning

---

'supplementation' has the same rationale as his use of 'metaphor' to designate both rhetoricity in general and a specific stage in the process of symbolization, as we shall see below.

[76] *Ecrits techniques*, pp. 59–61; *Papers*, pp. 48–50.
[77] MacCannell, *Figuring Lacan*, p. 165.

beyond appearances, metaphor cannot entirely negate the latter, ever retaining their traces.[78] The tree passage is meant to debunk the belief in an infinite value added to the subject through negation. The metaphoric concept, or 'significance', remains a cultural illusion which strives to repress the inter-human 'meaning' of the corporeal image.

Seen in the light of Lacan's later writings, the tree passage thus assumes an ethical and political dimension, in that it displays the fundamental limitations of the pretensions of the Law which rules any culture. In the mid-fifties, however, Lacan presented this emphasis on the material sub-structure necessary to the conceptual process as a matter of the relation of signifier to signified:

Le premier réseau, du signifiant, est la structure synchronique du matériel du langage en tant que chaque élément y prend son emploi exact d'être différent des autres ... . Le second réseau, du signifié, est l'ensemble diachronique des discours concrètement prononcés, lequel réagit historiquement sur le premier, de même que la structure de celui-ci commande les voies du second.

The first network, that of the signifier, is the synchronic structure of the language material in so far as in that structure each element assumes its precise function by being different from the others ... The second network, that of the signified, is the diachronic set of the concretely pronounced discourses, which reacts historically on the first, just as the structure of the first governs the pathways of the second.[79]

What is elsewhere glossed as 'phenomenality' is here explained as the 'diachronic', that is, the pure contingency of historical usage, which as such both opposes and interacts with the systematicity of the synchronic organization of language. In this conception, neither linearity nor systematicity dominates the other. Without abstraction – the systematic diacritical structuring principle of synchrony – language could not function at all; but without concreteness – the more or less random effects of historical usage adapted to local purposes – synchrony would be 'empty', having nothing to work upon. If we compare the

---

[78] As though responding in advance to MacCannell's assertion, Lacan said in *Encore*, p. 23: 'Ce qui est important, ce n'est pas que ce [le référent] soit imaginaire ... c'est proprement que le signifié le rate' [The important thing is not that it [the referent] is imaginary, but precisely that the signified misses it].

[79] *Ecrits*, p. 414; *Ecrits* Eng., p. 126.

diachronic to what is given in experience, and the synchronic to the 'forms of intuition' and the 'categories of the understanding' by which we organize our knowledge, we can recognize that this is a rather Kantian notion of the principle of linguistic functioning.

And it is precisely this notion of language in general that the tree episode is meant to exhibit. Lacan takes the (banal) word 'tree' precisely in order to show that every point in an utterance is connected 'vertically' to a set of historically attested contexts. And since it is this 'verticality' which constitutes the 'polyphony' of language audible in poetry, we can conclude that for Lacan language in general is poetic. In this sense it is indeed accurate to claim that for him poetry is the essence of language.

But this means not only that his is a theory of figurative language in general, but also and above all that the literal, the language of truth and reason, is itself the product of historical contingency:

Ce qu'on appelle logique ou droit n'est jamais rien de plus qu'un corps de règles qui furent laborieusement ajustés à un moment de l'histoire dûment daté et situé par un cachet d'origine, agora ou forum, église, voire parti. Je n'espérerai donc rien de ces règles hors la bonne foi de l'Autre, et en désespoir de cause ne m'en servirai, si je le juge bon ou si on m'y oblige, que pour amuser la mauvaise foi.

What is called logic or law is never more than a body of rules that were laboriously drawn up at a moment of history duly certificated as to time and place, by agora or forum, church, even party. I shall expect nothing therefore of those rules except [without] the good faith of the Other, and, as a last resort, will make use of them, if I think fit or if I am forced to, only to amuse [beguile, deceive] bad faith.[80]

The point of these remarks is not only that the rules of logical discourse are always open to manipulation, but that all such rules arise in specific, local, conditions tied to the interests and functions of particular social institutions. They have a concrete historicity, which means that they developed within a particular language and can be judged only from within some language. It is only the trust in language (the good faith of the Other), in the possibility of truth to emerge in language, that makes rules serviceable. There is no actual vantage point outside of the

---

[80] *Ecrits*, p. 431; *Ecrits* Eng., p. 140; my translations.

concrete, contingent, forms of a specific language from which to discern truth, but only the projection of such a place; that is, only a necessary illusion makes it possible to distinguish the literal, the transparent representation of reality, or the pure utterance of truth, from the figurative. In short, there is no assurance of truth outside of language concretely used other than the shared belief in such a guarantee.

To argue that all language is poetic is therefore to maintain that the process whereby the rules of logic are developed is the same as that involved in forming a metaphor. Every signifier, however exalted or humble, results from a concrete, historical process of 'vertical' linking with other signifiers, even such banal words as 'tree', or 'curtain'. Indeed, well before 'Agency', in an article entitled 'Remarks on Psychical Causality' first presented as a lecture in 1946, Lacan had already proposed a disquisition on the word 'curtain' which in many respects resembles the excursus on 'tree'. Although the earlier passage deals explicitly with the relation of truth to language rather than with the theory of rhetoric, as in 'Agency', yet the fundamental principle of linguistic functioning illustrated is precisely that of knotting, tying words together. 'Le mot n'est pas signe, mais noeud de signification' [The word is not a sign, but a knot of signification].[81]

As the tree recalls the resistance to the fixing of meaning through its anagrammatic relation to the bar (in French), so the curtain is synonymous with that 'veil of appearances', in Hegel's phrase, which allegedly blocks our access to essential reality.[82] When the discourse of the curtain tells us that a word is a 'knot' of signification, therefore, it is indicating the paradox of a meaning, a truth, a Thing-in-Itself that appears to be beyond the phenomenal world of appearances. As a pun this knot is also a

---

[81] *Ecrits*, pp. 166–7; my translation.

[82] In *Relation d'objet*, p. 742, Lacan makes this rapprochement explicit: 'Pour mieux nous faire comprendre, nous voudrions introduire ici l'image d'un voile, d'un rideau, placés devant un objet. Le rideau prend toute sa valeur d'être ce sur quoi se projette l'absence; il est l'idole de l'absence; ce qui est au-delà comme manque, s'y réalise comme image ... [In order to make ourselves better understood, we would like to introduce here the image of a veil, of a curtain, placed in front of an object. The curtain takes on its full value of being that upon which absence is projected; it is the idol of absence; what exists as lack beyond it is realized as image ...]. See references to the veiling effect of the phallus in the '*Hamlet* Seminars' and in 'La signification du phallus', discussed in chapter 3 below. See also Zizek, *Sublime Object*, p. 196; Pommier, *Exception féminine*, p. 152.

'not' (*noeud-ne*); the meaning of words has a necessary relation to nothingness as well as being, a point supported by the references to the radical ambiguity of Heidegger's truth as revelation and to the need for meaning to be 'unveiled'. A knot is also a tangle, an inextricable coming together of a series of strands, to form an impasse, to block further passage; these are the aporiae and abysses of the quest for truth, above all the difficulty of relating the particular to the universal. And a knot is a special kind of loop, one which not only ties several things together, but which, when its ends are pulled, presses all the more tightly against itself; it is an image of self-referentiality.[83]

In the tree passage, the '*noeud*' of signification has been replaced by the '*point*' of the signifying chain, the point where the latter is punctuated by a 'stitch' (another meaning of the French *point*) which ties together, on the vertical, the attested contexts. But this *point* is of course also the emphatic form of *pas*, of the not (*ne ... point*), a point attested in the last paragraphs of 'Science and Truth'.[84] The *point* indicates the essential tie of meaning and negativity through punctuation, a meaning reinforced by the visual pun in Lacan's formulae for metaphor and metonymy, where the minus sign $(-)$ used for metonymy resembles the horizontal line Lacan employs to symbolize the bar of resistance to meaning (linearity), which is crossed by the perpendicular line which completes the plus sign (+) in the formula for metaphor (verticality).[85]

The apparent incoherence of the sequence of items in the tree passage thus retraces the unpredictable and uncontrollable branching of the particularity of historical contingency. Their apparent coherence, on the other hand, arises from the more or less systematic, universalizing, order to which they are inevitably subjected in this retrospective presentation. Although no single meaning or essence unites all the attested uses of tree into a totality, certain insistent themes emerge to tie them together. The phallic senses of strength and majesty are quickly transposed into a preoccupation with destiny, first in the cross that became a sign for all Christians, then in the Y of the Pythagorean crossroads, which might suggest that most fateful crossroads faced by Oedipus, next in the chain of generations of the family tree, and

---

[83] *Ecrits*, pp. 166–7.   [84] Ibid., p. 877; 'Science and Truth', pp. 24–5.
[85] Nancy and Lacoue-Labarthe, *Titre*, p. 100; Gallop, *Reading Lacan*, p. 119.

then in the zig-zag pattern produced in the tortoise shell used for purposes of divination. The sense of a pattern to our lives made visible by a sudden flash of heat and light which would satisfy our desire to know our destiny is carried forth in the reference to Heraclitus-Heidegger's *Hen Panta* and the Hegelian overtones of Valéry's 'Plane Tree', whose 'No!' echoes the negativity of the *point* and the bar. Thus the curtain of phenomena is lifted momentarily when, as Lacan puts it later in 'Agency', the 'being' of the subject – Freud's 'nucleus of our being' – 'n'apparaît que l'éclair d'un instant dans le vide du verbe être' ['appears in a lightning moment in the void of the verb "to be"'].[86]

Neither whimsy nor logic, the tree is that which seems to subvert the opposition between logic and whimsy, just as it undermines the customary distinctions between the necessary and the contingent, the universal and the particular, scientific prose and poetic language. As Lacan states in a later text, 'Le signifiant introduit deux ordres dans le monde, la vérité et l'événement' ['The signifier introduces two orders in the world, that of truth and that of the event'].[87] Even while misleading us about Lacan's message, the wording of this text is precisely the message that the tree is trying to convey, between the lines and yet in the very words it uses: if poetry is an evocation of the dark spirits of the night, it is only in order to expose them to the flash of light that will send them packing, and it is the creative arrangement of the signifier in history, rather than theoretical discourse, which determines what we are.

La seule chose qu'il y a … à trouver [en analyse] … c'est le trope par excellence, le trope des tropes, ce que l'on appelle son destin … Le destin … est de l'ordre de la figure, au sens où ce mot s'emploie pour dire *figure du destin* comme on dit aussi bien *figure de rhétorique* …

The only thing to find [in psychoanalysis] … is the trope par excellence, the trope of tropes called one's destiny … Destiny is on the order of the figure, in the sense in which the word is used in saying 'figure of fate', the way you also say 'rhetorical figure' …[88]

For Lacan the power of poetry, as of psychoanalysis, consists in its ability to intervene precisely where prose discourse has failed,

---

[86] *Ecrits*, p. 520; *Ecrits* Eng., p. 160.
[87] *L'éthique de la psychanalyse*, p. 308; *The Ethics of Psychoanalysis*, p. 265.
[88] *Transfert*, p. 372.

or is lacking; but this is simply a new application of the same power which had earlier given rise to what subsequently came to be considered as 'prose discourse'. Metaphor is somehow involved in creating and filling the place where the discourses of family, society or theory have left a void. Lacan's theory of poetry is designed to explain how that is not only possible, but practical.

All the commentators we have considered struggle to trace the connections between two apparently irreconcilable requirements of Lacanian metaphor: that it be based on similarity, with all that that entails for the fixing of meanings in relation to reason, the literary and culture; and yet that it be somehow dependent on a metonymy which flatly contradicts the possibility of determinate meaning. To some it seems clear that he effects a radical separation between the two tropes, and that the one is ethically and politically good, the other bad. Others, on the contrary, strive to show that the relation between poetry and difference is not one of pure opposition, and that metaphor allows only a 'relative stabilization' of meaning.[89]

While Lacan's presentation of the rhetorical functions in 'Agency' at first sight does more to obscure than to clarify these issues, when it is read in the context of traditional definitions of the tropes and completed by the analyses in his other writings, a coherent and persuasive theory emerges which throws considerable light on the issues in dispute. Now, as we have already remarked, most theoreticians from Aristotle to Jakobson have asserted that metaphor is indeed the trope of similarity. Aristotle's example, the 'sunset of life' (the 'evening of life' in the translation Lacan uses), defines old age in terms of an analogical relation between life and day, which can be expressed in the form of a ratio: sunset is to day as old age is to life.[90] The resemblance remains hidden unless we put the latent term defined, 'old age', in relation to an unexpressed, fourth term, in this case 'day'. As the etymology of the term indicates, metaphor is supposed to be a transfer of meaning from one term to another which customarily does not take that meaning – *Sinnesübertragung* for Jakobson, *transfert de sens, transfert de signifié*, for Lacan – a shift based on a non-expressed similarity between two sets of terms.

---

[89] Weber, *Return to Freud*, pp. 3, 180.   [90] Aristotle, *Poetics*, 1457b, pp. 23–6.

As a matter of four terms related to each other by analogy, Aristotelian metaphor must depend on the primacy of the signified over the signifier. The analogical relation between sunset and old age can only be derived from the presupposition that the two terms share similar attributes, or meanings: for instance, both a day and a lifetime must be considered as natural temporal cycles whose end is equally natural. The attributes must have logical priority over the metaphoric process. They must be conceived as existing before the discovery of the more or less hidden analogy, so that metaphor thus has a fundamentally mimetic function.

As early as 'The Function and Field of Speech and Language in Psychoanalysis' (1953), however, Lacan protested vehemently against the assimilation of metaphor to comparison, because that conception supports the 'realistic' tendency to read images as pictures, as iconic symbols of things outside language. His denunciation in 'Agency' of 'les psychanalystes ... exclusivement fascinés par les significations relevées dans l'inconscient' ['psychoanalysts [who] were fascinated exclusively by the significations revealed in the unconscious'] is likewise directed against the mimetic conception of language.[91]

His most ample presentation of metaphor and metonymy, found in chapters XVII and XVIII of his seminar on the psychoses, also begins with the assertion that metaphor does not depend on a relation of similarity, but in addition to stating what it is not, here he also announces what it is: 'Il n'y a pas comparaison, mais identification' ['There is not a comparison, but an identification'].[92] And it is the 'structure of the signifier' which makes possible the transfer of meaning, and thereby the identification, understood in the psychoanalytic sense of the creation of a new identity of the subject. In Lacan's terminology, this is primarily a symbolic rather than an imaginary identification in that the controlling factor is the signifier rather than the meaning to be transferred. Lacan's assertion that metaphor is a matter of identification rather than of analogy is therefore the equivalent of his contention that the signifier takes precedence over the signified. The force of both claims is that metaphor has a non-mimetic function, and that this function is

[91] *Ecrits*, p. 513; *Ecrits* Eng., p. 162.
[92] *Psychoses*, p. 247; *Psychoses* Eng., p. 218.

non-mimetic precisely because metaphor is a constructive process. The symbolic transfer of signifieds involved in metaphor somehow creates new meanings, indicated by the (+)s of the formula for metaphor in 'Agency', rather than comparing ones that already exist. To the extent that these new meanings open up a new identity, a new mode of being for the subject, metaphor will indeed be the trope of tropes, the trope of destiny.

Lacan clarifies and justifies this claim in a lengthy discussion of the metaphor he drew at random from the Quillet dictionary, the line from Victor Hugo's 'Booz endormi' ['Boaz Asleep']: 'Sa gerbe n'était point avare, ni haineuse' [His sheaf was neither miserly nor spiteful]:[93]

Sans la structure signifiante, c'est-à-dire sans l'articulation prédicative, sans la distance maintenue entre le sujet et ses attributs, on ne pourrait qualifier la gerbe d'avare et de haineuse. C'est parce qu'il y a une syntaxe, un ordre primordial de signifiant, que le sujet est maintenu séparé, comme différent de ses qualités.

Without the signifying structure, that is, without predicative articulation, without the distance maintained between the subject and its attributes, the sheaf cannot be qualified as miserly or spiteful. It's because there is a syntax, a primordial order of the signifier, that the subject is maintained as separate, as different from its qualities.[94]

The logic of Lacan's argument is therefore as follows: In order for a metaphoric transfer of meaning to take place, the attributes customarily attached to a person or thing, a 'subject' in the grammatical sense, must first be detached from their usual mooring and then reattached to the new location. Now in 'nature', in our perceptual experience, attributes do not go wandering off from their sites: the green we see in leaves does not simply float away onto youth, evening does not affix itself to age, and spite does not adhere to sheaves of grain. These 'meaning effects', as Lacan calls them, can occur only within language, as a result of that peculiar syntactic order of the signifier which both separates subjects from their predicates (attributes) and enables them to acquire new ones. In short, the key to Lacanian metaphor is the function of predication.

---

[93] *Psychoses*, pp. 247–8; *Ecrits*, pp. 506–7.
[94] *Psychoses*, p. 248; *Psychoses* Eng., p. 218.

Logically prior to any given use or meaning, and therefore to all resemblance, the syntactic structure of predication subtends every metaphoric identification:

C'est par le fait que la gerbe est le sujet de *avare* et de *haineuse*, qu'elle peut être identifiée à Booz dans son manque d'avarice et sa générosité. C'est par la similarité de position que la gerbe est littéralement identique au sujet Booz.

It's by virtue of being the subject of *miserly* and *spiteful* that the sheaf can be identified with Booz in his lack of avarice and in his generosity. It is by virtue of the similarity of position that the sheaf is literally identical to the subject Booz.[95]

If Lacan has thus adopted a concept of similarity after all, it is not the resemblance of attributes traditionally used to define analogical metaphor, but Jakobson's notion of positional simi-larity.[96] A whole series of grammatically equivalent signifiers may be inserted along the 'vertical' axis of substitutions, because any actual, positive, language, such as French or English, estab-lishes and provides a syntagmatic structure, or 'horizontal' axis, consisting of specific signifying places, or positions, along which the chain (or string) of signifiers is aligned. Although these places are marked by word-order in the examples Lacan draws from French, in general it does not matter whether languages use case or other devices for this purpose, so long as they define such signifying places as subject and predicate. Likewise, the term 'signifier' here does not designate words only, but ranges from the level of set phrases to that of phonematic pairs and oppositions. It thus can include linguistic elements such as the prefixes, suffixes and endings that are used in many Indo-European languages to indicate case, tense and other syntactic relations.

'[Ce] qui fait la vertu métaphorique de cette gerbe, c'est qu'elle est mise en position de sujet dans la proposition, à la place de Booz' ['What gives this sheaf its metaphorical quality [is] that the metaphor is placed in the position of subject, in Booz's place.'][97] By occupying the same syntactic place in the syntagmatic chain, that of subject in the Hugo example, the sheaf and Boaz become

[95] Ibid.; *Psychoses* Eng., p. 219.
[96] Jakobson, 'Two Aspects of Language', p. 77. See also Grigg, 'Metaphor and Metonymy', pp. 59–60.
[97] *Psychoses*, p. 257; *Psychoses* Eng., p. 225.

one and the same; they are identified, not compared; that is to say, they are fused together, or condensed. Metaphoric identification is thus the equivalent of Freud's condensation. Instead of imagining that both share the same qualities, which the metaphor then discovers, Lacan emphasizes that the similarity in meaning (of their attributes) is created by means of the metaphoric process. It is language which makes this identification possible; it is the signifier that allows the poet to define the sheaf and the man in such a way as to establish their identity. Far from depending on similarity, metaphor is therefore the condition of possibility of analogy.[98]

In keeping with Jakobson's distinctions, Lacan calls this structure of the signifier the metonymic slope of language, since it involves relations of contiguity and articulation rather than of similarity. 'La métonymie est au départ, et c'est elle qui rend possible la métaphore' ['metonymy exists from the beginning and makes metaphor possible'],[99] because the positionality of language, the general rule that the linear juxtaposition of signifiers in a chain is taken to carry syntactic meaning, is the logical prerequisite for the propositional function of language.

When Lacan assimilates Freud's primary processes, condensation and displacement, to the metaphoric and metonymic 'slopes' of the signifier in 'Agency', he is asserting that the same positional relations govern the organization of the signifiers used in symptoms and dreams. Juxtaposition automatically takes on syntactic significance; signifiers that appear next to one another are joined together through positional links. Even the simplest dreams of children show that 'metonymy exists from the beginning', much like the 'primitive' predication that colonialist derision epitomized in the expression, 'Me Tarzan'. To illustrate this point, he recounts from memory (and with some distortion) Anna Freud's dream of eating strawberries which Freud discusses in chapter III of *The Interpretation of Dreams*. Lacan's metonymy is thus the hidden substructure of the signifier as such, which forms the 'heart of Freudian thought', since without it the primary processes of unconscious functioning – condensation, displacement and graphic representation [*figuration*] – could not exist.

---

[98] *Papers*, p. 238.   [99] *Psychoses*, p. 259; *Psychoses* Eng., p. 227.

That is the force of his dictum that 'the unconscious is structured like a language'.[100]

The example of the child's dream may show that predicative structure is one facet of unconscious thought, but it does not demonstrate that this structure is a necessary component of all such thinking. Confirmation of this claim must be sought in Lacan's argument about the first function of the signifying structure mentioned above, detaching the subject from its attributes. In rhetorical tradition and by etymology, metonymy connotes something other than contiguity, namely, a change of name. The precise expression Lacan uses – 'substitution for something that has to be named' – captures the peculiarity of the aphasics, whose word association tests Jakobson reports in 'Two Aspects of Language and Two Types of Aphasic Disturbances', the article whose definition of the axes of similarities and combinations no doubt stimulated the theory of rhetoric expounded in 'Agency'.[101] The primary symptom of their malady, like that of certain victims of stroke, is the inability to call up the names of familiar objects. They therefore have no other choice but to resort to metonymic substitutions such as 'thatch', 'dirtiness' and 'poverty' for the word that escapes them – 'hut'. The term Lacan uses to characterize this metonymic relation, which rhetoricians try to capture in speaking of the container (for the contained), the part (for the whole), or connection (lexical or real contiguity), is 'evocation', or 'allusion'.

In 'Agency' he refers to this process of 'word to word' connection as using 'cette structure de la chaîne signifiante ... pour signifier *tout autre chose* que ce qu'elle dit' ['the structure of the signifying chain ... in order to signify *something quite other* than what it says'].[102] Citing Quintilian's cliché example of the fleet designated by the expression, 'thirty sails', he points out that this meaning can be indicated regardless of the real circumstances. The meaning effect, the naming process, depends on the allusive capacity of language rather than on the real contiguity of the part (sail) with the whole (boat) as traditional rhetoric asserts; and that

---

[100] As we shall see, Lacan's later thought would require that this dictum be rewritten as something like: 'the unconscious is structured like a *knowledge* of language'.

[101] Grigg, 'Metaphor and Metonymy', pp. 58, 67.

[102] *Ecrits*, p. 505; *Ecrits* Eng., p. 155.

effect derives from the general rule mentioned earlier, that in a signifying chain mere juxtaposition entails significance. Even if each ship had several sails, in which case the number of ships would be so reduced as to make the notion of a fleet highly questionable, the phrase 'thirty sails' could still connote the latent signified, 'fleet'. To take a less archaic example, even if professors and middle-level managers wear shirts with blue collars, they can be designated as white-collar workers nonetheless. Just as it is the linguistic function of positional similarity that is relevant to metaphor, so it is the positional contiguity of the symbolic system that is operative in metonymy. It is the connection between the manifest signifiers, 'thirty' and 'sails', or 'white collar' and 'worker', whatever the historical origin of that link may have been, which evokes the latent meaning.

But if 'thirty sails' can mean 'fleet', and any expression may be used to signify something 'other than what it says', then clearly meaning does not inhere in signifiers. It may always be displaced, from one set to another. Metonymy is therefore the equivalent of the primary process mechanism of displacement. By the same token, it is this displacement which allows the numerical denotation to be subtracted from 'thirty', and 'white collar' to be divested of its reference to colour or apparel. In short, displacement/metonymy brings about the detachment of the subject from its attributes – the loss of meaning.

Metonymy is essential to the unconscious, because, at this stage of Lacan's thought, the unconscious is precisely that which escapes expression in language. 'Chaque fois qu'il y a refoulement ... il y a toujours interruption du discours. Le sujet dit que le mot lui manque' [Each time that repression takes place ... there is always interruption of discourse. The subject says that the word escapes him.][103] Repression is the 'lacking word'. The only way to designate that for which the word is lacking is to refer to it by another name, by allusion. The unconscious formations of normal life as well as of neuroses – slips, dreams and symptoms – depend first of all on displacement, because the entire structure of the signifier 'est l'instrument avec lequel s'exprime le signifié disparu' ['is the instrument by which the missing signified expresses itself'].[104]

---

[103] *Ecrits Techniques*, pp. 294–5; *Papers*, p. 268.
[104] *Psychoses*, p. 251; *Psychoses* Eng., p. 221.

Ultimately, Lacanian metonymy involves three distinct but interconnected movements: the installation of that structure of the signifier which creates the signifying places of which we spoke first; the resulting detachment or loss of meaning or object (*signifié*); the search for that lost signified, a pursuit which leaps allusively from one signifier to the next in the apparently endless round of 'the incessant sliding of meaning'. The first step he calls 'primary symbolization' [*symbolisation primordiale*], or affirmation (*Bejahung*) in Freud's vocabulary, which is logically prior to the use of language for discourse. This 'pure nomination', as Derrida put it, evokes, calls forth, the things so named. In Heidegger's description:

Naming does not come afterward, providing an already manifest essent with a designation and a hallmark known as a word; it is the other way around: originally an act of violence that discloses being, the word [later] sinks from this height to become a mere sign ... Pristine speech opens up the being of the essent in the structure of its collectedness.[105]

This is the level of judgements of 'being', or pure attribution (as opposed to the level of judgements of existence and non-existence), which precedes and makes possible conceptualization of the world and of experience. Only that which symbolization first 'lets be', to use the Heideggerian (and mystical) formula Lacan cites in this context, can then be represented and found in reality. Without this primary symbolization, the 'This, not that' of which MacCannell speaks, that is, the discursive negation of conceptual definition, or even denegation (*Verneinung*), could not come into play, for there would be no 'this' or 'that' to include or exclude.

Primary symbolization is metonymic in the sense that, as the first act of naming a previously nameless world, it must overcome the originary aphasia of the pre-linguistic state by utilizing the aphasic's compensatory mechanism of finding substitutes for everything to be named. In the Hegelian phrase Lacan cites in 'Function and Field', 'le symbole ... [est le] meurtre de la chose, et cette mort constitue dans le sujet l'éternisation de son désir' ['the symbol ... [is] the murder of the thing, and this death

---

[105] Heidegger, *Introduction to Metaphysics*, p. 144. 'Essent' means roughly 'the things that exist'. 'Collectedness' refers to the gathering function of *logos*, the capacity of naming to organize the flux of experience into groupings that give them a certain permanence, or being.

constitutes in the subject the eternalization of his desire'].[106] Just
as the signified (fleet) disappears in a standard metonymy (thirty
sails) – hence the minus sign in Lacan's formula in 'Agency' – so
the 'real thing' at which symbolization aims is removed from,
and replaced by, the symbol. As a result, human reality is the
reality of language. For this symbol is a signifier; that is, it gets its
meaning only through its difference from other signifiers. Once
inside language, we are caught in the vicious circle of 'reference
back', in that any given meaning can only be defined in terms of
other meanings; hence the *manque-à-être* [want-to-be], the eternalization of the desire to find the lost signified, the being of the
world and of ourselves, once again.

Language, the signifier, entails the 'lack-of-being', the loss of
that real 'nucleus of (our) being' supposedly outside of language,
which flashes forth in the void of the verb 'to be'. But it is
language which also institutes the notion of being, of a complete
self and of an 'object', a perdurable essence or noumenal self and
entity beyond mere existence or appearance, by its capacity to
assert, to predicate one thing of another through the juxtaposition
of signifiers in a chain linked together by the verb 'to be' in its
copular use of pure attribution or definition: 'This is that.' Lacan
refers to Heidegger in this context, contending that the latter's
analyses of the verb 'to be' are meant to introduce us to 'ce qui est
absolument irréductible dans la fonction du verbe *être*, la fonction
purement et simplement copulaire' ['that which is absolutely
irreducible in the function of the verb *to be*, the copular function
pure and simple'].[107] The attribution of this idea to Heidegger
seems untenable to me. While the latter does discuss the copular
function at length, he repeatedly disparages the 'superficial
theory of propositions and judgments [which] has deformed [the
meaning of the 'is'] to a mere "copula" '.[108] And he certainly
makes no bones about asserting that this copular notion of 'the
"is" ' derives from the interpretation of the *logos* as the logic of the
statement (proposition, predication), an interpretation he characterizes as a deplorable turn in the history of the West, indeed the
deplorable turn which launched western metaphysics.[109] To give

[106] *Ecrits*, p. 319; *Ecrits* Eng., p. 104.
[107] *Psychoses*, p. 339; *Psychoses* Eng., p. 301.
[108] Heidegger, *Being and Time*, p. 401.
[109] Heidegger, *Introduction to Metaphysics*, p. 168. To this he opposes the reading

the 'is' priority over the 'to be' is precisely a Kantian manoeuvre, as Heidegger acknowledges; it is therefore not surprising that one should find an excellent explanation of this move in the writings of the neo-Kantian philosopher and intellectual adversary of Heidegger, Cassirer.

that linguistic form which is fundamentally set apart from all substantial expression, serving solely as an expression of synthesis *as such*, of pure combination. Only in the use of the *copula* does the logical synthesis effected in judgment achieve its adequate linguistic designation ... For Kant, judgment meant the 'unity of action', by which the predicate is referred to the subject and linked with it to form a whole meaning, to form the unity of an objectively subsisting and objectively constituted relationship. And it is this intellectual unity of action which finds its linguistic representation and counterpart in the use of the copula.[110]

In his *Foundations of General Scientific Theory* [Fichte] postulated the proposition A *is* A as the first, absolute principle of all philosophy, and added that this proposition, in which the 'is' has the sole signification of a logical copula, says nothing whatsoever regarding the existence or nonexistence of A.[111]

This strictly copular use of the verb becomes possible only when the subject is considered to be a pure name, the indicator of a 'being' which serves as the support of various qualities or attributes. In other words, the predicative structure of language, which isolates the subject on one side of the copula and the predicates on the other, effects a separation of the subject from the qualities it has in perceptual experience. In this sense, the signifier adds a degree of freedom to thought by detaching it from what is given in 'natural' existence. In this sense, fixing meaning is liberating.

In sum, metonymy, the linguistic structure designed to name ourselves and the world, to designate the meaning of being, necessarily institutes the separation of subject from predicate, of meaning from being. The signifying structure – metonymy – thus

of *logos* as gathering, as unconcealment, which corresponds to Lacan's *symbolisation primordiale*, the act of bringing to light in which being and thinking are as yet undifferentiated, and which is thus the condition of possibility of the statement (see chapter 4 of *Introduction to Metaphysics*, especially pp. 101–2). Perhaps Lacan is confusing Heidegger with Aristotle here, for it is the latter who restricts the revelatory, or apophantic, function of language to the proposition. (See Aubenque, *Le problème de l'être chez Aristote*, p. 102.)

[110] Cassirer, *Philosophy of Symbolic Forms*, vol. I, p. 313.   [111] Ibid., p. 317.

empties the meaning out of being by the very process through which it makes the notion of pure being possible. That is the gist of Lacan's somewhat arcane explanation of his algorithm for metonymy in 'Agency':

la structure métonymique, indiquant que c'est la connexion du signifiant au signifiant, qui permet l'élision par quoi le signifiant installe le manque de l'être dans la relation d'objet, en se servant de la valeur de renvoi de la signification pour l'investir du désir visant ce manque qu'il supporte.

the metonymic structure, indicating that it is the connexion between signifier and signifier that permits the elision by means of which the signifier installs the lack-of-being in the object relation, using the value of 'reference back' possessed by signification in order to invest it with the desire aimed at the very lack it supports.[112]

Incapable of direct satisfaction through the process of naming, the desire 'to be' is installed in the connection between signifiers. The signifier shunts it along the rails of the closed system of signification by marshalling the latter's allusive power to refer meanings back to one other. The point in the distance at which the rails seem to converge is the imaginary locus of an ultimate meaning outside of the system, a god-term that would join meaning to being and bring the otherwise limitless circulation of meanings to a halt. It is the very attempt to muster 'a full language without [differential] syntax, the vocation of a pure nomination' which produces that incessant sliding of meaning characteristic of differential linearity. Many years after 'Agency' and the seminar on the psychoses, Lacan gave this pithy description of the essential paradox: 'le langage nous impose l'être et nous oblige comme tel à admettre que, de l'être, nous n'en avons jamais rien' [language imposes being onto us and forces us as such to admit that, as to being, we never have anything of it].[113]

It is left to metaphor to fill the gap in being opened up by language, by knotting signifiers together. Once the process of predicative detachment has begun, nothing can guarantee that subject and attributes will be reattached according to the principles and findings of observation, logic or science. Predication cannot be reined in by the mere force of 'realistic' thought, for the freedom to substitute any grammatically appropriate term in a

---

[112] *Ecrits*, p. 515; *Ecrits* Eng., p. 164; translation slightly modified.
[113] *Encore*, p. 44.

given syntactic place is an intimate and necessary mode of the functioning of language. The same operation that permits language to detach the 'naturally' existing qualities from an object can be reapplied to language itself; the lexical ties of subject and attribute that exist within language, in the form of the usages codified in a dictionary, can also be severed. The predicational function of signifying systems, which allows them to divest the materials they use of any previous connections, can now serve to redefine and redeploy those materials as signifiers in new, and perhaps untoward, signifying chains. Lacan found an amusing way to characterize the uncontrollable proliferation of metaphoric action in 'Metaphor of the Subject': 'l'enfant épelle les pouvoirs du discours et inaugure la pensée' by singing: 'Le chat fait oua-oua, le chien fait miaou-miaou' [The child spells out the powers of discourse and inaugurates thought by singing: 'The cat goes bow-wow, the dog goes meow-meow'.][114]

The complete metaphoric process is thus a 'double twist' or a 'double-triggered mechanism', as Lacan calls it in 'Agency', in which metonymy must be 'there from the start' in order to detach the subject from its predicate, emptying it of its sense, $(-)s$, before new meanings can be formed by reattaching the subject to new predicates, crossing the bar to give the $(+)s$. The process of reattachment requires that the signifier suppressed from the subject position retain some connection to the metonymic chain that appears.[115]

L'étincelle créatrice de la métaphore ... jaillit entre deux signifiants dont l'un est substitué à l'autre en prenant sa place dans la chaîne signifiante, le signifiant occulté restant présent de sa connexion (métonymique) au reste de la chaîne.

The creative spark of the metaphor ... flashes between two signifiers one of which has taken the place of the other in the signifying chain, the occulted signifier remaining present through its (metonymic) connexion with the rest of the chain.[116]

In the Hugo example, the sheaf has been emptied of its connections with crops, fields, agriculture, nature and so on, and has been reconnected to attributes which belong to human beings such as Boaz, that is, avarice and spite. But at the same time, by

---

[114] *Ecrits*, p. 891.   [115] See Grigg, 'Metaphor and Metonymy', pp. 68–9.
[116] *Ecrits*, p. 507; *Ecrits* Eng., p. 157.

virtue of its identification with the sheaf, the latent signifier Boaz takes on the fecundity attributed to the natural generosity of the sheaf. Condensed into a single unit, both the manifest and the latent terms function as the subject of the predication. The force of the metaphor arises from the fact that we understand that it is the aged Boaz who has acquired a newfound generosity and procreative power. As a symbol of the 'miraculous' overcoming of natural limits through divine intervention, the Hugo line stands as a metaphor of the non-natural, of the proliferative power of the signifier, of poetry; in short, it is the metaphor of metaphor.

And that is just what the algorithm for metaphor indicates. The metaphoric function, f, states that if you take a signifier, S (miserly, e.g.) and juxtapose it to another as predicate (sheaf), where this other signifier has taken the place of a third (Boaz), ($\frac{S}{S'}$), then a new set of signifying possibilities will emerge, S(+)s, through the emptying of one set of meanings, ($-$), and the attaching of the new set. If metonymy connotes the process of oblique naming whereby meaning is emptied from the subject, metaphor designates the function of predication whereby new attributes are attached to that subject. It is this process of tying signifiers together in new combinations which constitutes the 'knotting' or 'stitching' illustrated by the tree.

❖❖❖

3

A Being of Significance

❖❖❖

La poésie est création d'un sujet assumant un nouvel ordre de relation
symbolique au monde.   Lacan, *Les psychoses*

> But something other dearer still than life
> The darkness hides and mist encompasses:
> We are proved luckless lovers of this thing
> That glitters in the underworld: no man
> Can tell us of the stuff of it, expounding
> What is, and what is not: we know nothing of it.
>
> Euripides, *Hippolytus*

The foregoing exposition of Lacan's theory of metaphor and
metonymy would seem to put to rest the notion that 'metaphor
dominates, founds and precedes metonymy'. On the contrary, the
account of the relation between the two tropes given in the
seminar on the psychoses and reprised in 'Agency' leaves no
doubt that, and how, metonymy 'is there from the start', forming
the basis of the 'double-triggered mechanism' of metaphor.
Lacan's assertion that it is language which creates the presupposition of something before and something beyond itself[1] would
seem to sweep the ground from under the claim that the 'hole' or
the 'bar' forms the centre around which Lacan's system revolves.
The idea that the place of the centre is created by the system
rather than being defined in advance as its origin, ground and
truth apparently eliminates any remaining metaphysical or essen-
tialist connotations.

Yet it also seems doubtful that so many careful and intelligent
readers of Lacan would simply have misread his conception of
the relation between the two tropes and that between language
and reference. Thus Derrida criticizes the determinate lack
which allegedly controls Lacan's whole system as a reversion to

---

[1] *Encore*, p. 44.

metaphysics.[2] Implicit in *Titre*, explicit in 'Purveyor' as well as in the texts of MacCannell, Gallop and many others not discussed here, the lack in question is that of the phallus, more specifically the maternal phallus of psychoanalytic theory. The accusation is that metaphor, Lacan's 'paternal metaphor', not only compensates for the castration (the want-to-be) of his metonymy by reappropriating the full presence, the truth lost through the imposition of the signifier;[3] it also, and more importantly, occupies 'the *transcendental position:* the privilege of a term within a series of terms which makes it possible and which presupposes it'.[4]

For Derrida, then, being contained within the series does not prevent an element from also being the condition of possibility of that series, and it is from this standpoint that one can argue that the phallic metaphor dominates, founds and precedes metonymy. The series in question is, of course, that of the signifier, or the letter, and the effect of the phallus is to guarantee the unity, identity and permanence of the letter. At first Derrida entertains the possibility that this capacity might derive from the form of the letter, then he quickly decides that it must stem from the ideality of meaning. He concludes that Lacan found it necessary to graft Freud onto Saussure in order to guarantee this ideality of meaning by integrating phallocentrism with phonocentrism.[5] The Saussurean theory of the sign supplies the self-presence of the voice via the phoneme, while the Freudian phallus furnishes the guarantee of wholeness, of integrity, as a remedy against the disintegration of castration. It is in order to maintain this unity and identity that Lacan supposedly ignores all the 'uncanny' effects of doubling in Poe's 'Purloined Letter'. On the level of language, therefore, the function of the Lacanian phallus is to overcome ambiguity, to master and restrain 'dissemination', by

---

[2] Derrida, 'Purveyor of Truth', pp. 81–100.   [3] Ibid., p. 89.

[4] Ibid., p. 94, note 33. I would argue that this is, at best, an oversimplified view. While it is true that the 'transcategorial' may have this structure, as does Aristotle's essence [*ousia*] in the *Metaphysics*, it is also true that this God-term may be either immanent or transcendent. Derrida's characterizations of Lacan's concept of the phallus often seem to imply that this 'transcendentality' is in fact transcendent, that is, completely separated from and exterior to the series, and thus in a position of complete mastery over it, while Lacan maintains that it is a limit, and an illusory one at that ('Subversion of the Subject', *Ecrits* Eng., pp. 320ff.).

[5] Ibid., p. 94, note 33.

guaranteeing the controllable polysemy that has always been the ideal of philosophic language, of a univocal language of truth and presence.[6]

Derrida is obviously challenging the main claim of 'Agency' that since Freud, and from the standpoint of psychoanalysis, reason (language, logos) has taken on a radically new aspect. Beyond and before the agency of the traditional autonomous subject of religious and secular humanism, linguistic articulation remains unknown and unmastered in the unconscious,[7] operating within and beyond the control of that ego. According to traditional lights, this reason, which is imposed on the human being willy-nilly and which produces effects despite the subject, is downright irrational. Indeed a major portion of the ethics seminar is devoted to exploring the contradictions psychoanalysis uncovers between reason understood as the logos, the word, the signifier, and reason understood as the principle of rational conduct which directs people to act in accordance with their own best interests, or needs (whether the latter be understood in the utilitarian or the theological manner). This traditional reason is therefore not itself, at least not since Freud. To which Derrida retorts that this is not some new reason 'since Freud', but 'reason itself. Before Freud, under Freud and since Freud.'[8]

It is not possible to decide the status of the phallus, reason and truth in Lacan's thought without first understanding the process of the 'paternal metaphor', by means of which it becomes 'le signifiant destiné à désigner dans leur ensemble les effets de signifié, en tant que le signifiant les conditionne de sa présence' ['the signifier intended [whose role it is] to designate as a whole the effects of the signified, in that the signifier conditions them by its presence as a signifier'].[9] In a broad sense, this means that the phallus symbolizes the fact that the signifier as system of differences supplants the characteristics given in natural perception. Lacan goes on to describe meanings as the 'progéniture bâtarde de sa concaténation signifiante' ['bastard offspring of the signifying concatenation'],[10] thereby indicating that they are the effects of a non-natural system of signification. The institution of

---

[6] Ibid., pp. 101–13.   [7] Lacan, *Ethique*, p. 247.
[8] Derrida, 'Purveyor', p. 100.   [9] *Ecrits*, p. 690; *Ecrits* Eng., p. 285.
[10] *Ecrits*, p. 692; *Ecrits* Eng., p. 288.

the paternal metaphor therefore represents the passage from nature to culture.

Lacan is paraphrasing Lévi-Strauss here: 'Les symboles sont plus réels que ce qu'ils symbolisent, le signifiant précède et détermine le signifié.'[11] The precedence of the signifier is linked to the other main distinction between nature and culture, the prohibition against incest. In a famous passage, Lévi-Strauss designates the incest taboo as the phenomenon which both marks and undermines the borderline between nature and culture, for it belongs to both of the domains it would separate. As a universal human phenomenon, it participates in the natural; but as a law imposed onto nature, it partakes of the cultural.[12] Taking Lévi-Strauss's views as a starting-point, Lacan's theory of the phallic signifier and the paternal metaphor is designed to explain in detail how the passage from nature to culture takes place.

'Signification of the Phallus' gives what might be termed an outline, rather than a description or an explanation, of that theory. To a great extent that outline corresponds to the theory of metaphor described in *Psychoses*. In asserting that the phallus 'équivaut à la copule (logique)' ['is equivalent ... to the (logical) copula'],[13] Lacan makes it the agent which first isolates a subject separate from its attributes and then serves to reattach them. He thus claims that the birth of the subject coincides with the institution of the phallus. But once the subject is separated from its unity with nature, and this is always already the case, it can never find genuine completeness again. The phallus thus becomes the bar of repression, of resistance to (complete or natural) meaning, after its 'veiling' signals the disappearance of the 'signifiable'.[14] Disappearing behind a veil, the phallus becomes the Thing-in-Itself; it represents the completeness which henceforth can only be evoked indirectly but never be made genuinely present. In this way it comes to symbolize the metonymic process by which the content is evacuated from those things ('signifiables') that are to serve as signifiers, as elements of that 'primary language' of which Lacan speaks in 'Function and

---

[11] Lévi-Strauss, 'Introduction à l'œuvre de Marcel Mauss', p. xxxii.
[12] Lévi-Strauss, *Elementary Structures of Kinship*, pp. 8–11.
[13] *Ecrits*, p. 692; *Ecrits* Eng., p. 287.   [14] *Ecrits*, p. 693; *Ecrits* Eng., p. 288.

Field';[15] namely, the image of the constituents of the phenomenal world, and first of all, of the body.

The institution of the phallic signifier, like Lacanian metaphor, is a process involving several moments; that is why he can attribute apparently incompatible qualities to the phallus without genuine contradiction. It represents completeness, but only by virtue of symbolizing the process by which that completeness is irrevocably lost. In that sense, it is self-referential; that is, the phallus as signifier – the differential process of signification – represents the loss of the phallus as signified – the noumenon. Put in slightly different terms, the latter indicates that being beyond language which language both promises and withholds, whereas the former, the result of the logos used on itself, refers to a purely cultural being, created in and by language. In a similarly paradoxical manner, as the 'bar', the phallus represents both the impossibility of the sign based on natural affinity and the possibility of the purely cultural sign, the first resulting from the emptying of meaning, the second from the subsequent reattachment of meaning.

The key to these paradoxes is the process of iterated action, or what Lacan calls the signifier's composition with itself: the same operation is applied twice. When the primary process which makes all language 'metaphorical', in the sense of the figurative in general, is applied a second time to the language of primary symbolization that results from its first application, the result is 'metaphor' in the restricted sense. The sign takes shape when a second round of substitution supplements the lacking content emptied from the signifiable in the first place. Whether or not this iterative process constitutes the reappropriation of the literal that deconstruction claims it to be will depend on the specific description and rationale of metaphor Lacan supplies to flesh out this outline.

In the previous chapter, I have argued that Lacan adapted Jakobson's rhetoric by grafting it onto the theory of being and predication he had already developed in the thirties and forties on the basis of his reading of the German philosophical tradition.[16] But if predication forms the missing link between rhetoric

---

[15] *Ecrits* Eng., pp. 69, 81.   [16] See Roudinesco, *Esquisse d'une vie*, pp. 125–65.

and being, it does not by itself furnish an adequate explanation of the paternal metaphor as the passage from the state of nature to that of culture. It is always a good idea to take Lacan at his word, and the word he uses repeatedly in 'Agency' to describe the metaphoric spark is 'creative'. Neither an idealism nor a formalism, his theory of the signifier is a creationism.[17] The roots of this concept should be sought, therefore, in Heidegger, whom he connects to creationism in *Ethique*, and to whom he refers also in 'Agency'; and beyond him in the constructivist notions of the sign often characterized as Kantian or neo-Kantian, but which include certain contributions from the long tradition of controversy about metaphor and linguistic creativity which stretches from German idealism to European romanticism, symbolism and surrealism. It is here that metaphor is construed as the fundamentally creative function of poetry, language, culture and identity.

These notions derive in a distant way from Aristotle, who claimed that the ability to find metaphors was the mark of scientific as well as poetic genius; but for him 'a good metaphor implies an intuitive perception of the similarity in dissimilars',[18] whereas for creationist theories, as for Lacan, metaphor is independent of similarity. They also have some affinities with positivist and spiritualist conceptions, but their respective theories of metaphor are nevertheless quite distinct. In the positivist view, language is or should be the impartial representation of an objectively verifiable world of objects and events; this is the denotative function. Language becomes metaphorical when it deviates from its denotative function by including some indication of a purely 'subjective', emotional attitude toward, or colouring of, the objective fact; this is the connotative function.[19] According to the spiritualist version, metaphors 'arise from the fact that a word which originally signifies only something sensuous is carried over into the spiritual sphere'.[20] In a second

---

[17] *Ethique*, pp. 144–6, 251–3.   [18] Aristotle, *Poetics*, 1459a.

[19] Cf. Ayer, *Language, Truth and Logic*; Carnap, *Meaning and Necessity*.

[20] Hegel, *Aesthetics*, vol. I, p. 404. This statement in itself is of course peculiar neither to Hegel nor to spiritualism, but forms part of the common heritage of western metaphysics. Locke, for instance, makes the same point in Book Three, Chapter 1, of his *Essay Concerning Human Understanding*. Although he uses the word 'transferred' to describe this process, he does not call it 'metaphor'. Moreover, Hegel does not limit the direction of the metaphoric process, from the 'lower' to the 'higher', the inorganic to the organic, or the material to the spiritual. On the contrary, he stresses that the transfer can move in either

phase, the meaning of the metaphor, or symbol, is deemed not only 'spiritual', but absolutely inexpressible in language or any material form.[21]

Each of these doctrines posits a non-rational factor at which metaphor aims, but for the first it is irrational, while for the second supra-rational. Neo-Kantian theories differ from both in that they include the metaphoric or symbolic in the same domain of rationality as the logical or discursive use of language. Yet they also diverge from recent adaptations of the Aristotelian concept of metaphor in that they maintain the romantic distinction between the intuitive and the intellectual functions instead of collapsing metaphor into logic as these theories do.

Like so much in German idealism, and especially in German romanticism, the notion of creationism is a secularized version of Augustinian theology. For the latter, all 'creatures' must have been created by God out of nothing, since they are constantly changing, and change supposedly entails 'non-being'. To the extent that they 'are', they must have received this share of being from the one who is immutable, who is being through and through; from the one who said, in *Exodus*: 'I am that I am.' And of course the instrument of this creation, as the first lines of the Christian Bible proclaim, is the Word.[22]

The term 'creationism' was used particularly by the philosopher of science, Alexandre Koyré, with whose ideas Lacan became familiar as early as 1933,[23] and to whom he often referred throughout his career. For Koyré, 'creationism' referred not only to the notion of creation *ex nihilo*, but specifically to the anti-Aristotelian view, promulgated as early as the end of the thirteenth century, that God is free to make the natural universe behave in any way he wishes, regardless of (human) logic or

---

direction, and that the spiritual can come to stand for the material just as the material can refer to the spiritual.

[21] See 'The Romantic Crisis', Chapter 6 of Todorov's *Theories of the Symbol*, for a rapid summary of Goethe's distinction between 'allegory' and 'symbol', as well as a more detailed treatment of the development of anti-mimetic theories of metaphor among the German idealists and romantics. He traces the critical distinction between the logical, intellectual notion of the symbol and the intuitive, pre- or non-rational use of the term, to Kant's *Critique of Judgment* (pp. 207–8).

[22] Gilson, *La philosophie au moyen âge*, p. 132.

[23] Roudinesco, *Esquisse d'une vie*, p. 139.

reason.[24] For certain historians of science, such as Duhem and Koyré, diverse versions of this theological 'voluntarism' were instrumental in the formation of the modern scientific notions of space and the universe, especially that of Newton.[25] Freeing God from the constraints imposed by Leibniz's 'sufficient reason', the Newtonians were able to argue for the existence of an absolute space, time and motion which could never be experienced directly, but which conformed to the structure of the purely theoretical tenets of Euclid's geometry. Of course they maintained that in reality this conception made it possible to account for the observed facts of physical motion in a way that the competing theories could not.

In *Concepts*, Lacan argues that once this separation of the formal properties of space from its observable characteristics had been effected, the way had been paved for modern, formal geometries and topologies, conceived totally independently of any application to physical space. He therefore sees a parallel in this one respect between Descartes's voluntarism and Newton's creationism (although Newton and his followers of course argued strenuously against Cartesian physics and theology). In effect, anything was now possible, provided only that it conform to the logic of the signifier itself, i.e. the definitions, operations and rules of a formal mathematical system. The essence of the scientific revolution of the seventeenth century resided in this newly liberated signifier, which was now free to follow its own path of development, unconstrained by, because prior to, actual observation.[26] As a result of this autonomous creativity *ex nihilo* of the signifier, it was no longer necessary to presuppose the existence of a transcendent God.[27] The voluntaristic liberation of God had thus paradoxically made it unnecessary to postulate God's existence.

This view of the emancipation of the signifier, whether in the guise of the 'little letters' of Descartes's analytic geometry or those of Newton's mechanics, is thus Lacan's secularization of theology. It differs from that of romanticism or humanism in that, instead of transferring the creative power from God to the

---

[24] Koyré, 'Le vide et l'espace infini au XIVᵉ siècle', pp. 37–9.
[25] See Koyré, ibid., p. 38; Koyré, *From the Closed World to the Infinite Universe*, chs. 9–11; Duhem, *Etudes*.
[26] *Four Fundamental Concepts*, pp. 204–5.   [27] *Ethique*, pp. 251–3.

autonomous subject, Lacan has moved it onto the signifier itself. He thereby linked creationism simultaneously to modern, formalist notions of mathematics, such as non-Euclidean geometries, and to the formation of non-natural, social worlds, in that both function independently of perceptual experience, and thus of Aristotelian *connaissance* (knowledge), the one through the combination of the little letters of science, the other through the creative use of the letters of language.

As we saw in the previous chapter, Heidegger attributes to language the fundamentally creative role of 'disclosing being' in 'the structure of its collectedness'. This role he assimilates to the Greek *poiein* in his translation of a sentence from Plato's *Symposium*, 205b: 'Every occasion for whatever passes over and goes forward into presencing from that which is not presencing is *poiesis*, is bringing-forth [*Her-vor-bringen*].'[28] He explains the mode of this poetic functioning in terms of collectedness, the *Hen Panta* of Heraclitus, in the 'Logos' article which Lacan translated for the first number of the journal *La Psychanalyse* in 1956.

Hen is the unique One, as unifying. It unifies by assembling.
The Hen Panta lets lie together before us in one presencing things which are usually separated from, and opposed to, one another.[29]

Just after translating this article, at the 6 June 1956 meeting of his seminar on the psychoses, Lacan took up this notion of assembling opposites in a new unity in his invention of the *point de capiton*, his image of the process of knotting the signifier (discussed in the last chapter) by means of a 'quilting stitch'.

Lacan illustrates his concept by analysing the opening scene of Racine's tragedy, *Athalia*. He concludes that the entire play is played out when Joad the priest manages to transform Abner's zeal into fidelity. Abner enters the temple full of vague fears about Queen Athalia's machinations against the faithful, and full of an equally vague zeal with which he strives to offset those fears. He leaves the temple with the calm assurance of faithfulness that Joad passed on to him in the form of a particular signifier, the 'fear of God'. Unlike the fear of the gods, a feeling that is 'multiforme, confus, panique' [multiform, confused, panicky], the fear of God 'remplace les craintes innombrables

---

[28] Heidegger, *The Question Concerning Technology*, p. 10.
[29] Heidegger, 'Logos', pp. 70, 71.

par la crainte d'un être unique qui n'a d'autre moyen de manifester sa puissance que par ce qui est craint derrière ces innombrables craintes' ['replace[s] [mankind's] innumerable fears by the fear of a unique being who has no other means of manifesting his power than through what is feared behind those innumerable fears'].[30] This gathering together of a host of fears into one fear through the invention of a new signifier 'transforme, d'une minute à l'autre, toutes les craintes en un parfait courage' ['transforms, from one minute to the next, all fears into perfect courage'].[31]

By gathering the many into the (new) one, the dominant signifier, 'le signifiant arrête le glissement autrement indéfini de la signification'; ['the signifier stops the otherwise endless movement (*glissement*) of the signification'].[32] But by thus pinning meaning down, the *point de capiton* has succeeded in changing meaning, in this case into its opposite, and has thereby transformed the relation of the subject to his experience. As Zizek explains, far from constituting a point of supreme density of meaning, the *point de capiton* represents the agency of the signifier in the signified; it is a self-referential, purely performative element, whose signification coincides with its own act of enunciation.[33] Behind the supposed meaning of 'the fear of God', there is nothing but the tautological function of stating: 'the fear of God'.

Concentrating a whole series of elements into what appears to be a single totality of meaning which ostensibly controls the entire field and thus is easier for the subject to handle, in fact the unity of the *point de capiton* is not some over-arching meaning but a point of sheer non-sense. In describing the notion of creationism, Lacan refers to the pot, or vase, which Heidegger discusses in his essay on 'The Thing' (English translation in *Poetry, Language, Thought*). Speculating that pottery vases might well be the first artifacts created by humankind, Lacan treats them as possibly the original signifiers, in which case they would be significant of nothing other than everything significant, in other words, of nothing in particular, of no specific signified.[34] From Heidegger he thus takes the claim that the vase creates

---

[30] *Psychoses*, p. 302; *Psychoses* Eng., p. 267.   [31] Ibid., p. 303; ibid.
[32] *Ecrits*, p. 805; *Ecrits* Eng., p. 303.   [33] *Sublime Object*, p. 99.
[34] *Ethique*, p. 145.

emptiness, the void.[35] It introduces both emptiness and fullness, discontinuity and difference, at the same time, into what was previously the continuous plenum of the real. The vase as object represents the existence of that void at the centre of the real which is called the Thing; and this void presents itself as a *nihil*, as a nothing. That's why the potter creates the vase with his hand around the void, out of the hole, *ex nihilo*. There is an identity between fashioning the signifier and introducing a cleft [*béance*], a hole into the real.[36]

For Heidegger the poetic activity which creates both being and non-being is firmly opposed to the copular use of the verb 'to be', which he finds at the origin of the debased notion of language as representation that founds western metaphysics.[37] As a result, Heidegger's poetry by itself is inadequate to explain Lacan's notion of metaphor. Moreover, Lacan considers the *point de capiton* to be a diachronic phenomenon, depending as it does on retrospection, and therefore incapable of accounting for the basically synchronic functioning of metaphor.[38] In order to complete the theory, we must therefore turn to the neo-Kantian doctrines of the sign.

Lacan's view that metaphor is the basic principle of all linguistic functioning echoes the call, launched in 1936 by I. A. Richards, for a new rhetoric that would reject the idea that figurative language is a deviation from a normal or literal usage and would

---

[35] Heidegger, 'The Thing', p. 169; Lacan, *Ethique*, pp. 144–5.

[36] *Ethique*, p. 146.

[37] This difference bears witness to a radical disparity between Heidegger and Lacan. For Heidegger, modern science is one manifestation of the fall into metaphysics of the ancient Greeks (Plato and Aristotle); its conception of nature as a giant storehouse of energy derives from the general position that everything must give a rational account of itself, must 'render its reason', in the Leibnitzian phrase. Lacan, on the other hand, follows Koyré in claiming that the origin of modern science is not to be found in the Greek *mathesis universalis*, but in the Hebrew conception of infinitude, of the void within natural reality. Thus Heidegger sees poetic being, with its creation of the void, as the polar opposite of metaphysical, and especially scientific, being, whereas for Lacan the creation of the void is the condition of possibility of science. Hence Heidegger's reactionary hostility to the Enlightenment, as opposed to Lacan's nuanced espousal of Enlightenment rationality, with a healthy mistrust of the ravages of the pure concept and a rejection of the idea of progress in history.

[38] *Ecrits*, p. 806. In his later teaching, Lacan explains the *point de capiton* in terms of what he then calls the signifiers s1 and s2. I will treat this development in chapter 6, in my discussion of the Lacanian theory of the subject.

show instead that 'metaphor is the omnipresent principle of language'.[39] The possibility of misunderstanding that arises due to the ambiguity inherent in language is not a scourge to be hunted down and extirpated but constitutes the very basis of any possible understanding, as well as 'the indispensable means of most of our most important utterances – especially in Poetry and Religion'.[40] Although Richards is sometimes considered to be a logical positivist, and Lacan disparages him under that title in 'Agency', his theory of metaphor, which is at the same time a theory of meaning, is much closer to the constructivist than to the associationist conception. It leans heavily on the work of what seems to be a disparate group of thinkers – Coleridge, Bentham, Bradley and Freud, as well as Richards' colleagues Ogden and Empson – but it ties them together with a common thread: the basic Kantian hypothesis, or 'theorem' as Richards calls it, that 'things ... are instances of laws'.[41] All perception is a sorting. The reflective intellectual process of abstraction, whereby particular experiences are stripped of their individual circumstances in order to arrive at what they have in common is,[42] in this account, a secondary phenomenon. The primary mental function, by virtue of which meanings are formed, is a 'primordial generality and abstractness' which allows us (and other animals) to respond to present situations in terms of qualities used to classify past situations.[43] 'We *begin* with the general abstract anything, split it, as the world makes us, into sorts and then arrive at concrete

---

[39] Richards, *The Philosophy of Rhetoric*, p. 92. It is true that, at the end (and in the beginning), Richards lets himself be carried away by the tide of standard metaphysics, proposing that the goal of the new rhetoric 'should be a study of misunderstanding and its remedies' (p. 3). Despite his professed aim of discovering a principle of ambiguity, and other significant divergences as well, there is a remarkable convergence between the very wording of his theory of metaphor and Lacan's remarks on the topic in *Ecrits techniques*.

[40] Richards, ibid., pp. 73, 40. One piece of evidence Richards adduces to demonstrate the fundamental character of ambiguity is Freud's notion of the over-determination of dreams (p. 38).

[41] Ibid., p. 36. Richards does not mention Kant. Rather he gives us to understand that he came to this notion via the Hegelian Bradley, and he even uses Hegel's example of 'this bit of paper' (p. 31). Nevertheless, the 'theorem' as stated is of course the fundamental principle of *The Critique of Pure Reason*. I might add that Richards' book was no doubt also the inspiration for Perelman's *The New Rhetoric*, to which Lacan replies in 'Métaphore du sujet', the short piece from which I quoted above (see p. 55).

[42] Cf. Locke, *Essay*, Book Three, Chapter III, among so many others before and since.

[43] Richards, *Philosophy of Rhetoric*, p. 31.

particulars by the overlapping or common membership of these sorts.'[44] The categories thus act like signs, in that they link and stand for what the organism takes to be the causally effective aspect(s) of a series of complex situations. From the start, the meaning of experience is fundamentally ambiguous, since primordial abstraction requires 'two thoughts of different things active together',[45] the past and the present situations. Richards distils this theory of primary meaning in the phrase 'delegated efficacy'.[46]

Words operate in an analogous way among people, but they substitute for the 'absent cause and conditions' which form 'the missing part of the [causal] context' in which they are used.[47] Since they derive their meaning from the circumstances of their use, and since they always link at least two different situations (the property they inherit from primary meaning), words do not and cannot have a proper, literal or correct meaning.[48] Moreover, they acquire an additional dimension of ambiguity, and flexibility, from the fact that their meanings also depend upon their linguistic context, both that of the other words used in the utterance and that of the rest of the language which serves as a necessary background for the utterance.[49] Consequently, meaning must result from a process of interpretation, of inference and guesswork, which strives to take account of the entire context. The meaning of a word constantly shifts, and it is the unchanging possibility of such changes that constitutes metaphor as the 'omnipresent principle of language'.

By virtue of this principle language can develop a more complex set of connections among things than is possible through primordial abstraction alone. It becomes a completion of human experience rather than a mere copy of existence; its function is to construct an order rather than to imitate one that already prevails. Richards cites Shelley's 'Defense of Poetry' to the effect that

---

[44] Ibid., p. 31.   [45] Ibid., p. 93.   [46] Ibid., p. 32.   [47] Ibid., p. 34.

[48] Richards explains that the illusion of a proper meaning comes from the purely relative stability of certain social contexts in which the words are often used (p. 11). Furthermore, he emphasizes that the illusion serves the interests of the social class which tries to impose the belief in a 'correct' usage (pp. 70–1; 78–9). These two assertions together form the nucleus of the theory of meaning at which Derrida arrived in the 'Afterword' of *Limited Inc* some fifty years later.

[49] *Philosophy of Rhetoric*, pp. 55, 57, 64. Richards relied on Bloomfield's *Language* to reach conclusions identical to those Jakobson condensed in the syntagmatic and paradigmatic 'axes' he developed from Saussure.

'language is vitally metaphorical; that is, it marks the before unapprehended relations of things and perpetuates their apprehension'.[50] According to the context theory, all meaning functions metaphorically, for 'when we use a metaphor we have two thoughts of different things active together and supported by a single word, or phrase, whose meaning is a resultant of their interaction'.[51] It is this interaction which Richards intends to clarify by means of his famous distinction between 'tenor' and 'vehicle'. Both the latter are 'thoughts' which together constitute a metaphor; but while the tenor is the meaning of the vehicle, the force of the metaphor itself is neither the vehicle nor the tenor but the relation between the two.

The ambiguity of meaning leads to the perception of relations among things, and the power of linguistic meaning is to establish new relations beyond those that stem from perception.[52] When a certain Lord Kames, whose *Elements of Criticism* (1761) becomes the lightning-rod for Richards' keenest darts, wonders whether 'poets [have] a privilege to alter the nature of things, and at pleasure bestow attributes upon a subject to which they do not belong?' Richards therefore responds as Lacan would later do in 'Metaphor of the Subject', that 'most moderns would say "Of course, they have!"'.[53] If Kames cannot accept certain audacious images, it is because he, like all those in the Aristotelian tradition, fails to recognize that metaphors may be based on any sort of relation whatever, not just resemblance.[54] Richards' reference to

---

[50] *Philosophy of Rhetoric*, p. 90.   [51] Ibid., p. 93.

[52] This aspect of the theory is entirely consistent with the notion of metaphor Hegel formulated in the *Aesthetics* (pp. 403–8), and with the romantic concept of *Witz* that contributes to both Hegel and Breton. 'The simile, like the image and the metaphor ... expresses the boldness of the imagination which ... evinces its power to bind together things lying poles apart' (p. 411). Hegel's metaphor, however, and even his image and simile, fall short of what he calls the 'concept', whereas Richards' idea of linguistic meaning, when supplemented by that of Cassirer, traces out the path that leads to Lacan's notion of the phallus as, in a sense, the 'concept'.

[53] *Philosophy of Rhetoric*, p. 107.

[54] In fact, Kames proposes a second principle of figurative language to explain the specific images that provoke his question: they are due to the 'principle of contiguous association' (Richards, *Philosophy of Rhetoric*, p. 107)! Lest the identity of this proposal with Jakobson's metonymy seem too marvellous a coincidence or too great a mark of Kames' prescience, it should be recalled that by the mid-eighteenth century, Locke, Hume and Hartley had advanced the theory of the association of ideas, one of whose modes of functioning was precisely the principle of contiguous association, and that grammarians and rhetoricians had sought to integrate the principles of 'mental functioning' with

the 'moderns' includes the same surrealists whose theory of metaphor Lacan quotes in 'Agency'. Before Lacan, although not quite for the same reasons, Richards both approves and disapproves of Breton's idea that the highest aim of poetry is to bring together two objects as remote as possible from each other in a sudden and striking fashion. Although he does not accept remoteness as a criterion of poetic value, he does agree that the juxtaposition itself is of prime importance in metaphor, because it induces the reader's mind to strive to connect the two things, that is, to find some relation between them. No doubt Mallarmé said it best in 'Crise de vers': 'Instituer une relation entre les images exacte, et que s'en détache un tiers aspect fusible et clair présenté à la divination' [Institute a relation, with exactness, between the images; a third aspect will be the result, fusible and clear, offered to the divination].[55]

Lacan assents to Breton's idea that any two terms whatsoever may be joined in a metaphor, and that instead of the metaphor being determined by a pre-existing relation, of similarity, it is the juxtaposition which establishes the relation between the two. He likewise endorses Richards' claim that the effect of the metaphor is to stimulate the mind of the reader or listener to seek out possible connections between the two terms. That is why he attempts to accept Mallarmé's challenge by defining dream interpretation as a *mantique* [divination]. And although he rejects the basic theological (vitalist) premise they share with a Kant or a Hegel, a Shelley or a Coleridge, that the spark jumps from meaning to meaning (or from image to image), their constructive theory of metaphor furnishes him with a concept of linguistic functioning that, in some important respects, complements that of Heidegger's logos.

Both Heidegger and Richards draw from the modern traditions of idealism, romanticism and pragmatism – Richards cites William James in this context – the notion of a prediscursive level of primary symbolization. While Richards and James attribute

those of rhetoric. (See my entry on 'Metonymy/Metaphor' in the *Encyclopedia of Contemporary Literary Theory: Approaches, Scholars, Terms* for some brief remarks on this topic.) Here as so often Lacan manages to combine both theories, recognizing the distinctness of the contiguity relation via Freud and Jakobson, yet retaining the modernist idea that the metaphoric imagination is capable of joining any subject with any predicate.

[55] Mallarmé, *Œuvres complètes*, p. 365.

this function to the entire animal kingdom, Lacan follows Heidegger (and Hegel) in restricting it to the domain of human language. But whereas Heidegger posits a relation of opposition between that primordial synthetic use of the 'is' to signify what he calls the 'apophantic as', 'letting something be seen in *togetherness* [*Beisammen*] with something – letting it be seen *as* something'[56] – and copular or logical synthesis, Lacan endorses Richards' view that the secondary level of signification results from the iteration of the same signifying operation that defines primary symbolization. That is why metaphor plays a central role for Richards and Lacan but almost none at all for Heidegger.

Richards characterizes that operation as 'the delegated efficacy of signs by which they bring together into new unities the abstracts, or aspects, which are the missing parts of their various contexts'.[57] In that 'efficacy' we may hear not only the title of Lévi-Strauss's famous essay on 'The Efficacity of Symbols', but also Lacan's 'effects of the signified'. These effects are precisely the new order of relations among things made possible by the metaphoric capacity of language. Richards' metaphor means (non-intuitive, 'non-natural') relation. Now one of the functions of the signifier 'father', according to Lacan, is 'l'introduction d'un ... ordre mathématique, dont la structure est différente de l'ordre naturel' into the series of generations ['the introduction of ... a mathematical order, whose structure is different from the natural order'].[58] And since the phallus has always designated the possibility of sexual relations, it is an easy step to have it signify the general capacity to form this new order of human relations. That is why Lacan merges the pre-discursive use of the verb 'to be' with the copular function of the 'is', its function as marker of pure relation, or synthesis.

Ce qui fait le fond de tout drame humain ... c'est qu'il y a des liens, des noeuds, des pactes établis. Les êtres humains sont déjà liés entre eux par des engagements qui ont déterminé leur place, leur nom, leur essence.

Every human drama ... is founded on the existence of established bonds, ties, pacts. Human beings already have commitments which tie them together, commitments which have determined their places, names, their essences.[59]

---

[56] Heidegger, *Being and Time*, p. 54.   [57] *Philosophy of Rhetoric*, p. 93.
[58] *Psychoses*, p. 360; *Psychoses* Eng., p. 320.
[59] *Le moi dans la théorie de Freud*, p. 231; *The Ego in Freud's Theory*, p. 197.

This, in short, is the social tie so prominent in MacCannell's reading of Lacan. Connectedness is the first characteristic of that second type of being which the signifier institutes.

Richards' new rhetoric also goes some distance toward explaining why the relatedness produced by language should play its role only when veiled:

We rediscover that the world – so far from being a solid matter of fact – is rather a fabric of conventions, which for obscure reasons it has suited us in the past to manufacture and support.

Intense preoccupation with the source of our meanings is disturbing, increasing our sense that our beliefs are a veil and an artificial veil between ourselves and something that otherwise than through a veil we cannot know.[60]

The reality of the relations designated by language is that those relations are not 'real', i.e. matters of fact, but the 'conventional' productions of language. Language veils reality, separating us from it. But to the extent that we take anything designated by language as real, as independent of language, we are veiling the truth of language, what Richards calls, after Bentham, the fictionality of our world. In Lacan's terms, the phallus as signifier of the effects of the signified (these relations) can only operate when we accept the fact that linguistic relations replace 'real' or 'natural' ones.

On one level, the phallus represents the reality that language veils reality. It stands for the new order of human relations which it itself initiates and makes possible. Yet that order is not one of fixed meanings. Richards' doctrine of usage implies that all meaning is potentially ambiguous;[61] a meaning could be fixed to a word or phrase only if it were possible to reach the totality of its contextual usages, and that is precisely the kind of receding horizon imaged forth by the rails of Lacan's metonymy.

A word is always a cooperative member of an organism, the utterance, and therefore cannot properly ... be thought to have a meaning of its own, a fixed correct usage, or even a small number of correct usages

---

[60] Richards, *Philosophy of Rhetoric*, pp. 41–2.
[61] In fact, Richards wants to have it both ways: although his theory embraces ambiguity, he constantly attempts to reserve a zone of purely univocal terms, which he calls technical or scientific language (ibid., pp. 48–50). This is in keeping with his aim of 'remedying' ambiguity by establishing its law. It is this, the metaphysical side of logical positivism, which Lacan rejects (although this repudiation is qualified in his analysis of the 'letter').

unless by 'usage' we mean the whole *how* of its successful cooperations with other words, the entire range of the varied powers which, with their aid, it can exert.[62]

When Lacan claims that any metaphor must remain open-ended, he does so on the basis of this notion of contextual meaning:[63]

> Chaque fois que nous avons dans l'analyse du langage à chercher la signification d'un mot, la seule méthode correcte est de faire la somme de ses emplois ... La signification est donnée par la somme de ces emplois.

> Each time that we are obliged, in the analysis of language, to look for the signification of a word, the only correct method is to enumerate all of its usages ... The signification is given by the sum of these usages.[64]

Consequently, each word must refer to many 'things' (which Lacan calls the 'signifiable' in 'Signification of the Phallus'), and vice versa. This many-to-many relation is just what is meant by the Freudian term *Verdichtung*, or condensation,[65] which Lacan then identifies with metaphor.

The context theorem of meaning contributes an essential step to the logic of the (phallus as) signifier. Since all meaning is contextual – relational – each word must 'condense' at least two senses, and thus be potentially ambiguous. Meaning is therefore severed from words; the order of words must be separate from the order of signifiables. The institution of that relation of signification, represented by the phallus, forms words into signifiers and signifiables into signifieds; it constructs the sign-function. By applying the principle of contextualization a second time, a new set of relations is created, one which is autonomous with respect to those that obtain among the perceptions resulting from the first application of contextualization to sensory experience. Paradoxically, then, it is precisely the capacity to take on various meanings according to context which founds both the independence of word from context and the dependence of word on context. The autonomy in question is not the assertion of a meaning independent of any context,

---

[62] Ibid., p. 69.
[63] Augustine's *De locutionis significatione*, which Father Beirnaert brought to Lacan's attention much later in the year at the 23 June 1954 session of the seminar (see chapter xx of *Ecrits techniques de Freud*), is something of a red herring. Although Augustine does imply that meanings form a closed order, he offers no theory of contextual usage comparable to that of Richards.
[64] *Ecrits techniques*, p. 262; *Papers*, p. 238.   [65] *Papers*, p. 268.

nor of a context of all contexts, but of the rule of movement
from one context to the next – by which I do not mean a
specific rule that tells you how meaning will change from one
context to the next, but rather the general rule of predicational
ambiguity that meaning does in fact vary according to usage.
The historical (understood as concrete situational usage) and
the metaphorical (in which predication is conceived as depending on a first metonymic detachment of sense) necessarily
go hand in hand.

Exactly how they are joined still remains something of a
mystery, however, in Richards' theory: 'If we ask ... how a sign
comes to stand for an absent cause and conditions, we come up
against the limits of knowledge at once. No one knows.'[66] His
inability to answer this question stems at least in part from his
premise that linguistic ambiguity is a continuation of, rather than
a radical departure from, the process of sorting present experiences he attributes to all animals. Lacan adopts and modifies the
latter, Hegelian, view of ambiguity, which explains why, unlike
Richards, he includes both the pre-discursive and the discursive
within the field of language. Even though historical usage plays a
pivotal role in Lacan's conception of the metaphorical creation of
meaning, his theory is not purely and entirely contextual like that
of Richards.

At various times, Lacan called the radical break instituted by
language 'primordial symbolization', the 'signifying cut' (*la
coupure signifiante*), and a 'rim' (*bord*), in the topological sense of
the term. This pre-discursive level of sheer naming is the metaphorical cut of which Zizek speaks, and which he claims must
precede metonymy, when that word is understood to designate
the endless slippage of meaning. Lacan attempted to answer
Richards' question in his repeated discussions of the '*fort/da*'
game Freud reports in *Beyond the Pleasure Principle*. In fact, so
often does Lacan return to this game – at least nine times between
1938 and 1964 – that one cannot help suspecting he became
caught up in the very process of repetition he was trying to
elucidate.[67]

---

[66] Richards, *Philosophy of Rhetoric*, p. 34.
[67] He discusses the game in the following articles and seminars: 'La famille',
'Function and Field', *Papers*, the 'Introduction' to the 'Seminar on "The

Although his interpretation of the operation and his conception of the purpose of the game varied considerably over the course of the years, the idea that it concerned the problem of absence, loss and death remained constant. As is well known, Freud interpreted the child's game of throwing away and reeling in a spool as its attempt to come to grips with its mother's absence. In 'La famille', one of his earliest writings, Lacan integrated his interpretation of the *fort/da* into an analysis of the situation of fraternal jealousy described by Augustine in *Confessions*, vol. I, section VII, in order to bring out what he took to be the intimate link between the loss of the mother and the loss of self, that is, the child's desire for death. The experience of weaning arouses in the infant a tendency toward death represented as the maternal imago, a nostalgia for wholeness that can take many forms but always consists in a more or less sublimated return to the womb. The game of *fort/da* is the reproduction of the malaise of weaning, an attempt to overcome the deprivation of separation by actively reproducing the trauma, in which the subject appears twice, once as the one who has the object, once as the one who has renounced it. His jealousy and his imaginary murder of his nursing brother result from his identification with the brother and thus the reactivation of his own desire for death. It is a kind of imaginary suicide that represents his primordial masochism. In the reprise of this analysis he gives in *Concepts*, Lacan decides that the proper term for Augustine's *invidia* is envy, not jealousy, for

l'envie est communément provoquée par la possession de biens qui ne seraient, à celui qui envie, d'aucun usage ... l'image d'une complétude qui se referme ... de ceci que le petit *a* ... peut être pour un autre la possession dont il se satisfait ...

envy is usually aroused by the possession of goods which would be of no use to the person who is envious of them ... by the image of a completeness closed upon itself ... the idea that the *petit a* ... may be for another the possession that gives satisfaction.[68]

It is the identification with the other in his apparent fullness which opens up the path toward the symbolization of absence, of one's own sense of loss, because this identification supplies a

Purloined Letter" ', 'Direction of the Cure', 'Formations de l'inconscient', *Ethique*, and *Concepts*.
[68] *Concepts*, p. 106; *Concepts* Eng., p. 116.

representation of the self. Only this imaginary reduplication of the subject, by endowing him with a minimal distance from himself, enables him to objectify and thus symbolize himself as both complete and incomplete – weaned – and it is the difference between the two states, effected by his action of throwing the spool away, which comes to represent absence.

Lacan soon renounced the notion of primordial masochism, emphasizing instead that the game gives rise to that 'naissance du symbole' [birth of the symbol] which institutes 'la maîtrise de déréliction [du sujet]' ['mastery of [the subject's] dereliction'].[69] The subject's action, his game of making the object appear and disappear, 'destroys' that object by making it a mere support for the game. The game itself, the anticipation of presence and absence, is the subject's new 'object'. His desire has been raised 'to a second power' in that he no longer wants to have the object of satisfaction, but rather to control the interplay of its presence and absence. But this interplay, in which the experience of the presence of an object is based on the possibility of its absence and vice versa, is precisely the mark of the symbolic 'initial negativation' or 'annihilation' of the thing;[70] the nature of the spool is a matter of indifference to the child, and none of its qualities destines it to play the symbolic role he gives it. Hence, the game is now suited to inscription in the system of differences of an already extant language (German), of which the syllables *fort* (/o/) and *da* (/a/) are the embryonic form. It is this aspect of symbolization, the cancellation, or evacuation, of the thing as a set of attributes, occurrences or experiences and its replacement by the pure difference of an interplay of presence and absence that Richards ignores.[71]

It is the same destruction which 'ouvre le monde de la négativité' [opens up the world of negativity],[72] i.e., the world of subjectivity, in which the subject may deploy his action. He reverses his previous relation to the object, for now he calls upon the object to disappear (and throws it away) when it is present before him and calls it back (and reels it in) when it is absent. The utterance 'away' coincides with its opposite in reality, that is, with the presence of the object, while the 'here' is pronounced when it is in fact absent. Inverting his relation to presence and

[69] *Ecrits*, p. 318; *Ecrits* Eng., p. 103.   [70] *Papers*, p. 174; *Psychoses*, p. 168.
[71] *Psychoses*, pp. 170–1, 188.   [72] *Ecrits techniques*, p. 196; *Papers*, p. 174.

absence is thus a performative rather than a constative utterance; when he says *'fort'* or *'da'*, the subject is 'calling to', or 'provoking' the object rather than making a statement of 'fact'. Negativation is the instrument of the subject's liberation from the 'natural' situation in which he finds himself – the presence or absence of the object of his needs – and thus the source of his mastery. It is this liberation from the immediate, practical situation which Hegel takes to be the essence and goal of the symbol.[73]

Now the relation to the ideal ego, represented by the replete suckling brother in the Augustinian analysis of envy, must find its place within the symbolic system. Once in language, the subject can no longer find satisfaction in the physical presence of the object that would fulfil its needs (the mother's breast in this case), for the presence he now seeks is that of another subject, one who exists within the world of language and whose presence is therefore always mediated by language. When the subject now calls to a real or imaginary partner, that other will also disappear, undergoing the symbolic death of passing from the status of being to that of symbol. But, for the Lacan of the early fifties who still took his cue from Hegel, that death into language provides the milieu in which communication can take place, so that the child can produce in it 'la provocation du retour qui le [son partenaire] ramène à son désir' ['the provocation of the return that brings the partner back to his desire'].[74] Moreover, the existence in language, as name for instance, lifts the other out of the flux of experience and bestows upon her a certain duration; symbolic existence is the 'seule vie qui perdure et qui soit véritable, puisqu'elle se transmet sans se perdre dans la tradition perpétuée de sujet à sujet' ['the only life that endures and is true, since it is transmitted without being lost in the perpetuated tradition of subject to subject'].[75]

By the mid-sixties, this optimistic view of the force of the language game had been overshadowed by the darker implications of the *fort/da*. Lacan had shifted the emphasis in his interpretation of the notion of linguistic mediation from the capacity to bring the other back to the impossibility of ever doing

---

[73] *Hegel, Aesthetics*, pp. 417–18.   [74] *Ecrits*, p. 319; *Ecrits* Eng., p. 104.
[75] Ibid., p. 319; ibid., p. 104.

so completely, from the opening of the channel of communication to its obstruction. If any response of the other must now be transmitted through language, the subject's only contact will be with the barrier of the symbol that seems to separate them, a circumstance Lacan will refer to as the non-presence of the Other. By calling to the other in language, the child reinforces its own isolation instead of remedying it. Furthermore, in trying to overcome the dependency on the other, in trying to control the other's presences and absences, the subject submits himself to a new form of subjection, dependency on the response of the other for recognition of the subject's desire. Thus the original desire, to escape solitude, to bring back the mother, has become eternalized in a game the player cannot win, has become eternalized precisely because the player cannot win the game.

Since the presence of the Other is needed to guarantee the wholeness of the self, the linguistic barrier also undermines the presence and mastery of the subject. In *Concepts*, the spool represents loss in the form of what Lacan's latest theory called the a-object, 'c'est un petit quelque-chose du sujet qui se détache tout en étant encore bien à lui, encore retenu' ['a small part of the subject that detaches itself from him while still remaining his, still retained'].[76] He now condemns as 'idiotic' the idea that the oppositional function of the phonemes in the *fort/da* allows the subject to attain mastery. On the contrary, 'dans les deux phonèmes, s'incarnent les mécanismes proprement de l'aliénation' ['in the two phonemes are embodied the very mechanisms of alienation'].[77] No subject can master, can grasp the 'radical articulation' of the *fort/da*, for, in coming to speak, the subject is spoken from the field of the Other, locus of the signifiers. The subject passes from the state of pre-linguistic non-existence (*fort*), in which he obviously has no mastery, no control, no choice as to his action, to the alienated state of reified meaning (again *fort!*), in which he is 'free' only to let himself be defined by the terms of the Other's signifying system. It is the hole or lack introduced by this 'radical vacillation of the subject' that the child's game allows him to represent.

This vacillation is the Lacanian *vel*, the forced choice between being and meaning that ushers the subject into language.

---

[76] *Concepts*, p. 60; *Concepts* Eng., p. 62.   [77] Ibid., p. 216; ibid., p. 239.

Nous choisissons l'être, le sujet disparaît, il nous échappe, il tombe dans le non-sens – nous choisissons le sens, et le sens ne subsiste qu'écorné de cette partie de non-sens qui est ... ce qui constitue, dans la réalisation du sujet, l'inconscient ... ce sens ... [est] éclipsé par la disparition de l'être, induite par la fonction même du signifiant.

If we choose being, the subject disappears, it eludes us, it falls into non-meaning. If we choose meaning, the meaning survives only deprived of that part of non-meaning that is ... that which constitutes in the realization of the subject, the unconscious ... this meaning [is] ... eclipsed by the disappearance of being, induced by the very function of the signifier.[78]

The implication of the last sentence quoted is that the limited share of freedom available to the subject is somehow contained in the non-meaning of the unconscious. It is this margin of freedom that is to be recovered in the operation Lacan now dubs 'separation' (see chapter 5 for an analysis of this concept). Whereas the earlier version of the theory stressed the liberating effects of replacing the subject's embedding in a situation (what Richards called the 'causal context') with his involvement in the new relations made possible by language (Richards' 'literary context'), the later version plays up the subject's oscillation between the subjective death of pre-linguistic embedding and his equally deadly subjection to the rules of the linguistic system.

Although the relation between meaning and freedom has apparently shifted from one version to the other, the function of the signifying cut as the symbolization of absence persists. Between the time of 'Function and Field' and that of *Concepts*, Lacan's new formulations of the *fort/da* permit a more fully developed and specific response to Richards' question. The spool no longer represents the object, the mother insofar as she has been forfeited through weaning; now it stands for that part of the self which has been lost and has not yet been symbolized. This lacking part of the subject forms the nucleus, as it were, of the 'object', which would satisfy the subject, making it whole and happy. By itself, however, the spool could only represent something for someone as a *sign*, in a relation of three terms – the spool, what it designates (the missing part), and the person for whom the sign functions as such (the child). Starting with the 'Introduction' to 'The "Purloined Letter" Seminar' (1955), Lacan

[78] Ibid., p. 192; ibid., p. 211.

insists that, in order for the spool to become a signifier in a game embodying the pure opposition of presence and absence, a minimum of four elements must operate together, in synchrony. In 'Les formations de l'inconscient', he lists these as the two words, or phonemes, the speaker and the addressee.[79] In the *fort/da* game these would correspond respectively to the *fort*, or /o/, the *da*, or /a/, the child who pro-vokes, and the spool to which he calls.

This is the second component of Lacan's response to Richards' problem. Meaning is a relation, as Richards states, but in order for 'things to be instances of laws', one must go beyond the tripartite organization of the sign to the 'quadratic relation' of symbolization.[80] Curiously enough, however, Lacan is no more certain of the specific nature of that relation than Richards is of the means of representing absence. In *Ethique*, Lacan makes a vague gesture in the direction of Heidegger's *Geviert*, whereas in the 'Seminar on "The Purloined Letter"' he groups together the letter plus the three 'characters', or subjective positions – the king, the queen and the minister. The 'Introduction' to the latter article juxtaposes four terms in what are known as Markov chains, which Lacan invokes to demonstrate the existence of symbolic laws prior to any reality (Richards' 'theorem'), and his own L-schema in which the signifying chain moves among four poles – the unconscious subject (s), the Other (A), the ego (a) and the imaginary other (a').[81] To these we might add the four terms of the Aristotelian ratio for metaphor, since Lacan states that the child's relation to the mother's body involves not two but four terms governed by 'l'activité métaphorique de substitution signifiante, ressort de tout progrès symbolique' [the metaphoric activity of signifying substitution [which is] the mainspring of all symbolic progress].[82] And there are the four discourses Lacan introduced in the late sixties – of the master (philosophy), the hysteric (science), the analyst and the university (knowledge for

---

[79] *Formations*, vol. 12, nos. 2–3, p. 188.   [80] *Ecrits*, p. 48.

[81] *Ecrits*, p. 53. See chapter 9 of Allouch's *Lettre pour lettre* for an illuminating discussion of the significance of this mathematical analysis to an understanding of the psychoanalytic process, especially of the relation of the Markov chains to the L-schema and to transference. I will return to this topic in my discussion of interpretation and historicity in chapter 6.

[82] 'Le désir et son interprétation', 13.6, p. 334.

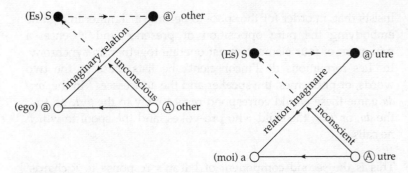

its own sake), each of which has four letters – s1 (the master signifier), s2 (knowledge), a (surplus enjoyment), $/$ (the divided subject) – and four places –

Speaker	Listener
agent $\longrightarrow$	other
truth	production[83]

Roudinesco has shown that Lacan first made use of a quadripartite system when, in 'Le mythe individuel du névrosé', he applied one of Lévi-Strauss's kinship laws to the development of a neurosis from generation to generation in the family of Freud's 'Rat man', and to that of Goethe in *Dichtung und Wahrheit*.[84] The four elements of the system in this case were the paternal function, the ego, the subject and the experience of death. The idea that symbolization in general requires four terms, however, is to be found in the constructivist theories of E. Cassirer and his pupil S. Langer, which straddle the British and the continental philosophical traditions.[85] Langer's *Philosophy in a New Key* presents a theory of signification which precisely differentiates

---

[83] Lacan discusses the four discourses in his seminar, *L'envers de la psychanalyse 1969–1970*, esp. pp. 31–42, and p. 196. See chapter 2 of Bracher's *Lacan, Discourse, and Social Change* for a valuable summary of their significance.

[84] Roudinesco, *Esquisse d'une vie*, pp. 284–5.

[85] Henri Delacroix refers to Cassirer's *Philosophie der symbolischen Formen* repeatedly in the 1930 edition of *Le langage et la pensée*, to which Lacan referred in his 1931 article, 'Folies simultanées'. Ogden and Richards also refer to the Cassirer in their *Meaning of Meaning* (p. 44), a book with which Lacan was presumably acquainted, since he criticizes it in 'Agency' (*Ecrits* Eng., p. 150). Although I have not yet found concrete testimony to that effect, it seems more than likely that Lévi-Strauss would have had contact with Langer's thought while in the United States during the second World War, via Jakobson and through their contacts in psychoanalytic circles in New York and Boston.

the three-term sign characteristic of animal intelligence from the four-term symbol essential to human thought. What makes this common insistence on the same criterion of symbolization appear to be more than coincidence is the fact that for Langer as for Lacan it forms part of a general theory of signification which expressly relates philosophy, symbolic logic and psychoanalysis by means of the principle of metaphor.

Langer draws primarily on the work of Whitehead (to whom the book is dedicated) and Russell as well as that of Cassirer in formulating her theory of the four terms necessary to the symbol.

In an ordinary sign-function, there are three essential terms: subject, sign, and object. In denotation, which is the simplest kind of symbol-function, there have to be four: subject, symbol, conception and object.[86]

Of course Lacan does not retain the same four terms. For one thing, the conception (his signified) and the object are one and the same in the Hegelian perspective. For another, Langer's formula omits the pure difference of opposition so important to Lacan. For a third, he introduces the function of the addressee into the relation. But Langer does not claim that all symbols utilize just these four elements; nor does Lacan settle on one particular set. On the contrary, his specification of the four terms involved in symbolization floats considerably; they remain neither fixed nor consistent in the different variations he propounds. The only aspect of his theory which does stay fixed and consistent is precisely the general rule enunciated by Langer, that there must be a minimum of four terms in any symbolic relation.

The new key of Langer's title is the concept of symbolization which makes it possible to consider symbolic logic and psycho-analysis as two aspects of the same phenomenon.

One conception of symbolism leads to logic ... [the] theory of knowledge ... science ... The other takes us in the opposite direction – to psychiatry, the study of emotions, religion, fantasy, and everything but knowledge.

---

[86] Langer, *Philosophy in a New Key*, p. 52. Langer's description seems to be an extension of the 'triangle of reference' Ogden and Richards sketch out in *The Meaning of Meaning* (p. 11) to include the subject along with their symbol, thought and referent. They object to the term denotation, which probably comes to Langer via Russell and Whitehead, but they do treat the subject, in the roles of listener and speaker, at some length, although as an entity separate from the symbol-function. Lacan, by the way, does not use the term 'referent' until much later, e.g. in the passage from *Encore* to the effect that the important thing is that the signified misses the referent (p. 23).

Yet in both we have a central theme: the *human response,* as a constructive, not a passive thing. Epistemologists and psychologists agree that symbolization is the key to that constructive process.[87]

Symbolization, the transformation of experience into symbols, is a primary human need. Since symbolism is the material of all thought, the mind must have a tendency to produce new symbols constantly, even when asleep: 'the brain is following its own law; it is actively translating experiences into symbols, in fulfillment of a basic need to do so. It carries on a constant process of ideation'.[88] Dream, ritual and superstitious fancy are all 'primitive' forms of symbolistic thinking. And 'the great contribution of Freud to the philosophy of mind has been the realization that human behavior [such as ritual] is not only a food-getting strategy, but is also a language'.[89] Langer is able to assimilate the psychoanalytic concept of these 'lower' forms of thinking into the mainstream of thought about language because she has adopted Cassirer's fundamental insight that 'symbolization is pre-rationative, but not pre-rational'.[90] Both the 'lower' and the 'higher' forms of intellection function according to the same principle, although in different ways.

Like Richards and so many others, she emphasizes the capacity of symbols to represent absent objects, but unlike Richards she also stresses their power of retaining messages rather than merely transmitting them. Borrowing the image of the telephone exchange from L. Troland (*The Mystery of the Mind*), she characterizes this force as the ability whereby messages may be relayed, stored up, answered by proxy, *'noted down and kept'*.[91] This last expression is synonymous with the one that Lacan uses in *Psychoses* to pinpoint his notion of the 'isolation of the signifier as such': 'Il y a usage propre du signifiant à partir du moment où ... au point d'arrivée du message, on prend acte du message' ['There is appropriate use of [proper, specific to] the signifier whenever ... at the message's point of arrival one makes a note of it.'][92] This process of 'writing down', as he phrases it a few lines later, or inscription, is the starting-point of the order of the signifier as distinct from that of the signified, in that one need not understand

---

[87] *New Key*, p. 19.   [88] Ibid., p. 33.   [89] Ibid., p. 41.   [90] Ibid., p. 33.
[91] Ibid., p. 24; L. Troland, *The Mystery of the Mind* (New York: D. Van Nostrand, 1926).
[92] *Psychoses*, p. 213; *Psychoses* Eng., p. 188; my translation in inner brackets.

the message in order to take note of it. Underlying this inscription, which is produced during the subject's history and duplicates all her acts, is what Lacan calls the 'permanent discourse', a running commentary on one's life that corresponds to the process of continuous ideation Langer describes.

Langer makes a similar move in her discussion of verbal symbols. Conceptualization rather than communication being the primary linguistic function, it follows that the best materials for the formation of symbols should be perceptions that have no practical significance, no use-value, no direct tie to wants and needs. 'The more barren and indifferent the symbol, the greater is its semantic power.'[93] The more purposeless they are, the less natural significance they possess, the better they will be suited to annexing the conventional meanings of language. Hence the importance of sounds, 'interesting little phonetic items that can acquire conventional meanings because they carry no natural messages'.[94] From this anti-utilitarian stance, which takes meaninglessness as the criterion for symbols, to Lacan's theory of the metonymic detachment and metaphoric reattachment of meaning, is only a short step.

For Langer it is the human tendency to play with inherently meaningless sounds, combined with that of grouping perceptions in 'dreamlike associations of ideas', which produce the conditions necessary for the advent of language. Because 'an articulate sound is an entirely *unattached item* ... it is the readiest thing in the world to become a symbol when a symbol is wanted'.[95] Thus it can easily become linked to any emotionally charged object experienced by a child: 'the next deeply interesting experience that coincides with hearing or uttering the vocable, becomes fixed by association with that one already distinct item'.[96] At this point the sound would operate as a sign, in a three-sided relation. In

---

[93] Langer, *New Key*, p. 61. Langer's emphasis on conceptualization over communication, which was to play such a leading role in structuralism, follows a long tradition that goes back to Humboldt, e.g. in *Über die Verschiedenheit des menschlichen Sprachbaues*.

[94] *New Key*, p. 96.   [95] Ibid., pp. 101–2.

[96] Ibid., p. 102. Lacan uses a similar vocabulary when specifying the four elements required for the process of symbolization in his seminar on unconscious formations, in a passage to which we have already referred several times. He speaks of the two *vocables*, and of the image already in a symbolic relation, as is attested by the game of presence and absence tied to distinct [*discrets*] signifying elements ('Formations', p. 188).

order to reach the level of a symbol, a fourth term must be added, the objective denotation whereby the object of the child's experience can be shared with others. And 'denotation is the essence of language, because it frees the symbol from its original instinctive utterance and marks its deliberate *use*, outside of the total situation that gave it birth'.[97]

According to Langer, it is none other than metaphor which makes this passage from sign to symbolic naming and conception possible.

The use of metaphor can hardly be called a conscious device. It is the power whereby new words are born ...

If ritual is the cradle of language, metaphor is the law of its life. It is the force that makes it essentially *relational*, intellectual, forever showing up new, abstractable *forms* in reality, forever laying down a deposit of old, abstracted concepts in an increasing treasure of general words.[98]

In her theory of metaphor, adopted from P. Wegener's *Untersuchungen über die Grundfragen des Sprachlebens*, the essence of symbolic transformation is catachresis.[99] It will be recalled that Aristotle describes one category of metaphor in which analogy is used to designate a thing which has no name of its own. His example in *Poetics* 1457b is the action of the sun in casting forth its flame. The word 'leg' in English, when applied to a piece of furniture, is such a catachresis.

Metaphor is the basic principle of linguistic development because it allows the conceptualization of new experiences, ones not heretofore named, by means of analogy with meanings already fixed onto words.

Where a precise word is lacking to designate the novelty which the speaker would like to point out, he resorts to the powers of *logical analogy*, and uses a word denoting something else that is a presentational symbol for the thing he means ...

In a genuine metaphor, an image of the literal meaning is our symbol for the figurative meaning, the thing that has no name of its own. If we say that a brook is laughing in the sun ...[100]

---

[97] Langer, *New Key*, p. 108.   [98] Ibid., p. 115.

[99] I should point out that neither Langer nor Wegener explicitly uses the word catachresis.

[100] Langer, *New Key*, p. 113; italic added. There is a remarkable resemblance between Langer's example and the one that Lacan uses both in *Psychoses* (p. 257) and 'Agency' (*Ecrits* Eng., p. 158): 'Love is a pebble laughing in the sun.' Langer also offers an excursus on the cross similar to Lacan's curtain and

Language evolves by a process of accretion and metaphoric generalization. After a word has accumulated several analogic applications, one can discover what they all have in common. This is the general meaning, or concept, which is thus free from any particular situation. Once the denotation has been fixed through constant figurative use, the word becomes what Wegener calls a 'faded metaphor'. Since the meaning of a word can be determined only in relation to the context in which it is used, a new, metaphorical usage must be a 'novel predication' occurring within an utterance whose other terms are used in their now literal, 'faded', sense.

All words, therefore, which may be logical subjects (of predications) ... have acquired this capacity only by virtue of their 'fading' in predicational use ... So the process of fading ... represents the bridge from the first ... phase of language to the developed phase of a discursive exposition.[101]

If catachresis is the foundation of Langer's theory, the 'presentational symbol', or image, is its capstone. Like Richards, she asserts that our mental images have the same characteristics as our symbols: they are not copies of experience but have 'been "projected" ... into a new dimension', acquiring a stability, unity and identity which allows us to call them up 'freely', that is, independently of the natural (or social) reality in which we find ourselves and of the practical needs that bind us to that situation.[102] In short, they have the capacity to 'mean things', giving us the power to conceptualize, remember and relate to things *in absentia*. 'But the best guarantee of the symbolic function of images [such as that of a rose, or of fire] is their tendency to become metaphorical.' Langer concludes that 'images are, there-

---

tree passages but which antedates them both (*New Key*, pp. 231–2). All three in fact imitate Richards' description of the many uses accumulated by the word 'book' (*Philosophy of Rhetoric*, p. 74). No doubt there are other models I have not discovered; the point I wish to stress is that none of them are the least bit mysterious, fraudulent or magically 'symbolist'. All support the argument that poetic power is an extension of the power inherent in language, not a bizarre or decorative deviation from it.

[101] Cited in Langer, *New Key*, p. 114. This idea seems to be derived from the notion that language is a 'faded mythology', found in Herder's *Über den Ursprung der Sprache* and Schelling's 'Einleitung in die Philosophie der Mythologie'.

[102] Ibid., p. 117.

fore, our readiest instruments for abstracting concepts from the tumbling stream of actual impressions'.[103]

Like words, images can enter into concatenations. The latter, which we call stories or fantasies, represent the features we abstract from temporal processes, happenings which never recur in exactly the same way twice. In short, fantasies form the basis of laws for events, the way predication does for things. Consequently, fantasies also have the capacity to be used metaphorically, as catachreses for the innumerable new experiences that constantly threaten to overwhelm us. For example, 'an arriving train may have to embody nameless and imageless dangers coming with a rush'. Langer finds the ultimate proof of this contention in 'the fact that the lowest, completely unintentional products of the human brain are madly metaphorical fantasies ... I mean the riotous symbolism of dreams'.[104]

In dreams, as in infancy and 'primitive' thought, the images derived from the sense impressions of those things – food, breast, etc. – that fulfil one's needs are used to symbolize the experience of being alive, especially the unknown powers that control the satisfaction of needs and thus sustain life. They 'have to serve for the whole gamut of [one's] desires, for all things absent'. In dreams, as in all 'primitive' presentations, however, the mind has not yet become capable of differentiating a literal, conceptual meaning from a metaphorical sense, of 'distinguish[ing] the figure from its meaning'. That is why the symbols themselves, bereft of any meaning and thus not yet true symbols as far as the dreamer can tell, 'seem to command our emotions'. The *sacra*, or holy articles of early civilizations, function in an analogous way and serve a similar purpose. 'The study of dreams gives us a clue to the deeper meaning of these bizarre holy articles; they are phallic symbols, and death-symbols.' The gods are 'emblems of the creative power', but this power resides in fact in mankind. It is the 'power of conception – of "having ideas"'. 'The practical efficacy attributed to sacra is a dream-metaphor for the might of human ideation.'[105]

---

[103] Ibid.   [104] Ibid., pp. 119–20.

[105] Ibid., pp. 120–3. The link between phallic symbols, the unconscious, the sustenance of life and the genitals is of course an ancient one, as the following passage from Schopenhauer indicates: 'The genitals are properly the focus of will, and consequently the opposite pole of the brain ... The former are the life-sustaining principle ensuring endless life to time. In this respect they were

The logic and the terminology of this argument help to illuminate some of the darker recesses of Lacan's teachings. The capacity of symbols, as opposed to signs, to relay messages becomes the power of retransmission, which Lacan uses to distinguish human language from that of the bees in 'Function and Field'. The 'new dimension' in which the image acquires the function of a presentational symbol corresponds to that 'other scene' which Freud adopted from Fechner, and which Lacan took to indicate the symbolic dimension of the unconscious. The fading subject Lacan describes in *Concepts*, like Wegener's, is one that has become literalized, reified, petrified, reduced to being nothing more than a signifier. While most theories of rhetoric envisage a process of 'dying' or 'falling asleep' whereby through time and over-use metaphors lose the novelty, intensity or expressivity associated with their figurative status, Wegener's notion of fading highlights the simultaneity of the formation of the concept and the loss of mobility. Lacan's use of the term 'fading' therefore accentuates the contrast between the reified subject of the concept and the open-ended subject of metaphor.

The Langer–Wegener theory throws the most light, however, on Lacan's explanation of the phallus as metaphoric signifier. The ambiguous word 'conception' serves as one of the links that join the share of the logos – Langer's conception as symbolization, 'having ideas' – to the advent of desire – conception as the unknowable power of life.[106] Uniting the two thus means recognizing that this unknown is precisely the creative power of a purely negative trans-individual and trans-biological subjectivity, the 'nucleus of our being'. The attempt to symbolize this nameless, because unnameable, thing, initiates a kind of originary catachresis. If repression is the 'lacking word', as Lacan claims in *Papers* (see previous chapter), and if metaphor intervenes when 'the precise word is lacking', as Langer–Wegener maintain, then

worshipped by the Greeks in the *phallus*, and by the Hindus in the *lingam*, which are thus the symbol of the assertion of the will' (*World as Will and Idea*, p. 426).

[106] Jung makes a similar connection in his article, 'Psychological Aspects of the Mother Archetype', first published in German in 1938, in English in 1943: 'There is no consciousness without discrimination of opposites. This is the paternal principle, the logos, which eternally struggles to extricate itself from the primal warmth and primal darkness of the maternal unconsciousness' (p. 125).

this first symbolization of and by the phallus (conception) must constitute the primal repression (*Urverdrängung*). As a presentational symbol, the image of the phallus has not yet separated from its meaning; it remains a signifier without a signified. It is the very action of 'noting down', of recognizing it as such that gives the phallus a meaning; thus it becomes the bar, separating the two sides of the sign from each other in a self-referential movement of conception.[107]

Quelque chose est signifiant … pour autant que quelque chose qui constitue un tout, le signe, est là justement pour ne signifier rien. C'est là que commence l'ordre du signifiant en tant qu'il se distingue de l'ordre de la signification.

It's to the extent that something constituting a whole, the sign, exists and signifies precisely nothing. That is where the order of the signifier, insofar as it differs from the order of meaning, begins.[108]

The phallus is first of all the catachretic signifier without a signified; then it comes to signify its own status as signifier without a signified. Like Richards, Lacan has a bounce-off theory of metaphor which nevertheless avoids the pitfall of deviation theories, since it is not based on a literal or proper meaning. It differs from Richards' view, however, in that it starts not from a causal context or situation as presences but from the very lack of meaning. At the same time, it escapes from the spiritualist idea that metaphor involves a transfer from 'the sensuous to the spiritual sphere'.

Conceptually, the constituents of this process may be divided into three levels involving the four minimal terms of any relation: the basic lack, or nameless thing; the catachresis that names it; the metaphor that designates the catachresis and thereby institutes the level of the literal, of the concept. If we adopt the notational convention for the sign Lacan takes from Saussure,

$\underline{S}$ (Signifier)
s (signified)

---

[107] In an important article on the relation of narcissism and signification in Lacan, Chase has teased out the catachretic function of the identification with the phallus via her reading of de Man, Kristeva and Hegel ('Butcher's Wife', pp. 1004, 1009).

[108] *Psychoses*, p. 213; *Psychoses* Eng., p. 189. In later versions, this meaningless signifier will be the empty, or null set of Russell and Whitehead's set theoretical foundation of numbers.

and call the image of the phallus P and the unknown signification x, then the first catachresis can be written as

$$\frac{P}{x}$$

Letting the newly created symbol be S_n, the entire relation becomes

$$\frac{S_n}{P} \quad \frac{P}{x}$$

which is homologous to the algorithm for metaphor Lacan writes in 'On the Possible Treatment of Psychosis':[109]

$$\frac{S}{\mathcal{B}'} \cdot \frac{\mathcal{B}}{x}$$

This process, which launches the subject into language, can be called either metaphorical, since it involves two layers of substitution, or metonymic, since it requires a first-level of non-meaning.[110] Regardless of the name assigned, the crux of Lacan's argument is that the signifying cut must precede the slippage of meaning, for without this first catachresis there would be no meaning to slip. Without the belief, or rather the illusion, that there is something behind the signifying chain, there would be no point in moving from one signifier to the other.

Written according to this algorithm, the paternal metaphor becomes:

$$\frac{\text{Nom-du-Père}}{\text{Désir de la Mère}} \cdot \frac{\text{Désir de la Mère}}{\text{Signifié au sujet}} \rightarrow \text{Nom-du-Père} \left(\frac{A}{\text{Phallus}} \right)$$

$$\frac{\text{Name-of-the-Father}}{\text{Desire of the Mother}} \cdot \frac{\text{Desire of the Mother}}{\text{Signified to the subject}} \rightarrow$$
$$\text{Name-of-the-Father} \left(\frac{O}{\text{Phallus}} \right)[111]$$

The basic sense of this formula is that the induction of the phallus in the

---

[109] *Ecrits*, p. 557; *Ecrits* Eng., p. 200.

[110] As we shall see in chapter 6, Miller argues that both statements are true, that each precedes the other in what is basically a circular, although non-reciprocal, movement ('Suture', p. 34). Hence the perfectly reasonable disagreements among knowledgeable commentators.

[111] *Ecrits*, p. 557; *Ecrits* Eng., p. 200.

Other $\left(\dfrac{O}{\text{phallus}}\right)$

provides a tenable resolution to the Oedipal situation. Armed with our understanding of the catachretic function of Lacanian metaphor, we are now in a position to explain how and why it should be metaphoric substitution which leads to this induction effect. Like Freud before him, Lacan assumes that, when the child of either sex becomes aware of itself as an entity separate from its mother, it supposes that it and the mother together originally had formed a single unit, complete and entire unto itself. The child thus identifies with that which would complete the mother. The trauma occurs when s/he realizes that the mother desires, and hence lacks, something other than him or her.[112] The child now desires the mother, but in order to fulfil this desire he wishes to be the 'desire of the mother', i.e. what the mother desires. He therefore tries to figure out what the meaning is of what she says and does to indicate her desire. The 'Desire of the mother' is thus a set of signifiers, but their meaning, the 'Signified to the subject', remains an enigma to the child. At this point, the child is basically a slave to mother's signifiers: to imagine that she is definitively lacking is to risk his own death, since he identifies with her lack. He therefore must be ready to do anything at all in order to guarantee her wholeness. In terms of signification, the child will seek its being all along the endless rails of the metonymic chain, ceaselessly looking for the missing meaning.

This missing signified of the desire of the mother, which Lacan would later call the unknown *jouissance* of the mother, thus plays the role of the 'nameless thing or experience' of which Langer speaks. As Miller insists, the secret of the paternal metaphor is that it 'is not the substitution of one signifier for another, but the substitution of a signifier for something which is not a signifier'.[113] The two expressions on the left side of the arrow in the algorithm inscribe this iterative substitution as a relation between four terms: a, the Name-of-the-Father, is to b, the Desire of the Mother, as c, the Desire of the Mother, is to d, the Signified to the subject. But, and this is the crucial point, the fourth term remains indeterminate, an x, not a d. In 'The Metaphor of the Subject'

---

[112] Pommier, *L'exception féminine*, pp. 26–7.
[113] Miller, 'To Interpret the Cause', p. 46.

(1961), Lacan accepts the Aristotelian view that metaphor consists of a relation among four terms, but as usual he gives his precedent a peculiar twist, in this case emphasizing that there is a fundamental difference between the first three terms, which are signifiers, and the fourth one, which is a signified.[114] Whereas the first three are well defined – old age, evening and life, in Aristotle's example – the fourth one cannot be pinned down to a single, determinate, term, but can take on a whole range of values. There is no way to limit the fourth term to the calm that falls at the end of the day. The signified of the evening might be beauty, coolness, brightness, violence, blood, despair and so on, rather than tranquillity.

It is Kant's discussion of the 'analogies of experience' in *The Critique of Pure Reason* which furnishes the model for this adaptation of the Aristotelian schema. Kant distinguishes between mathematical, or quantitative, analogies, and those he calls 'philosophical', or qualitative. In the former, when a, b and c are given, then d is completely determined by the analogy. If you start with '3 is to 4 as 6 is to what', the only answer is '8'. The mathematical principle is constitutive. On the other hand, a philosophical analogy is only regulative. When a series of real events is involved rather than mathematical entities, the elements are heterogeneous, beyond our control. Here if you have a given relation between two events, e.g. the one caused the other, knowing the third term does not allow you to specify what the fourth will be, i.e. what the specific effect of the third term as cause will be. The regulative analogy only allows you to infer the relation of the third term to the fourth, in this case that of causality. 'The relation yields, however, a rule for seeking the fourth member in experience, and a mark whereby it can be detected.'[115] If you know how the principle of causality functions in general, then you will know how a specific effect is related to a particular cause. In sum, this type of analogy only indicates to us the type of relation that exists between the given and the unknown terms (c and d, or rather x). Such rules make it possible to anticipate the rule or law according to which the sequence of phenomena will occur, but without actually determining in advance what will happen.[116]

---

[114] *Ecrits*, p. 889–900; 'Metaphor of the Subject', p. 11.
[115] Kant, *Critique of Pure Reason*, p. 211.   [116] Ibid., pp. 208–12.

That is why, in addition to the four terms of the 'analogy', Lacan's formulae for metaphor include a second set of terms to the right of the congruence sign, or the arrow. This latter indicates the rule or law inferable from the metaphoric relation, without specifying a particular signified. We can now describe the entire process. The signifier of the father in his role as prohibitor of incest – the Name-of-the-Father – replaces the signifier of the mother as object of the child's desire in the chain of signifiers that constitute the child's being. More specifically, it invokes a law to replace the signifier of the desire of the mother, whose signified had remained an enigma to the child, which is why the 'Signified to the subject' occupies the place of the x in our formula for the originary catachresis. The result of the substitution is to supply a new signifying expression on the right side of the arrow, namely the phallus, which can now serve, in Hamlet's words, to give a 'name and local habitation' to the enigmatic meaning of the mother's desire. There is now a rule which allows the subject to anticipate the appearance of the signifier of his or her desire.

What the subject is looking for is a guarantee that the chain of signifiers which constitute its being have an end, and therefore a sense; in short, a God-term. In fact, there can be no such signifier, precisely because the signifier gets its value from its opposition to all the others in the set. It must remain an unnameable symbol, because to name it is to introduce it into the set of signifiers dependent on each other, and thus to cancel it as guarantee of the system.[117] But you can name the absence of this signifier, and the phallus, which Lacan designates by capital phi (Φ), symbolizes this signifier missing from the set that he calls the Other. In Lacan's now famous phrase, it becomes the signifier of the point where the signifier is lacking.[118] The phallus (Big Phi) can become an actual signifier, because, in addition to acting as the sign of desire to someone, in the human world it also acts as the sign of someone, of the subject's 'real presence' beyond all processes of signification, thus making the subject into a signifier.[119] As the guarantor of a 'real presence' reminiscent of theology, this capital phi does indeed occupy a transcendental position, as Derrida maintains. But insofar as it is in fact impossible, and thus non-existent, its status is at best paradoxical.

---

[117] *Le transfert*, p. 277; see also *Ecrits* Eng., pp. 316–17.
[118] *Le transfert*, p. 273.   [119] Ibid., pp. 306–7.

In a sense, this desired real presence beyond representation is the nameless x that the catachresis of the paternal metaphor is designed to make accessible. But since that is impossible, the subject has recourse to the realm of representation in order to localize his desire in an object. It is only in order to evade the perception that the sole valid response to its question, 'What am I?' is 'Let yourself be', that the subject tries to give the object of its desire some solidity by forming a fantasy based on what Lacan calls the small phi (more precisely, minus small phi), that is, the representation of the penis, the imaginary phallus.[120]

Le rapport innommé, parce que innommable, parce que indicible, du sujet avec le signifiant pur du désir se projette sur l'organe localisable, précis, situable quelque part dans l'ensemble de l'édifice corporel. D'où ce conflit proprement imaginaire, qui consiste à se voir soi-même comme privé, ou non privé, de cet appendice.

The unnamed, because unnameable, because ineffable, relation of the subject to the pure signifier of desire is projected onto the localizable, specific organ that can be situated somewhere in the totality of the corporeal edifice. Whence the strictly imaginary conflict, which consists in seeing oneself as deprived, or not deprived, of that appendage.[121]

As a symbol, the phallus is separable from the body. To the extent that the subject is willing to part with that symbol, to look for it in the Other, he can superimpose it onto that which is lacking in the Other, namely the meaning of desire. Thus the imaginary phallus (minus little phi) comes to symbolize what is lacking in the (m)Other, the mystery of (her) desire.[122] It is this term which constitutes the x of the paternal metaphor.

But if the phallus thus acts as a barrier to metonymic sliding, it does not do so by fixing meaning per se. On the contrary, in the section of *Papers* where he takes up the creative function of speech, Lacan argues that metaphor cannot be controlled by the function of comparison precisely because it is impossible to contain the meaning of the metaphor in a single term, even if that is what the speaker 'wanted to say'. 'La première émergence à l'être du rapport métaphorique ... implique tout ce qui peut s'y attacher par la suite, et que je ne croyais pas avoir dit' ['The original emergence of the metaphorical relation to being [which is equivalent to that "Let yourself be" cited above] ... implies

---

[120] Ibid., pp. 278ff.   [121] Ibid., p. 287.   [122] Ibid., pp. 259–60.

everything which will come to be linked with it in the future, and which I do not believe to have said'].[123] For this reason a new metaphor, whether it be new for an individual, a group, or an entire language, opens up that host of new meanings, which Lacan indicates by the (+)s in his formula for metaphor in 'Agency'. Localizing the x of the signified in a signifier is not the same as simply assigning it a particular meaning. Otherwise, the whole process of metaphor would be superfluous. The latter implies that there is no foundation on which to base the truth of one's being, and that in itself is a kind of truth; namely the paradoxical truth that the truth of meaning is built upon something meaningless, or better, on the (mis-)recognition of the lack of meaning.

The 'Introduction' to the 'Seminar on "The Purloined Letter"'' and the lecture on 'Psychoanalysis and Cybernetics', reprinted in *The Ego in Freud's Theory*, take up the same problem of the emergence of sense from non-sense from the perspective of the mathematical analysis of chance occurrences. Randomness is synonymous with lack of meaning in that it represents the absence of any rule, regularity or law. Lacan refers to Markov chains in order to show that any sequence of purely random events, or symbols, will assume a certain regularity provided the elements of the sequence be regrouped in sets of three or four. In other words, if a second set of elements is formed consisting of groups of the original, randomly arranged, elements, then the succession of the new set's elements will no longer be meaningless. An order will have been established.

Now the procedure which institutes this law is entirely homologous to that of metaphor, in that in each case new elements are formed as symbols of symbols.[124] Each element of the second set stands for a group of elements from the first, just as the metaphor stands for the interaction of vehicle and tenor. Both mathematical symbolism and verbal metaphor are metalanguages in this sense.[125] Likewise, as with the metaphoric law, the syntactic order will arise only through the attempt to discover some sort of

---

[123] *Ecrits techniques*, p. 262; *Papers*, p. 238.

[124] Cf. Ogden and Richards, *The Meaning of Meaning*, pp. 88, 213.

[125] *Psychoses*, p. 258. Indeed, Miller argues that at this time Lacan did believe that the Law played the role of the Other of the Other – that is, of a guarantee of alterity – so that his later rejection of the notion of metalanguage was in fact a criticism of his own earlier position ('Extimité', p. 78).

meaning in the random sequence of symbols which confront the subject. The latter must be operative at least in its most reduced form, as the subjective function which Lacan calls 'pure anticipation', by which he means the disinterested expectation that something will or will not happen, beyond any consideration of use or interest to the subject.[126] Focussing on a series of outcomes, rather than on just one, is the equivalent of grouping the results together to form the set ordered according to a syntax. It is this focussing, or punctuating, that Lacan would later call 'reading'.

Where deconstruction tries to eliminate the subject entirely, or to make it into an unendable sequence, and positivism can only account for its role in recognizing similarities among presences, Lacan's various algorithms for metaphor represent the production of meaning out of non-sense by means of anticipation and retrospective punctuation of the signifiers that constitute the unconscious self. As explained above, this reading entails the institution of a relation, whose expression requires at the least four terms involved in the process that simultaneously institutes linguistic meaning and the reading of the self, and these terms arise from the reflexive application of the (catachretic) sign to itself. In mathematical symbolism as in verbal metaphor, the relation is formed by the process of composition (iteration) in which the signifier of a first sign becomes the signified of the second.[127]

Unlike classical theories of reflexivity, however, this bending back onto oneself does not create a state of self-consciousness, since it is produced solely by the action of a set of symbols upon

---

[126] *Ego*, p. 305.

[127] The analogy between the verbal and the mathematical processes can be seen in the basically catachretic theory of the proper establishment of mathematical concepts formulated by Georg Cantor, the inventor of the modern mathematics of infinite sets:

> We posit a thing without properties, which is at first nothing else than a name or a sign A, and give it in order different, even infinitely many, predicates, whose meaning for ideas already present is known, and which may not contradict one another. By this the relations of A to the conceptions already present, and in particular to the allied ones, are determined; when we have completed this, all the conditions for the awakening of the conception A, which slumbers in us, are present, and it enters completed into 'existence' in the first [mathematical] sense; to prove its 'existence' in the second sense [in physical reality] is then a matter of metaphysics [science].

> (*Grundlagen*, pp. 45–6; translation by P. Jourdain, *Contributions*, p. 67.)

97

itself. The subject is first of all an 'it', an impersonal combination of symbols: 'He is ... constituted by relations of ... thoughts to each other and to the body. It would be better to say "it thinks in me", like "it rains in here"; or better still, "there is a thought in me".'[128] Reduplicating the operation allows an 'I' to be formed where formerly only the 'it' was, but this 'I' is not a fixed consciousness of a previously existing truth of the self; rather it will vary according to the particular punctuation essayed. While Derrida criticizes Lacan for ignoring the uncanny effects of doubling, the latter in fact concludes, in the 'Parenthèse des parenthèses' added to the 1966 version of the 'Seminar on "The Purloined Letter"', that the subject arises precisely through a process of doubling.

> La structure du sujet (s de notre schéma L) ... implique un redoublement ou plutôt cette sorte de division qui comporte une fonction de doublure.

> The structure of the subject (s in our L schema) ... implies a doubling or rather the kind of division which entails a function of lining.[129]

Consideration of the Langer–Wegener theory has allowed us to bring out several of the more obscure connections linking metaphor, unconscious processes, identity and the phallus. That theory accepts, however, the traditional notion that metaphor is based on analogy, the very contention which Lacan's analysis begins by calling into question. If metaphor is to create meaning and identity, it must operate according to other principles. If the identity created is to differ from the traditional metaphysical concept, then something other than the abstract determination of

---

[128] This passage, which sounds so Lacanian, comes in fact from Bertrand Russell's 1922 work, *The Analysis of Mind*, p. 18. Lacan refers to the French translation of this work in 'Remarks on Psychic Causality', although for quite different reasons (*Ecrits*, p. 183). Similarly, the role of anticipation and retrospective punctuation in reading a string of signs is emphasized in Richards' *The Philosophy of Rhetoric* (pp. 48–50). (For instance: 'In most prose ... the opening words have to wait for those that follow to settle what they shall mean – if indeed that ever gets settled' (p. 50).) Despite his genuine disagreements with logical positivism, and well before his explicit incorporation of the formalizations of symbolic logic into his theories, Lacan owed British philosophy an enormous debt. More on this topic shortly.

    I should perhaps add that Lacan's general emphasis on anticipation as a constitutive function of the subject no doubt stems from Heidegger's analysis of temporality in *Being and Time*, which we will discuss in chapter 6.

[129] *Ecrits*, pp. 54–5.

what a set of experiences have in common must be in play. If the phallus is to escape from its traditional transcendental role, then its position in relation to the signifying system must have shifted in some way.

It is here that the writings of Langer's teacher, Cassirer, can provide valuable assistance. His argument in *Sprache und Mythos*, first published in 1925 and translated as *Language and Myth* by Langer in 1946, culminates in the assertion that 'the basic principle of verbal as well as mythic "metaphor" is not one of mere analogy, but of a real identification'.[130] Whereas analogy is the principle of discursive thought, metaphoric identification is the root of all linguistic and mythic conception as well as the prerequisite for discourse.

Cassirer's theory of metaphor is his answer to the fundamental question of how it is possible to bridge the gulf between the specific perceptions of everyday life and the general concepts of science. He claims that most theories beg the question by covertly presupposing the existence of the very general categories whose formation the theory is supposed to explain. He approaches the problem by adapting the hypothesis of a scholar named Usener to the arguments furnished by Kant's notion of the formative or creative function of the subject. In his 'Essay toward a Science of Religious Conception' Usener conjectures that the principle of 'the processes of involuntary and unconscious conception' is that language 'causes the multitude of casual, individual experiences to yield up *one* which extends its denotation over more and more special cases, until it comes to denote them all, and assumes the power of expressing a class concept'.[131] It is Usener's description of the formation of this 'one' which strikes Cassirer as being applicable to the formation of words as well as of gods.

When external reality is not merely viewed and contemplated, but overcomes a man in sheer immediacy, with emotions of fear or hope, terror or wish fulfillment: then the spark jumps somehow across, the tension finds release, as the subjective excitement becomes objectified, and confronts the mind as a god or a daemon.[132]

That one thing, the immediate experience of one sensible impression which totally absorbs the mind, becomes objectified

---

[130] Cassirer, *Language and Myth*, p. 92.
[131] Cited in Cassirer, *Language and Myth*, p. 16.   [132] Ibid., p. 33.

as the image of a god without any recourse to, or mediation by, a general or abstract concept. Cassirer proposes that the sounds in language may perform the same function as the image of the god.

As soon as the spark has jumped across, as soon as the tension and emotion of the moment has found its discharge, a sort of turning point has occurred in human mentality: the inner excitement which was a mere subjective state has vanished, and has been resolved into the objective form of myth or of speech. And now an ever-progressive objectification can begin.[133]

The word (sound) now confronts the person as an external reality, and fixes the impression. The subject is thus unaware of the role his own activity has played in the formation of god or word. The initial fixing of intuitive meaning derives from an impulse toward concentration and compression, as opposed to the expansive tendency of comparing various experiences in order to find their common attributes. With the word as with the god, this isolation of the impression from mundane experience produces 'the highest degree of *condensation*'.[134] It will come as no surprise to the reader who has followed me to this point that this same condensation will end up as Cassirer's metaphoric principle.

All unconscious ideation leads to the hypostatization of its own products, resulting in the identification of the word or image with the thing. The 'almost violent separation and individuation' of mythic ideation and primitive verbal conception gives rise to so exclusive a focus that nothing outside the one thought seems to exist.

Its mere presence is the sum of all being. At this point, the word which denotes that thought content is not a mere conventional symbol, but is merged with its object in an indissoluble unity ... Whatever has been fixed by a name, henceforth is not only real, but is Reality ... In place of a more or less adequate 'expression', we find a relation of identity, of complete *congruence* between 'image' and 'object', between the name and the thing.[135]

I have highlighted the word 'congruence' in order to suggest the possibility that this passage may have given Lacan the idea of using a congruence sign in his algorithms for metaphor and metonymy in 'Agency'. Be that as it may, Cassirer goes on to say

---

[133] Ibid., p. 36.   [134] Ibid., p. 34.   [135] Ibid., pp. 57–8.

that this process of concentration on a single point makes it possible to find and extract 'the particular essence ... which is to bear the special accent of "significance"'.[136] Such an 'essence' is a punctiform unit, in that one particular aspect of the thought or experience is identified with the whole, 'not merely as [a] mediating aid to reflective thought, but as [a] genuine presence which actually contain[s] the power, significance and efficacy of the whole'.[137]

It is at this point that Cassirer reiterates his rejection of analogy in favour of identification. While recognizing the conscious use of metaphorical substitution and translation of one concept for another, Cassirer underscores the necessity of establishing those ideas and the words attached to them before such a discursive process can occur. What he is interested in here, therefore, is that 'genuine "radical metaphor" which is a condition of the very formulation of mythic as well as verbal conceptions', which involves 'not only a transition to another category, but actually the creation of the category itself'.[138] Here we have come back to the level of Heidegger's word as that which lets something come into being, except that the word 'back' is somewhat inappropriate since this book was published a few years before *Being and Time*.[139]

Cassirer finds this basic principle whereby categories are created and fixed to be that of the part for the whole. At first sight this notion appears to oppose both rhetorical tradition, which of course makes the *pars pro toto* the defining quality of metonymy (or synecdoche), and the Heideggerian logos, which gathers and collects. Indeed, Lacan does call this naming phase of the linguistic process metonymy, as we have seen. But the term metonymy seems to be a comparatively late invention – apparently no mention of the word as a rhetorical term has been found before the *Rhetorica ad Herennium* (82 BCE) – whereas Aristotle lists the substitution of species for genus, or vice versa, clearly a

---

136 Ibid., p. 90.   137 Ibid., p. 92.   138 Ibid., pp. 87–8.
139 Heidegger of course objects to the 'constructivist "standpoint"' for allegedly defining all signification as relation, thus presupposing rather than explaining the condition of possibility of the subject/object split that defines western metaphysics (*Being and Time*, pp. 88, 107–14). Adjudicating the relative merits of this dispute is a matter for professional philosophers. The important point for us is that Lacan's theory of metaphor describes the level that precedes the subject/object split; that is the force of his assimilation of Freud's primary affirmation to Heidegger's logos.

part-whole relation, as one type of metaphor. And the mythical, indeed magical, assimilation of the part with the whole that constitutes the punctiform units of significance does result from a process of pre-discursive verbal 'collection' in Cassirer's theory, since he surmises that 'this sort of concentration occurs by virtue of several experiences'.[140] Where the same 'inner significance' is isolated from two or more perceptual complexes, there a linguistic name will emerge. Moreover, since the unnamed simply does not exist in language, the differences among complexes will be effaced, so that 'whatever things bear the *same* appellation appear absolutely similar'.[141] As a result, in pre-discursive as well as post-discursive poetic thought:

> Every characteristic property which once gave a point of departure to qualifying conceptions and qualifying *appellations* may now serve to merge and identify the *objects* denoted by these names.[142]

The crucial move in this argument is the Kantian reversal whereby, rather than associating together similar objects, without realizing it the subject imposes similarity on objects through the use of names.[143] The assumption, for which Cassirer finds evidence in early mythic and religious thought, is that primordial experience consists of undifferentiated totalities such as the 'qualitative contrast of light and darkness', which mythic conception 'treats ... as one essence, one complex whole, out of which definite characters only gradually emerge'.[144] Referring to Freud

---

[140] Cassirer, *Language and Myth*, p. 95.   [141] Ibid., p. 95.   [142] Ibid., p. 96.

[143] Delacroix traces the history of the application of Kant's notion of the unity of 'apperception' to linguistics in the theories of Herbart and his disciples, Steinthal and Lazarus, on through Wundt and Cassirer (*Le langage et la pensée*, pp. 34–42; 56–60).

> Lier sous l'unité du mot la diversité des sensations, représenter la totalité d'une situation psychique par un de ses moments privilégiés, choisi pour la nomination, tel est le rôle du langage ... Nous contractons en une vue d'ensemble, en une image totale, en une unité complexe et confusément aperçue tout ce qui s'est déroulé en détails, en succession bigarrée: d'un drame, d'une scène, d'un tableau il nous reste une impression condensée.
>
> (p. 37)
>
> Connecting the diversity of sensations in the unity of the word, representing the totality of a psychic situation by one of its privileged moments chosen for naming, that is the role of language ... We contract into an overall view, into a total image, into a complex unity perceived confusedly, all that has occurred in details, in a multicolored sequence: of a drama, a scene, a picture, we retain [only] a condensed impression.

[144] Cassirer, *Le langage*, p. 14.

and Nietzsche, Lacan uses this same example of the light/dark or day/night (*jour/nuit*) opposition in *Psychoses* to make the point that light and dark are 'beings' which precede human experience and language in that each aspect of the whole exists only in contrast to the absence of the other.[145] Cassirer inserts this mythical and verbal (metaphoric) thought into a series of levels of religious and secular conception that range from undifferentiated ideation, which he likens to the mythic consciousness of *mana*, to the infinite notion of a God beyond all characterization.

What makes this series especially pertinent for an understanding of Lacan is that each level stands to the next in a dialectic relation based on varieties of predication. The development of mythico-religious consciousness and the evolution of language are thus inextricably intertwined. Ethnologists and scholars have been unable to find a good translation for *mana* because they have assumed that its unity must be on the level of a specific predicate, an attribute. Cassirer claims, on the contrary, that its coherence resides in 'a peculiar and consistent *form of predication*'.[146] It is the kind of attention directed to the object that counts, that which distinguishes the sacred from the profane; mana is the originary act of differentiation which operates in the religious sphere like the radical metaphor already described does in the mundane: '[It] make[s] the positing of attributes possible'.[147] The statement that something has or is mana translates the subjective sense that a vague, impersonal, divine power is present.

Only against the background of this first distinction can specific divinities, or demons, arise. The first type of these Usener calls 'momentary gods'. They are images 'born from the need or the specific feeling of a critical moment, sprung from the excitation of mythico-religious fantasy'.[148] Once an experience has been fixed in the form of an image, the new deity becomes separated from the moment of its origin, taking on the name and attribute of the activity involved in satisfying the initial need (e.g. the discovery of a spring by a thirsty person may lead to the formation of a god of well-digging). As the language evolves in time, the name of the god loses its denotation, thus becoming available to designate the god herself, that is, a personal being rather than an activity or

---

[145] *Psychoses*, pp. 168–70.   [146] Cassirer, *Language and Myth*, p. 66.
[147] Ibid., p. 67.   [148] Ibid., p. 62.

attribute. This new personal god can now take on a whole series of attributes, as names or appellations.

Once again, so Cassirer's story goes, the mythic mind seeks a unity in this multiplicity: 'It strives for a concept of being that is unlimited by any particular manifestation, and therefore not expressible in any word, not called by any name.' This new concept of the divine must be beyond all attributes, since any attribution implies negation and thus limitation. It is thus beyond language, as the writings of the mystics show, but it is speech itself which has prepared the way for its own transcending by laboriously developing 'two fundamental, linguistically grounded concepts – the concept of "being", and the concept of the "Ego"'. Whereas for a Kant, this development leads to the realization that being can no longer be a predicate of a thing but only the expression of a pure relation (our old friend the copula), for mythic consciousness, 'being is not only a predicate, but ... actually becomes the Predicate of Predicates ... allow[ing] one to subsume all the attributes of God under a single rubric.' The next stage is attained when this unity is transferred back from the objective realm of being to the subjective essence 'of the Person, the Self'. This new phase finds its expression in 'the form of "self-predication", of self-revelation of the god through a constantly reiterated "I am ..." which reveals the various aspects of his unified being'. The ultimate form of self-predication is that which excludes all others, all mere attributes, and simply reiterates itself in the Judaic 'I am that I am.' 'The only instruments of speech that remain ... are the personal pronouns.' The final step of the dialectic integrates the two lines of thought, that of objective being and that of subjective Self, in the religious thought of India represented by the Upanishads. By uniting the two, as Brahma – the power of the Word as such, 'being-in-being' – and Atman – the absolute, unchangeable, immortal Self – this thought once again breaks 'the bounds of language. For words can no longer grasp and hold this unity of "subject" and "object"'. They are left at the threshold of the infinite. Once again, the word is lacking.[149]

---

[149] All passages cited in this paragraph are from Cassirer, *Language and Myth*, pp. 73–9. I believe that this is the reason for which Lacan insists that it is so important for any genuine atheism to keep talking about God (see *Encore* and *Sinthome*). Likewise, the before and beyond, the two aspects of the illusion created by language according to Lacan (*Encore*, p. 44), correspond to Cassirer's (and Kant's) indefinite and infinite.

Like his pupil Langer, Cassirer puts this whole development under the sign of Kant's 'Copernican revolution'; symbolic forms are 'spontaneous law[s] of generation ... each of which produces and posits a world of its own'.[150] Cassirer's history of the evolution of religious thought is a kind of survey of what Lacan would call the various Names-of-the-Father. In speaking of the divine, it actually tells us about the creative power of language: the ability of metaphor to fix and determine the attributes of objective being, and the capacity of predication to separate the individuality and formative powers of the subject from those attributes. Cassirer's dialectic thus articulates the point of conjunction between metaphor and predication in a more viable way than any of the theories we have considered: radical metaphor both precedes predication (relation) and makes it possible by determining being, isolating subject and attribute through a series of applications of its own law, the law of 'conception' Lacan associates with the phallus. In the seminar on ethics, Lacan reads the 'I am that I am' as the expression of the symbolic law itself: that is, on the one hand, as pure speech from which all imaginary content – all attributes – has been eliminated; on the other, as the rule of its own functioning, pure predication.[151]

In a sense, then, the radical metaphor of the phallus, which Lacan terms its metonymic aspect, is the mediator between the immediacy of sensible experience – the imaginary – and the mediation of symbolic – relational or referential – thought. It marks the relation of the subject to the signifier as the separation of subject from attribute, which means not only that an experience is identified by condensation with an attribute, but also that the subject, and especially a human subject, is identified with a name. The latter possibility is embodied in the moment of mythic consciousness in which the common name of the activity represented by the deity, by the process of 'fading', becomes the proper name of a personal god. The metaphoric identity of the word with what it names, which characterizes the pre-referential use of language and underlies magical practices, serves a real linguistic function: 'The unity and uniqueness of the name is not only a mark of the unity and uniqueness of the person, but

---

[150] Cassirer, *Language and Myth*, p. 8.   [151] *Ethique*, pp. 98–9.

actually constitutes it; the name is what first makes man an individual.'[152]

Despite the common understanding of structuralism, or now poststructuralism, it is this capacity to constitute the unique individuality of the subject that forms the heart of Lacan's phallic signifier and consequently of his ethical teaching. Nowhere is this expressed more clearly than in his analysis of Sophocles' *Antigone*, in the seminar on the ethics of psychoanalysis. Lacan points out that Antigone justifies her position on the basis of the unwritten laws of the gods, the horizon determined by a structural relation. Once the words of language are used, once the signifier has fixed the changing flow of life in a name, her argument is that her brother is who he is, and nothing else. He is the only one who can be that. By her position, Antigone represents that radical limit which, beyond any content of Polynices' life, maintains the unique value of his being, a value which is essentially linguistic, since it is the proper name alone which makes it possible to separate his being from his accomplishments and sufferings. The pure being thus established results from 'la coupure qu'instaure dans la vie de l'homme la présence même du langage' ['the break that the very presence of language inaugurates in the life of man'].[153]

It must be noted that this uniqueness is as different from the radical individualism of the ego of bourgeois ideology as it is from the collectivism of structuralist and Marxist ideology. Far from being an autonomous agent, this individual is dependent upon the impersonal operation of language for its constitution. For that very reason, it remains a pure limit, a horizon to which language points but which it can never define, because all its terms, even 'I', 'here' and 'now', are necessarily universals, as Hegel's analysis of 'this bit of paper' reminds us. The individuality of this subject can be maintained only as long as no attributes, which are universal by definition, are attached to it. In other words, the uniqueness of the subject persists only as long as it remains free of content, meaningless. The metaphor of the subject must thus begin by at least implicitly positing a subject separate and distinct from, in short beyond, all attributes, like the personal god. When this implicit positing becomes explicit, as

---

[152] Cassirer, *Language and Myth*, p. 51.   [153] *Ethique*, p. 325; *Ethics*, p. 279.

with the god of the mystics, then you have reached the level of the concept.

The position taken in *Ethique* contrasts with that of the early fifties. At that time, Lacan asserted that the completed metaphor, the conceptual reconciliation of the universal with the particular, was the goal of psychoanalysis. In 'Function and Field' he cites the same Upanishads to which Cassirer refers to illustrate this point, and in his first seminar he quotes a passage from the German mystic, Angelus Silesius, to designate the end of the analytic process, when 'la contingence se perd et l'essentiel subsiste' ['the contingent falls away, but Essence, that stands fast'].[154] If repression is the 'lacking word', then the goal of analysis must be to supply that word, to fill the gap with the catachresis of the nameless thing. The subject needs to receive this word from the Other, from a representative of society, in order to guarantee recognition of her being.

By the end of the decade, at the time of his seminar on ethics (1959–60), Lacan had abandoned the universalizing ideal of analysis as the perfection of communication and the ratification of a social mandate. Its goal had become the isolation and confrontation of the meaningless core of the symbolic rather than the attachment of a symbolic meaning to the traumatic, because meaningless, unsymbolized, contingent, imaginary. Hence his emphasis on the metonymic in the seminar on ethics, the mean-ingless being constituted by the name of Polynices.

The full-blown theory of metaphor expounded in 'Agency' and the seminar on psychosis seems to stand midway between these two extremes. In his critique of *Titre*, Lacan complains that the being he describes in 'Agency' is not the eternal uncreated God of metaphysical ontology, but rather a 'being of significance'.[155] While this negation and this affirmation are consistent with Heidegger's presentation in *Being and Time*, Lacan's elaboration of this concept of being cannot be fully explained in Heidegger's terms. Although, as Lacan states in *Ethique*, the proper name abstracts being from the flux of time, instead of constituting the perdurable identity of traditional ontology, the signifier merely gives rise to 'un étant dont l'être est toujours ailleurs, comme le montre le prédicat' [a being whose being is always elsewhere, as

---

[154] *Ecrits techniques*, p. 258; *Papers*, p. 232.   [155] *Encore*, pp. 67–8.

is shown by the predicate], a subject that 'n'est jamais que ponctuel et évanouissant' [is never anything but punctual and vanishing].[156]

The notion of such a transitory being is found precisely in Usener's theory of the 'momentary god', which serves as the point of departure for Cassirer's idea of metaphoric identification.

It is something purely instantaneous, a fleeting, emerging and vanishing mental content … [Whenever] spontaneous feeling invest[s] the object before him … with an air of holiness … the momentary god has been experienced and created. In stark uniqueness and singleness it confronts us … as something that exists only here and now, in one indivisible moment of experience.[157]

This evanescent (another possible translation of Lacan's *évanouissant*) experience in the realm of mythic thought is identical to the punctiform unit of significance that constitutes the originary metaphor of verbal ideation. It is this conception that fleshes out the import of that 'spark that jumps across', in Cassirer's words, or of Heraclitus' 'lightning' quoted in Heidegger's 'Logos' article. That is why Lacan speaks in 'Agency' of the 'creative spark of the metaphor' and of 'cet être qui n'apparaît que l'éclair d'un instant dans le vide du verbe être' ['the "being" … which appears in a lightning moment in the void of the verb "to be"'].[158] And that is why this identification is necessarily historical, originating at a certain moment and lasting for only a finite amount of time.

The paradox of meaning is that once the symbol is abstracted from the temporal flow and fixed in an image or word, by virtue of the metaphoric process as described in Usener's and Cassirer's account of the development of mythico-religious conception, the meaning attached to that objectification becomes a variable, available to any number of values. The chief postulate of Lacan's notion of signification, apparently adopted from Cassirer, is the assertion that the same detachability and variability also characterizes the relation of subject to predicate, that is, identification. Meaning thus is not a being or a state, nor even a relation when that word is taken to mean the association of one term with another on the grounds of an attribute held in common as in a

---

[156] Ibid., p. 130.   [157] Cassirer, *Language and Myth*, p. 18.
[158] *Ecrits*, p. 520; *Ecrits* Eng., p. 168.

proposition, but a function in the logical and mathematical sense of the term.

Once again it is Cassirer who paves the way for Lacan, this time by specifically linking metaphor to Russell's logical definition of a 'propositional function'. He does so not in *Language and Myth*, to be sure, but in *The Phenomenology of Knowledge*, volume III of his monumental *Philosophy of Symbolic Forms*, first published in German in 1929 and translated into English in 1957. Starting from the traditional Aristotelian definition of metaphor as a transfer of meaning and the Hegelian view that the liberation of the subject consists in her independence from the immediate situation, Cassirer argues that it is precisely metaphor, the ability to take the same word in more than one sense, which gives rise to that freedom. The ability to move from meaning to meaning involves the capacity to envisage other contexts, to change 'viewpoints' or 'systems of reference'. Building on the theory developed in *Language and Myth* and further elaborated in volume II of *Symbolic Forms, Mythical Thought,* he repeats that metaphor is not primarily a matter of resemblances, and concludes that it signifies 'the essential detachability of the sign from the things for which it functions as a sign'.[159] By this means it can effect identification, imposing similarity onto the things to which it is applied. His theory thus synthesizes key points of Richards' description and Lacan's interpretation of Freud's *fort/da*; taken in conjunction with Langer's notion of the phallus, Cassirer's view of metaphor renders explicit the meaning of the phallus as that which institutes the sign by separating signified from signifier.

Cassirer's aim in this treatise is to show how one can take the second step, from the notion of various objects to the universal concept of logic, mathematics, science and knowledge in general. He rejects the widely held idea, one representative of which we saw in the Langer–Wegener theory, that the concept is a generalization based on an attribute common to all instances of a given object.

What holds together the various structures which we regard as examples of one and the same concept is not a unity of a generic image but the unity of a rule of change, on the basis of which one example can be derived from another and so on up to the totality of all possible examples.[160]

[159] Cassirer, *The Philosophy of Symbolic Forms*, vol. III, pp. 332–3.
[160] Ibid., p. 291.

Such a 'rule of change' can apply even to an infinite class, all of whose members therefore could never be compared to determine whether they possessed some attribute in common. On the contrary, membership in the class is determined, imposed, by the rule.

A rule with the properties described is what Russell defines as a 'propositional function':

an expression containing one or more undetermined constituents, such that, when values are assigned to these constituents, the expression becomes a proposition. In other words, it is a function whose values are propositions.[161]

Algebraic equations and ordinary statements containing the explicit or implicit quantifiers 'all', 'any', 'some', 'one', etc., are examples of propositional functions. Such statements include as subject a variable, an x (sometimes called an 'argument') that is quantified – 'for all x', 'there exists an x' – and the function itself, equivalent of a predication (phi of x) – 'such that x is mortal'. A universal concept would be a propositional function with the universal quantifier, 'for all x'.

Several important consequences flow from this manner of comprehending the concept. Universals are no longer conceived as substances – independently subsisting, durable entities, as in realism – but they are not simply empty words either, as in nominalism. Rather they are functions; their unity is the rule or law which logically precedes and enables the action of its application. They are not predications, since the latter result only when actual values are substituted for the variable. And they are not objects in a world; they are not on the same level as the values which can occupy the place of the x. A class defined by a propositional function might very well be impossible, its members non-existent, yet the concept would be meaningful. Just as metaphor makes it possible to move into frames of reference that do not exist as present realities, whether in the form of

---

[161] Ibid., p. 295. The quote is from Russell's *Introduction to Mathematical Philosophy*, pp. 155ff. Cassirer also refers to Russell and Whitehead's *Principia Mathematica*. The most complete presentation of the mature theory is found in 'Mathematical Logic as Based on a Theory of Types' reprinted in Russell, *Logic and Knowledge*, pp. 59–102. This is the article in which Russell gives his solution to the paradox of the Cretan liar. An excellent non-technical explanation of propositional functions is found in 'The Philosophy of Logical Atomism', also collected in *Logic and Knowledge*.

memory, imagining, hypothetical world, or future possibility, so the concept is the projection of a pure meaning, as in Fichte's A = A, independent of any consideration of existence.

As is well known, Lacan designates the phallus as a propositional function, or even a 'phunction', phi(x), but this practice appears to begin in the mid-sixties. Nevertheless, without falling prey to the retrospective illusion he often warned against, I think we can find evidence that he held at least an embryonic form of this notion as early as 'Agency'. In explaining the allusion to the Greek *enstasis* (exception) he embedded in the title word translated as 'Agency' – *Instance* – he does employ the notion of propositional function as developed by Russell.[162] And the algorithms for metaphor and metonymy in 'Agency', despite the fact that they designate 'metaphysical' rather than mathematical 'analogies', are written in the form of functions.

If the phallus is, or rather becomes, a general propositional function, it must be a class, not a value of x or a 'term within a series of terms' as Derrida puts it. To be sure, the phallus is designed to guarantee a 'beyond' of representation – real presence – but that beyond is in fact an illusion, and the phallic function is nothing in itself, a mere schema, as Russell calls the propositional function.[163] Hence, although it is the condition of possibility of signification, as Derrida claims, it is not 'transcendental' in any of the customary metaphysical senses of the term. Although it is difficult to pinpoint the precise moment of the change, it is clear that some time after the *Psychoses* seminar, Lacan's analysis of the phallus and the subject shifted from the paradigm of Aristotelian logic dependent upon grammatical predication to that of modern set theory which relies on Frege's and Russell's notions of function and argument. This move allowed Lacan to eliminate any vestige of the idea of the subject as a substance. In propositional logic, the subject is merely a variable which may or may not exist, since a universal propositional function may be valid even though in fact no value of x makes the proposition true. A predicate is no longer an attribute in the classic sense of the term, since one no longer posits a preexisting subject to which it is attached; rather the predicate defines a possible class, which may or may not have any

---

[162] *Encore*, pp. 65–6; 93–4. We will return to this matter in chapter 4.
[163] Russell, *Logic and Knowledge*, p. 234.

members.[164] As a result, all vestiges of the Rousseauist, Hegelian, or Lévi-Straussian notion of the birth of the subject as the separation of culture from nature could be abandoned, the whole process now being capable of formulation in terms of the creative power of the signifier. As we will see in chapter 6, this change will enable Lacan to distinguish between 'subjectivity' in its ordinary senses, and what he will call 'subjectivation' in his full-blown theory of the subject.

Now, since existence can be asserted or denied only of classes, or propositional functions, not of individuals,[165] in order to ensure his own existence, the subject must first safeguard the existence of the Other, the phallic function. This seems to be the source in logic of Lacan's explanation of the all-too-human temptation to use sacrifice, scapegoating, as the bond that holds social groups together. Finally, the phallus serves as the general proposition one must assume as an unproven premise in order to arrive at any general fact.[166] In order to assert the order, or rule of meaning, whereby signifier (or subject) can be attached to signified (attribute) in (human) reality, the phallus must remain an unfounded function, equivalent therefore to the non-rational assumption of the rationality of the world. The paradox of the logos as truth is that the most rational course is to acknowledge the non-rational, purely assertorial, 'basis' of rationality.

Richards, Cassirer and Langer all see symbolization (representation) as the key to culture. While Richards and Cassirer take the Enlightenment, and metaphysical, stance of playing up only the potential for scientific progress, Langer, writing during the Second World War, stresses that symbolism also opens up the possibility of oppression, for we control incipient behaviour with symbols. 'And more than that; the power of symbols enables us not only to limit each other's actions, but to command them ... to *constrain*'.[167] Here is the source of duty, and of slavery. If Lacan recognizes the creative and reconciling potential of the phallic metaphor in 'Agency', *Psychoses*, and other texts, he consistently rejects the belief in progress that characterizes the Enlightenment

---

[164] Porge, *Se compter trois*, p. 171.
[165] Russell, *Logic and Knowledge*, pp. 233–4.   [166] Ibid., p. 235.
[167] Langer, *New Key*, p. 233. Lacan will call this power of the signifier to command, the imperative mode, the root of the discourse of the master and of ontology [*le discours du maître, du m'être*] (*Encore*, p. 33).

and Hegelian conceptions of History. He often accentuated the violent effects of symbolization also, and 'the obscenity of the superego' becomes the focus of his attention in *L'Ethique* and later seminars.

What this means in concrete terms is that the individual must identify with the representative of this rule in order to accept the promise that one's culture holds out the possibility of future satisfaction of desire. And this acceptance depends on the assurance, and the threat, of the existence of an Other that can supply a specific value for the x in the phallic function to produce one's vanishing and punctual being. Since, as Richards had already emphasized, the meaning of metaphor results from the process of reading by another, the being of the subject so determined lies in the hands of that interpreter.[168] Lacan's theory of metaphor can only be completed, therefore, through examination of his concept of the letter in its relation to that connection to the Other which psychoanalysis calls transference.

[168] Lacan, *Ecrits*, p. 892.

4

From Logic to Ethics: Transference and the Letter

But whence comes this striking preference for ambiguous speeches in *Gradiva*?
Freud, *Delusion and Dream*

All general propositions deny the existence of something or other. If you say 'All men are mortal', that denies the existence of an immortal man, and so on.

Russell, 'The Philosophy of Logical Atomism' in *Logic and Knowledge*

'*Point de capiton*', Lacan protests in the preface to the Points edition of *Ecrits*, is his translation of the Stoics' *lekton* – the 'expressible' – a verbal function which forms the joint between the Stoics' logic and their ethics.[1] The example from Racine he used when introducing the expression *point de capiton* shows that it was not primarily a matter of theory, truth and falsehood, but of a kind of ethical action, in this case the conversion of fear into courage. Historians of philosophy specify that this 'expressible' is always an action, a fact or an event, never a state, a potentiality, or a concept. Bréhier points out that in Stoic logic, 'A body is warm' was an incorrect judgement; the proper form was, 'A body warms up', since they did not accept the idea of a property, 'warmth', that would be attributed to the subject.[2] For them, warming up was rather an occurrence which befell the body in question. The lekta thus introduced into the real of material bodies, or beings apprehensible through the senses, a series of relations that existed only in language and were expressible as verbs or the combinations of verbal expressions we call compound and complex sentences. The subject being the result of connections among signifiers – 'the signifier represents the subject for another signifier', as Lacan's famous dictum puts it – reorganizing the relation among the signifiers that constitute the

---

[1] *Ecrits 1*, Points edition, vol. I, pp. 10–11.
[2] Bréhier, *Théorie des incorporels*, pp. 20–1.

subject, introducing new 'master signifiers', as Lacan called them in the sixties, is one mode of activity whereby analysis can literally change the subject, helping her to modify her relation to herself, her desires and other people. As the radical metaphor, the Name-of-the-Father, which gives rise to the phallic function, must be considered in its ethical dimension as an action that introduces something new into the real and opens up a certain margin of freedom.

In psychoanalysis it is the function of transference (*Übertragung*) which provides the link between theory and practice, language and action, the way the lekton connects logic and ethics for the Stoics. Lacan reminds us in 'Agency' that Freud initially used the term 'transference' to denote the specific function of connection and substitution performed by the signifier which Lacan formulated in his algorithms for metonymy and metaphor. Only later did Freud apply the word to the description of the motive force linking analyst and analysand in the psychoanalytic situation.[3] By juxtaposing the two apparently disparate functions which Freud designated by the name transference, Lacan implies the existence of some more or less hidden connection between them. The etymological and lexical resonances of the term furnish one such link, to be sure, for like *meta-phorein Übertragung* signifies some sort of 'carrying across'. The precise nature of the transfer operative both in metaphor as signifying process and in transference as intersubjective link remains to be defined.

The general idea of a tie between rhetoric as an activity aimed toward establishing existential human relations such as persuasion, threat or suggestion, and rhetoric understood as the use of figurative language, was of course developed by the sophists and codified in Aristotle's *Rhetoric*. It was Richards, however, who as far as I can tell was the first to contend that such a connection can be demonstrated in the particular field of psychoanalysis. In language prefiguring that in which Lacan describes his *point de capiton*, Richards had argued:

Words are the meeting points at which regions of experience which can never combine in sensation or intuition, come together. They are the

---

[3] *Ecrits* Eng., p. 170. In fact, Freud used the word 'transference' to designate one aspect of the relation between analyst and patient at the end of 'Studies on Hysteria' (pp. 301–4), that is, as early as 1895.

occasion and the means of that growth which is the mind's endless endeavour to order itself.[4]

And since language is essentially metaphorical according to his new rhetoric, bringing these diverse regions together makes it possible to transfer patterns of behaviour from one to another.

The psycho-analysts have shown us with their discussions of 'transference' – another name for metaphor – how constantly modes of regarding, of loving, of acting, that have developed with one set of things or people, are shifted to another.[5]

We interpret a new situation in our relations with other people in terms of our previous relations with the members of our family; the old situation functions as the vehicle, whose tenor is the new one. Pathology, like poor reading, arises when the tenor completely dominates the vehicle, that is, when the relation between the two is limited to strict resemblance. Health, on the contrary, stems from a free interaction of the two, analogous to the creation of new relations between tenor and vehicle essential to good metaphor. In the domain of behaviour also, then, metaphor (transference) is an identification rather than a comparison. Richards concludes his discussion of transference by expressing the very Lacanian 'dream' 'that with enough improvement in Rhetoric we may in time learn so much about words that they will tell us how our minds work'.[6]

Although Richards does not make the connection explicitly, his vehicle and tenor correspond to Freud's manifest and latent contents of the dream, while his 'whole metaphor' coincides with what Freud calls the essence of the dream, the 'dream-work', or specific manner in which the two constituents are brought together. The pathology of reading which he decries is thus equivalent to the mistake committed by those psychoanalysts Freud admonishes for confusing the latent meaning, the so-called dream thoughts, with the dream.[7] Now Freud's early conception of transference, the one to which Lacan alludes in 'Agency', involves precisely the relation between what Richards would call the tenor and the vehicle.

An unconscious idea is as such quite incapable of entering the precon-

---

[4] Richards, *Philosophy of Rhetoric*, p. 131.
[5] Ibid., p. 135.   [6] Ibid., p. 136.
[7] Freud, 'Interpretation of Dreams', pp. 506–7.

scious and ... it can only exercise any effect there by establishing a connection with an idea which already belongs to the preconscious, by transferring its intensity on to it and by getting itself 'covered' by it. Here we have the fact of 'Transference'.[8]

Lacan can describe this transference-function as a signifying, metaphoric, process, because it is precisely a matter of substitution, one signifier – the unconscious idea – getting itself covered by another signifier – the preconscious idea or day-residue. The two are thus connected by an unspecified relation of reference, about which one can only say, as Lacan does of the line from Hugo's 'Boaz Asleep' (see pp. 55–6), that the latent signifier controls the selection and configuration of the manifest elements.

In his *Introductory Lectures on Psycho-Analysis*, Freud offers a perspicuous analysis of this process as it operates in a young woman's dream. The manifest dream places her at the theatre with her husband where she mentions her friend and the latter's fiancé, who could only get bad seats for 1 florin 50 kreuzers. The dream analysis showed that the woman had just learned of her friend's engagement, and that she had quite recently tried to get tickets to a play but had bought them too early. The dream as it actually appeared was thus a quilt stitched together out of these recent occurrences. In fact, however, the particular choice and organization of those elements were controlled by the latent dream thoughts, the young woman's questions about her own haste to get married and her wish to engage in sexual seeing.[9] Just as the string of words that actually appears in the line from Hugo's 'Boaz Asleep' involves the disconnecting of the sheaf from its usual lexical ties and their reconnection to ones emanating from the latent signifier 'Boaz', so the signifiers of the young woman's recent experience – the news of her friend's engagement, going to the theatre – were detached from their customary signifieds in order to be reattached to others determined by her question and her voyeuristic curiosity, her wondering whether she might have found a better husband if she had not been in such a hurry to marry.

The first definition of transference as the relation of the manifest to the latent content would appear, therefore, to be nothing other than the notion of meaning itself. Freud explains

[8] Ibid., p. 562.
[9] Freud, *Introductory Lectures on Psycho-Analysis*, pp. 122–5.

the parallel relation between unconscious and (pre-)conscious in the case of the symptom precisely as a matter of meaning:

[The hysterical symptom] cannot occur more than once – and the capacity for repeating itself is one of the characteristics of a hysterical symptom – unless it has a psychical significance, a *meaning*. The hysterical symptom does not carry this meaning with it, but the meaning is lent to it, soldered to it, as it were; and in every instance the meaning can be a different one, according to the nature of the suppressed thoughts which are struggling for expression.[10]

The hysterical symptom, Dora's aphonia for example, uses a physical state to signify her wishes and reproaches in just the same way that the theatre-goer's dream uses the events of the previous day to cover her questions and desires. Here as with the dream, the realities of history and body have been removed from their customary contexts and reinserted into a new signifying system.

At first sight it would seem that Freud has simply rediscovered, or renamed, the famous arbitrariness of the sign heralded by commentators from Aristotle to Saussure. Additional thought, however, shows that the parallel is by no means complete. Whereas the sounds of language have no inherent meaning, as Langer insisted, the elements put to use by the dream and the symptom do have meaning in a non-linguistic context, as images of the body or of events. In addition, while the 'arbitrary' linguistic couplings of sound and sense are given relative stability through social convention, dream images obey no such conventions. It is for these reasons, of course, that Freud has so often been criticized for the alleged capriciousness of his, or his disciples', interpretations.

Lacan recognized, however, that the relation between the two levels of these 'unconscious formations' as he called them, is not simply that of signifier to signified, but simultaneously that of signifier to signifier. In a dream, both the manifest images and the latent thoughts are signifiers, since the latter are always a series of words. The example of such a signifier–signifier relation that lies nearest to hand is that of writing, which is why Freud repeatedly likens the dream 'language' to a system of writing. And that is also the primary motivation for Lacan's theory of the

---

[10] Freud, 'Studies on Hysteria', pp. 40–1.

letter and its 'agency'. If the dream is a rebus, as Freud and Lacan claim, it is because, as with the pictographs of hieroglyphic writing, its images can be used to indicate the sounds that compose the names of the objects depicted. These sounds then function like the alphabet, or syllabary, of a writing system, in that the images can be juxtaposed to form the sounds of other words – those which constitute the dream thoughts. When Lacan introduced his distinction of the symbolic, imaginary and real in his inaugural speech to the Société Française de Psychanalyse, he adduced the example of the syllable 'po', a homophone for the word *pot*, which means jar, or small vase. The image of the jar can be combined with other syllabic representations to construct words such as *police* or *poltron* (coward).[11] Lacan can therefore gloss Freud's initial definition of *Übertragung* as the use of day-residues to form 'signifying material':

Le matériel signifiant, qu'il soit phonématique, hiéroglyphique, etc., est constitué de formes qui sont déchues de leur sens propre et reprises dans une organisation nouvelle à travers laquelle un sens autre trouve à s'exprimer.

The signifying material, be it phonematic, hieroglyphic, etc., is consti-tuted out of forms which have forfeited their own meaning and are taken up again in a new organization, thanks to which another meaning finds a means of gaining expression.[12]

This definition of the letter brings out its affinity with both the commonplace and the technical notions of metaphor. Whether the trope be based on similarity or create new relations, its concept requires the existence of terms which already have some meaning. The transfer of meaning always entails both using and suppressing the 'customary', or 'proper' or 'literal', meaning in order to apply the term otherwise, as the signifying material of a different situation. Just as the image of the jar must first be understood as being a *pot* before it can then be utilized to signify the syllable 'po', so the meaning of the term to be suppressed must be taken into account in order for an expression to be recognizable as a metaphor. In the case of *Übertragung*, Lacan adopts a catachresis theory similar to that of Langer, one which

---

[11] Allouch, *Lettre pour lettre*, p. 173. The choice of the *pot* here is guided by Heidegger's discussion of the vase in relation to being and the void, in the article entitled 'The Thing' cited in chapter 3, pp. 66–7.

[12] *Ecrits techniques*, pp. 269–70; *Papers*, p. 245.

also, as Cassirer explains, typifies the mystics' attempt to grasp the divine without using any attributes, since the latter entail negation and therefore limitation. According to these accounts, metaphor functions to symbolize that which is beyond or before symbolization; similarly, the unconscious desire is essentially ineffable, unexpressible, until it finds the signifying material offered by the day residues that have been divested of their sense.

As the term 'signifying material' suggests, materiality condenses out of experience through the constitution of the letter; that is, by emptying (imaginary) meaning from it. Lacan argues that any other concept of matter, which would make of it an autonomous principle or substance, must needs remain as much an idealism as any spiritualism. The combined affirmation and negation involved in the metaphoric construction of the letter is thus a kind of material *'Aufhebung'*, as Lacan calls it in 'Signification of the Phallus'. Unlike the Hegelian 'sublation', which implies that its terms are raised to a higher level of synthesis, Lacan's version of sublimation as the production of the letter consists of the very process of transformation itself, with no implication of an elevation or a teleology.

The second motivation for his use of terminology drawn from the field of writing is thus an appeal to the Pauline opposition between the letter and the spirit. In 'Function and Field', Lacan had declared that the unconscious is the censored chapter of the subject's history, whose truth 'le plus souvent ... est écrite ailleurs' ['usually ... has already been written down elsewhere [e.g. in symptoms]'].[13] He developed the sense of this definition of the unconscious in 'Agency', contending that the letter 'produit tous ses effets de vérité dans l'homme, sans que l'esprit ait le moins du monde à s'en mêler' ['produces all the effects of truth in man without involving the spirit at all'],[14] because it is precisely a series of signifiers without meaning for the subject. Insofar as the spirit means living consciousness, and consciousness has always meant consciousness of meaning, the unconscious can be defined as a letter that produces meaning effects beyond any conscious intention, without being understood.

If the letter is a signifying material bereft of any meaning, then it is difficult to perceive the difference between the letter and the

---

[13] *Ecrits*, p. 259; *Ecrits* Eng., p. 50.
[14] Ibid., p. 509; Ibid., p. 158.

signifier as Lacan defines it, for instance, in *Psychoses*. Yet in late texts such as 'Lituraterre' and *Encore*, he insists that it is a mistake to equate the two. In the fifties, the distinction between them rested primarily on their functions rather than on their properties. In order to speak of 'a' signifier, it must be possible to discriminate one from another; that is, there must be stabilized units or elements of significance. Now Lacan agrees with Richards that in non-literate societies the boundaries between words often remain uncertain.[15] Writing facilitates the separation of the register of the signifier from that of the signified by helping to punctuate speech, interrupting its flow at certain points and grouping sounds together to form words (and, potentially, other elements). Writing becomes the name of the process whereby speech can be codified into stable signifying units that exist separately from their meanings. Both the letter and the pure signifier are meaningless, but the crucial distinction between them is that the letter makes it possible to purify the signifier, to bar it from the signified. 'Writing down', or inscription, as Lacan indicated in *Psychoses*, opens up the register of the signifier by making us realize that meaning has nothing to do with hearing.[16]

If the signifier refers to the audible sign insofar as it bears meaning, the letter becomes that part of the sign that having no meaning, is pure material. It is the sign considered as an object, rather than as a producer of meaning, a thing which can undergo all sorts of fates long after the sound of the signifier has been dissipated, and which can therefore have a different addressee from that of the signifier.[17] But if it were simply a matter of the capacity of being stored away, torn up, passed along and so on, like any other material object, Lacan's letter would not have any special theoretical interest, nor would it have become the centre of so many controversies. What marks it as special is that 'cette matérialité [du signifiant] est *singulière* en bien des points dont le premier est de ne point supporter la partition' ['the materiality of the signifier ... is *odd* [*singulière*] in many ways, the first of which is not to admit partition'].[18] This is the quality which arouses

---

15 See Richards, *Philosophy of Rhetoric*, p. 47.
16 *Encore*, p. 34.
17 *Ecrits*, p. 495; *Ecrits* Eng., p. 147. See also Miller, 'Préface', in Jacques Aubert, ed., *Joyce avec Lacan*, p. 10.
18 *Ecrits*, p. 24; *Purloined Poe*, pp. 38–9.

Derrida to protest: *'This "materiality", deduced from an indivisibility which is not found anywhere, corresponds in fact to an idealization'*, before concluding that Lacan considers the letter only as 'determined ... by its meaning-content' transmitted by the self-presence of the voice.[19]

How indeed is it possible to reconcile the apparently incompatible traits of materiality and indivisibility? Lacan's answer depends on his definition of the letter as a localized unit or element. He claims, for instance, that

un élément essentiel dans la parole elle-même était prédestiné à se couler dans les caractères mobiles qui ... présentifient valablement ce que nous appelons la lettre, à savoir la structure essentiellement localisée du signifiant.

an essential element of the spoken word itself [the phoneme] was predestined to flow into the mobile characters which ... render validly present what we call the 'letter', namely, the essentially localized structure of the signifier.[20]

In linking Saussure's phoneme to the letter understood as the meaningless element of significance, he is adopting the Aristotelian definition of the *stoicheion*, which means both letter and element, as the ultimate constituent of language, 'an indivisible sound of a particular kind ... that may become a factor in an intelligible sound'.[21] This reference has induced Derrida to accuse the Lacan of the fifties of 'incessantly subordinat[ing] writing, the letter and the text' to the *phonè*, the self-present voice of the logos, even when he speaks of rebuses and hieroglyphs.[22] In this context Derrida cites an especially trenchant passage from 'Situation de la psychanalyse et formation du psychanalyste en 1956':

Une écriture, comme le rêve lui-même, peut être figurative, elle est toujours comme le langage articulée symboliquement, soit tout comme lui *phonématique*, et phonétique en fait, dès lors qu'elle se lit.

A [piece of] writing, like the dream itself, may be figurative; it is always articulated symbolically like language, that is, *phonematic*, exactly like it, and in fact phonetic, as soon as it is read.[23]

While Derrida takes this as evidence that Lacan's writing

[19] Derrida, 'Purveyor of Truth', pp. 84–5.
[20] *Ecrits*, p. 501; *Ecrits* Eng., p. 153.
[21] Aristotle, *Poetics*, 1456b.
[22] Derrida, 'Purveyor of Truth', p. 82.   [23] *Ecrits*, p. 470.

requires passage through the voice, which indeed it does, he ignores the significant phrase that closes the sentence: 'as soon as it is read'. The statements surrounding these lines show that the first step necessary in 'reading a rebus' is to pronounce the names of the objects pictured in it, not in order to attach a meaning to them in self-consciousness, but, on the contrary, in order to hear the sounds of the name shorn of any meaning, as pure signifiers, or phonemes specific to the language(s) called upon in the particular rebus. Only when those sounds are rearranged, that is, punctuated and regrouped into another set of signifiers, will the puzzle yield its solution. Freud gives a marvellously concise example of this process in *The Interpretation of Dreams*. A young man dreamt that his uncle gave him a kiss in an automobile. The solution is: auto-eroticism.

Lengthier and more intricate strings of signifiers of course demand more elaborate modes of reading: in addition to sounds and phonemes, one must take into account 'des mots, des locutions, des sentences, sans y omettre pauses, scansions, coupes, périodes et parallélismes' [words, locutions, maxims, without omitting pauses, scansions, breaks, periods and parallelisms].[24] The principle of reading, however, remains the same; it is still a matter of attending to what Valéry called 'the Voice in action', that is, 'the concrete [*sensible*] characteristics of the language, sound, rhythm, accent, tone, movement'.[25] For Valéry and other symbolist and formalist thinkers, the poetic capacity consists precisely in the ability to discern and appreciate the formal and musical qualities of the material aspect of language (as distinct from its meaning), whether in conjunction with or apart from their relation to that meaning.

This characterization of the analyst's capability is utterly consistent with Freud's definition of the dream:

At bottom, dreams are nothing other than a particular *form* of thinking, made possible by the conditions of the state of sleep. It is the *dream-work* which creates that form, and it alone is the essence of dreaming – the explanation of its peculiar nature.[26]

The conjunction of Freud and Valéry is by no means fortuitous.

---

24 Ibid., p. 471.
25 Valéry, 'Poetry and Abstract Thought', p. 72.
26 Freud, *Interpretation of Dreams*, p. 507.

Like so many formalists before him, Valéry interpolates music as the *tertium comparationis* linking the poetic state to that of dreams; things form unusual combinations, variations and substitutions in both, corresponding with each other 'harmonically', as though they had become 'musicalized'. As a result, verse constitutes 'strange discourse as though made by someone other than the speaker and addressed to someone other than the listener. In short, it is a language within a language.'[27] This other discourse, which is at the same time a discourse of and for the Other, owes its strangeness to the fact that, like music, it is organized according to the principles of an intelligible order. Poetry isolates homogeneous elements out of discourse the way music extracts tones out of the dimension of sound. Once they had been so extracted, physical science was able to rearrange and codify the relations among them in accordance with a principle of measure. As Jakobson explains in detail, the key to the structural understanding of verse is the recognition that it imposes a grid of measurable units upon discourse.[28] In French prosody, for example, the important thing about a syllable is that it counts as one unit in a line defined by the total number it contains; the syllable is thus a unit of measure, like the centimetre or the minute. His famous definition of the poetic function as the projection of 'the principle of equivalence from the axis of selection onto the axis of combination' says nothing else than that all aspects of discourse may be so treated in poetry, whether it be sound, rhythm, time, length, syntax or meaning.

When Freud lays down the rule that the analyst must break a dream down into its elements before embarking on its interpretation, he is imposing the same principle of measure onto the discourse constituted by the dreamer's account of the dream. And the law of the parallelism of the signifier, to which Lacan refers at the end of his excursus on the tree in 'Agency', is a specific application of the same general rule. Lacan's claim that the phoneme was predestined to assume the role of letter thus rests on its function as a metric unit, rather than on its alleged superiority or precedence over writing. Just as a syllable in French verse acquires metric significance simply because it is one

[27] Valéry, 'Poetry and Abstract Thought', pp. 63–4.
[28] Jakobson, 'Linguistics and Poetics', p. 96.

unit, regardless, therefore, of the particular sounds from which it is formed, so a phoneme constitutes an element of speech, regardless of its audibility or proximity to the speaker. The letter manages to separate the signifier from the signified by breaking the former down into a series of 'ones' whose value is defined by their unicity rather than by their reference. That is why, contrary to the old adage, you can compare apples to oranges, as Lacan was fond of repeating.

In fact, even in his Saussurean period of the fifties, Lacan does make explicit mention of the oneness that the letter crystallizes out of the flux of experience, whether vocal or other. 'Mais une fois la chaîne symbolique constituée, dès lors que vous introduisez, sous la forme d'unités de succession, une certaine unité significative, n'importe quoi ne peut plus sortir' ['But once the symbolic chain is constituted, as soon as you introduce a certain significant unity, in the form of unities of succession, what comes out [of a game of presence and absence, of chance] can no longer be just anything'].[29] The source of this oneness is thus the same process of grouping ('unities of succession') we examined in the previous chapter. The reason why the Lacanian letter cannot be partitioned has nothing to do with the etheriality of intentions or the ideality of meaning, but with its constitution through the process of grouping together into units. To divide such an entity into parts would be to divest it of its existence as a primordial element of significance, for the lower level elements from which it is formed are defined precisely as being random, as lacking the regularity characteristic of a unit. Lacan emphasizes this unicity in the 'Seminar on "The Purloined Letter"' in several places: he translates the word 'odd' in the Poe text as *singulier*, 'singular', asserts that 'le signifiant est unité d'être unique, n'étant de par sa nature symbole que d'une absence' ['the signifier is a unit in its very uniqueness, being by nature symbol only of an absence'], states that the 'true subject' of Poe's tale is 'la singularité de la lettre' ['the singularity of the letter'],[30] in addition to maintaining that it brooks no partition.

When Lacan declares that Dupin is able to locate the purloined letter because he is a poet, his reference is to the capacity to perceive the singularity of phenomena and language. While he

[29] *Le moi*, p. 227; *Ego*, p. 193.
[30] *Ecrits*, pp. 24, 29; *Purloined Poe*, pp. 39, 43.

contends that Dupin is wrong to imagine that mathematical truths claim to be applicable to all situations, he nevertheless agrees with Dupin's point that it requires a science of the particular to unearth the missing letter. Instead of resorting to a general principle in his search for the letter, as the Prefect of Police had done, Dupin's 'measures were adapted to [the Minister's] capacity, with reference to the circumstances by which he was surrounded'.[31] Dupin had already given evidence of his adeptness at properly noting and evaluating particulars in 'The Murders in the Rue Morgue', when he was able to divine the idiosyncratic chain of associations which led the thoughts of the narrator of the story from an encounter with a fruit merchant to the idea of a fellow named Chantilly who had failed in his attempt to begin a career as an actor. He summarizes this 'peculiar analytical ability' as the capacity to make a host of 'observations and inferences'.[32] But what characterizes Dupin most strikingly is his ability to recognize the particularity of alterity. It is this capacity which enables him to figure out that the perpetrator of the murders was an ape, for he alone grasps the fact that what appears as a different foreign language to each witness must in fact be that which escapes all attempts to capture it in a system of meaning, otherness its(non-)self; as in 'The Purloined Letter', Dupin has been able to locate the true place of the subject, the utterly meaningless noises of the totally alien (animal). Like the Minister, Dupin combines the creative with the analytic when he uses a process akin to the Kantian 'analogies of experience' to guide his inferences: 'The material world ... abounds with very strict analogies to the immaterial ... [there is some truth] to the rhetorical dogma, that metaphor or simile may be made to strengthen an argument ... '.[33] (One might also think of Swedenborg or Baudelaire in this context.) In the case of the purloined letter, the analogical principle in question is that of 'simplicity', which leads Dupin to conclude that the Minister has 'hidden' the letter in plain view.

This principle has a strictly objective basis in that, according to Lacan, it correlates the letter with the concept of place, which can only be introduced by, and understood in terms of, the signifier.

[31] Poe, 'The Purloined Letter', pp. 343–4.
[32] Poe, 'Murders in the Rue Morgue', pp. 191–7.
[33] Poe, 'The Purloined Letter', p. 344.

Dupin points out that signs whose letters are spread out over a large area are much more difficult to discern than those written in a more compact space. The space defined by the signifier is thus different from, even if in a sense coincident with, that of other objects. Since we know that for Lacan the institution of the signifier is concurrent with that of the phallus, it follows that he should describe its function on the imaginary level (little phi) as the unit of measurement of the various objects of desire. They are treated as equivalents in what we might call 'signifying space', and thus capable of being measured by the same unit, to the extent that the fantasies built around them are all designed to remedy the fading, or lack of being, of the subject by filling the place of the real presence.[34] The unicity of the phallic signifier is thus the symbol of the absence, or want-to-be, of the subject. It is precisely that uniqueness symbolized by the proper name (Polynices) which we discussed in chapter 3.

In his seminars of the early sixties, on *Le transfert* (1960–1) and *L'identification* (1961–2), Lacan developed a more complex and comprehensive theory of the singular materiality of the letter, which was designed to give a detailed account both of the history of the development of the various human writing systems and of the logic of the condensation of letters out of speech, that is, out of the stream of the signifier. At the same time, this argument made a clearer distinction between the letter and the signifier, and it showed more specifically how the one leads to the other. In 'Situation de la psychanalyse', Lacan had already proposed that linguists should jettison the term 'ideographic' writing, for it implies the existence of a direct connection, presumably one of resemblance, between the image and the thing represented. In 'Agency' and the seminar on 'Identification', he supported that recommendation by demonstrating that even in the two scripts that have long served in the west as prime examples of ideographic writing, Egyptian hieroglyphics and Chinese characters, sound plays an essential role. Champollion was able to decipher the Rosetta stone only when he recognized that many of the letters of Egyptian hieroglyphics rely on the same principle as rebuses: a pictograph serves not to designate its object but the

---

[34] *Transfert*, pp. 297–304.

sound of the object's name, its initial vowel, consonant, or syllable. Having studied Chinese during the Second World War,[35] Lacan also claimed that many Chinese characters are constructed in a similar way: compound characters are composed of signs for objects, the sounds of whose names form the syllables that are joined together to constitute the word designated by that character. Although both systems are figurative in a sense, they are at the same time phonematic and strictly dependent on the forms of the individual language.[36] If no script can be entirely phonetic, as Derrida rightly claims, it is also true that no writing system is completely non-phonetic either.[37]

But the mere fact that sound necessarily intervenes in the constitution of writing systems means neither that writing is phonematic in nature nor that sense is directly present in that sound. Employing evidence gathered by Février, Lacan argues in *L'identification* that the letters of the actual writing systems developed in divergent societies did not undergo a progressive evolution from image to phonematic mark by a process of abstraction and stylization, as many scholars have conjectured. The history of peoples around the world shows that the marks which eventually came to be used as letters existed already, before they had any relation to the voice.[38] Although their specific origin and use vary from culture to culture, all were distilled out of a particular discourse, such as the trademarks on Egyptian pottery that became Phoenician letters, or the lines on tortoise shells employed for divination in ancient China. Even the so-called artificial scripts of mathematics and symbolic logic were precipitated out of pre-existing discourses.[39] In short, all writing arose through the same process of evacuating and reattaching meaning as characterizes both metaphor and transference in the first sense.

According to Lacan, these marks developed into letters by

---

[35] See Roudinesco, *Histoire de la psychanalyse*, vol. II, p. 161.

[36] Allouch, *Lettre pour lettre*, provides an intelligent analysis of these claims, including detailed examples and extensive quotes from the seminar on 'Identification' in which Lacan elaborates his concept of writing. See especially his chapter 8.

[37] I am referring only to systems for writing actual languages that are spoken (as opposed to machine languages), and of course I am not considering pure mathematical notations such as the binary system.

[38] Julien, 'Le nom propre et la lettre', p. 36.

[39] *Encore*, pp. 36–7.

virtue of three processes, negation, naming and homophony.[40] The first of these consists in subtracting from the object all those qualities that appeal to our senses, inscribing a 'single stroke', or unitary trait, to represent its unity and uniqueness, its 'oneness', as I have called it above. In 'Group Psychology and the Analysis of the Ego', Freud used the expression 'single stroke' (*einziger Zug* in German, *trait unaire* in Lacan's French) to designate one mode of identification, especially with the ego-ideal.

As with his theory of rhetoric, Lacan revamped the expression even as he adopted it, in *Transfert* redefining Freud's single stroke in terms similar to those of the Usener–Cassirer theory of the 'radical metaphor', or 'condensation', according to which, it will be recalled, a 'punctiform unit', a '*one* ... extends its denotation over more and more special cases, until it comes to denote them all, and assumes the power of expressing a class concept'. 'Mais ce qui est défini par cet *ein einziger Zug*, c'est le caractère ponctuel de la référence originelle à l'Autre dans le rapport narcissique' [But what is defined by this *ein einziger Zug* is the punctual character of the original reference to the Other in the narcissistic relation.][41] Lacan explains that by 'punctual' he means that this kind of identification eschews any attempt to include the total reality of the person, generally a paternal figure, who plays the role of ego-ideal; it ignores the manifold qualities that constitute the Other and concentrates instead on isolated traits each of which is unique, and by virtue of this unicity partakes of the nature of the signifier. Yet the unitary trait is a sign rather than a signifier; unlike the signifier, which can function only in opposition to other signifiers, it operates alone, without entering into relation with a 'battery of signifiers'. By reducing the diversity of experience to the one, however, the unitary trait acts as the 'primordial symbolic term', the first step which prepares the way for the entry into the symbolic.

Before becoming a full-fledged signifier, the ego-ideal regulates the subject's relation to external objects, whether in groups or in individuals. Hence the function of the *einziger Zug*:

---

[40] Hartley, whom Richards refers to as the main proponent of associationism in the eighteenth century, gives a somewhat similar conjecture as to the origins of writing, although without the emphasis on homophony. See *Hartley's Theory of the Human Mind*, pp. 123–4.

[41] *Transfert*, p. 414.

C'est pure et simple affaire d'essai métaphorique que de donner à tous les objets un trait commun, pure affaire de décret que de fixer un trait commun à leur diversité.

It's a pure and simple matter of a metaphoric exercise to give all objects a common trait; a pure matter of decree to affix a common trait to their diversity.[42]

In short, it operates according to Kant's principle of 'apperception' as modified by Cassirer's notion of metaphor, imposing a series of unities onto the diversity of experience, and thereby preparing the contents of perception to become objects of knowledge (see chapter 3, note 28). But in psychoanalytic terminology, 'objects' of course refers also to objects of love; Lacan is thus arguing that all love has a narcissistic root in that the subject draws upon her fund of narcissism to confer every 'unitary trait' on the love-object by means of the metaphoric process. As we shall see in the next chapter, this contention forms an important part of his theory of transference.

The reduction of sensory qualities entailed in this first step of forming the letter resembles the Russian formalists' notion of 'algebraization' or 'automatism', which they thought it was the function of art to combat through defamiliarization.[43] Consequently, it might appear that Lacan has simply reversed the formalists' position: where they see the perceptual fullness of the object as the mark of its individuality and 'life', Lacan takes the perceptual impoverishment of the object, its universalization into the pure numerical quality of oneness, as the representation of its uniqueness. In a sense, that is true: as we shall discuss in chapter 6, according to Lacan the fullness of what was perceived at any given time can never be recovered. But it is for that very reason that a distinctive mark is required. This negation, the equivalent of the metonymic minus discussed in chapter 2, introduces an entirely non-natural type of knowledge which is the necessary prerequisite for the second phase of the process, naming. This latter process will lead, in turn, to the new form of materiality of the letter. Once produced, the future letter, like any other object, is given a name that designates the object it embodies. Now the name of the object – the signifier – can be

---

[42] Ibid., p. 458.
[43] Shklovsky, 'Sterne's *Tristram Shandy*', pp. 12–13.

taken to designate the sign that represents the object pictographi-cally. One can say of the sign for a loaf of bread, 'This is a loaf of bread.' It is just this ambiguity that Magritte plays upon in his famous painting, 'This is not a pipe.'[44] The mark that will constitute the letter is thereby also identified with the thing, the way a proper name is supposed to label a single entity directly, independently of the linguistic system of differences.

The third and crucial step in the institution of writing is the use of the name of the mark to indicate a different object from the one denoted by the sign, one whose name has the identical sound. In Egyptian hieroglyphics, for instance, the name of the scarab and the verb 'to become' having the same consonants (kh+p+r), the pictograph of the insect was utilized to write the verb. The capacity to designate an other object is precisely the metonymic function. This use of homophony, which is the key to the rebus, reverses the identification effected in the previous step. The letter now stands neither for a thing nor an image, but for one or more sounds which constitute a name that can henceforth be trans-ferred onto other things. Name and thing have been sundered; the effect of the letter is to separate the signifier from the object. The 'other object' is thus other in two senses: it is different from the first object denoted by the noun; and it is separate from the name. An entire order of the signifier has been detached from that of the signified, so that there is no longer any specific relation between the two.

Even while instituting the referential relation, homophony thus makes it possible to attend to the signifier without regard to the referent, that is, to attend to the pure sound of language. This non-referential attention to language gives rise in turn to the scrutiny of linguistic structures or forms, such as grammatical and syntactic categories. Now the phonematic, grammatical and syntactic systems of a language are, in most respects, specific to that individual language, and it is this specificity made manifest by the letter which constitutes its 'materiality' for Lacan. Only when the letter has done its work of separation does this materiality of the signifier emerge, and what appears thus is just what Valéry called the voice in action. Homo-phonè is therefore the link that connects the voice to the letter.

[44] Cited in Allouch, *Lettre pour lettre*, p. 159.

Via this route Lacan rejoins the formalist tradition that stretches back to Kant and German idealism. When, instead of highlighting perception of the object, Shklovskian defamiliarization serves to lay bare technique, as in his analysis of *Tristram Shandy*, it fulfils the same function as Lacan's homophony. If the first step of the process 'algebraizes' the object, the last step reinstates the importance of sensory qualities, but they are those of the letter as object rather than those of the things in the perceptual world. Lacan's notion of the materiality of the letter thus resembles the definition of the artistic 'sign' proposed by the majority of formalist critics, including Valéry and Shklovsky. In contrast to the alleged 'transparency' of the symbols of practical and scientific language, in which the sign itself disappears in order to permit direct access to the meaning, the artistic 'sign' is supposed to be 'opaque', that is, it 'calls attention to itself'. One might therefore be tempted to ask whether, like so many formalists, Lacan thereby makes the signifier into the signified.[45] In one sense, the answer is clearly no, because homophony does not become an end in itself, or the 'truth' of language, the way literariness does for a Shklovsky, form for a Rousset, or style for a Spitzer. In other ways, however, the reply to this question cannot be so unambiguous. Lacan's analysis of uniqueness in *Antigone*, which parallels those of metonymy and of the letter in many ways, is surely formalist in that, like the other two derivations, it depends on the emptying of content through a self-referential process. Yet in each of these cases Lacan gives his argument a final deconstructive twist that both maintains and undermines the formalist edifice. Polynices' uniqueness remains both unexpressible and inaccessible, and can only be realized through an act. Metonymic loss of meaning can only be supplemented by metaphoric production of sense. Having been definitively severed from the signified, the signifier no longer bears any trace within itself whereby the lost signified might be reconstructed. Language can no longer be conceived as a means of finding or constructing the unity of the objects of experience, but as the

---

[45] This formula summarizes the gist of Derrida's early critique of Rousset in *Writing and Difference*, as well as of Felman's reading of Lacan in 'Turning the Screw of Interpretation' (see pp. 30–1). Some have interpreted Derrida's assessment of Lacan in 'Purveyor' in these terms, but that is certainly a gross oversimplification of his argument there.

mark of the irretrievable gap between conscious identity and the unconscious that undermines it.[46] The homophony of the letter thus becomes the royal road to the paradoxical truth of the unconscious.

In his first seminar, Lacan claims that the meaning of Freud's discovery of the unconscious is that 'Dans l'analyse, la vérité surgit par ce qui est le représentant le plus manifeste de la méprise – le lapsus, l'action qu'on appelle improprement *manquée*' ['in analysis, truth emerges in the most clearcut representation of the mistake – the slip, the action which one, improperly, calls *manquée* [missed, failed, abortive]'].[47] There is a fundamental ambiguity in the term Freud used to designate failed actions – *Fehl/ leistung* – as in the French translation – *acte manqué* (or *action manquée*) – for it is not only an act that fails to achieve its goal, or a performance that is not brought off properly, but also a stand-in for a performance that is lacking but whose lack is indicated by that very failure. In all those failed acts in which Freud saw the operation of the unconscious – slips, dreams, symptoms, jokes, free associations – there is a truth striving to appear. But this truth can only manifest itself as an interruption of discourse, in the form of a mistake, precisely because, when it comes to stating the truth of the subject, the word is always lacking. Only homophony, the same 'mistake' that gives rise to the letter, can ensure the possibility of transference in the first sense of the term, which allows the otherwise ineffable to reach a kind of expression.

The general idea that error forms the necessary condition for the emergence of truth can be found in the writings of the later Heidegger, after the 'turn', for example in 'On the Essence of Truth'. What distinguishes Freud from Heidegger in this context is that the psychoanalyst developed a method for analysing unconscious formations, and thus succeeded in bringing the phenomenon of error into the field of scientific study.

If the agency of the letter governs the unconscious lapse, it is now clear that the primordial mistake – and hence vehicle of truth – is homophony, which exploits the fundamental ambiguity of language. The radical nature of this contention can only be appreciated against the background of western metaphysics

46 Butler, *Subjects of Desire*, pp. 190–3.
47 *Ecrits techniques*, p. 292; *Papers*, p. 265.

which, at least since Aristotle, has considered homophony to be the arch-enemy of that unity of signifier to signified presumed necessary to philosophy, science and truth. In his ground-breaking study of the problem of being in Aristotle, Aubenque proposes that the Greek philosopher developed his theory of homonymy in response to challenges from the sophists.[48] How is it possible to defend opposite sides of the same proposition equally, as the sophists claimed to do? Or rather, where is the flaw in their arguments that allows them to give the illusion of doing so? These are the questions which led Aristotle to reflect on language and the process of meaning. His answer is that the meaning of one or more words changes in the course of the argument; in other words, that they rely on what he calls homonymy in the first sentence of the *Categories*. But if a single word can take on several meanings, then language cannot be the closed order of being in which word and meaning are one, as the sophists claimed. This kind of homonymy shows that word and meaning are separate entities, and that there must exist between them a relation of reference not based on resemblance (since the same word may refer to two things which have no common attributes at all and thus cannot possibly both 'resemble' that same word). Language is meaningful only if one can know to which thing a given word refers in a particular discourse. There-fore communication and thinking require the possibility of speci-fying the single meaning operative at a given time.

Since thought and communication do in fact exist, such a reduction of ambiguity must be possible, at least in the case of sophistical arguments. But language is subject to a more funda-mental type of equivocity: words being universals, each must refer to a multiplicity, and perhaps even an infinity, of individual things. Aristotle's solution is that language can refer to things only via meanings, and that these meanings are, or should be, the essence of the thing. This solution will succeed, however, only if there is a fundamental unity of essence; otherwise the problem of homonymy will simply have been displaced from one level to

---

[48] The following summary is drawn primarily from chapters 3 and 4 of Aubenque's *Le problème de l'être chez Aristote*. In order to save space, I have condensed Aubenque's thesis considerably, omitting several steps in his argument and oversimplifying others. I am indebted to Weber's *Rückkehr zu Freud*, recently translated as *Return to Freud*, for leading me to discover Aubenque's treatise.

another. This unity must exist at the level of the proposition, of a statement of the form x is y (provided it be a definition of essence and not the attribution of 'accidental' properties). The copular 'is' thus becomes the equivalent of the One, of unity; whence arises the problem of (the unity of) being.

Aubenque's thesis is that Aristotle affirms both the irreducible heterogeneity of being and the necessity of presupposing that such a unity does exist. Without unity there could be no knowledge at all, since whatever one asserted might be false as well as true. But the various categories of attribution (and the Greek *categorein* means 'to attribute'), such as quantity, quality, time, place, process, etc., have no common denominator; there is no principle or rule which would make it possible to relate each to the others, or to make one of them the source of the others. There is thus no unity of being of the things of this world. The word 'being' suffers from a fundamental homonymy, since it may refer to any of the categories of being ascribed to a subject in a proposition. Aristotle's theory of being is aporetic, in that it both requires and denies the unity of being. Indeed, 'predication itself ... is aporetic, since it consists in saying that the same *is* other'.[49] The synthesis effected by predication entails a prior division, which itself is an indication of the lack of self-identity of the things in a world of movement and change.

Homonymy is therefore the enemy of truth not just because the possibility of changing meanings in the course of an argument might lead to mistakes in logic, but because it undermines the very existence of identity. To make of the mistake the source of truth is thus the most violent reversal of tradition possible. But it is still a reversal, that is, it retains the notion of truth and identity as a necessary, even if inaccessible, horizon, unlike the Derridean deconstruction which renounces truth altogether, in theory if not in practice. Insofar as Lacan's homophony specifically designates the voice, it opposes even more radically the Augustinian conception of the relation between sound and sense that dominates the Middle Ages and is still influential in the nineteenth century, as one can see in a poet like Lamartine or a theoretician such as Freud. In this view, sound is the incarnation of the 'true word', an unfortunately necessary externalization, in the form of the 'mate-

[49] Aubenque, *Le problème de l'être chez Aristote*, p. 448.

rial voice', of the inner voice of God, of truth.[50] Although the comparison to the incarnation is of course honorific, Augustine and his successors nevertheless draw the conclusion that sound is not merely a detour necessary for human beings, but the occasion of a necessary loss, the purity of the inner word being corrupted by its ejection into the externality of material sound.

This loss is a fall from the universal to the particular, whether that of a specific language such as Greek or English, or that of a group or individual employing the language. Although the ultimate ideal of such a theory is the sheer transparency of telepathic communication, philosophic ideas of language have generally taken as their aim the more realizable goal of what in his later writings Lacan called the discourse of the master (and thus of being, *maître – m'être*), and which early on he termed a 'well-made language', one which is precisely 'privée de toute référence à une voix' ['deprived of all reference to a voice'].[51] In the context of his discussion of the emergence of truth from error, this deprivation signifies positively the univocity of a one-to-one correspondence between words and things, of which homonymy is the antithesis, and negatively the elimination of any partial or particular point of view. After citing Hegel's notion of absolute knowledge as the totalization of discourse through the removal of all contradictions, Lacan intimates that the existence of many discordant discourses regarding diverse arenas of human interaction, such as religion, law, science and politics, betrays the obstinate resistance of particularization to the law of the universal. What is at stake ultimately in this ideal of a unified science is the elimination of language entirely, for reasons Cassirer ably describes:

Language can never definitively leave and break through this sphere [of possible perception]; for even where as discourse, as objective logos, it is directed toward something absolutely nonsensuous, it can only designate this nonsensuous something from the standpoint of the speaker ... All living speech contains within it this dichotomy, this polarity of subject and object ... This inward participation of the ego in the content of what is said is expressed in innumerable subtle shadings, in changes of dynamic accents, in changes of tempo, rhythm, and melody ... In [science's] symbolic signs and concepts everything which possessed any

---

[50] Augustine of Hippo, *The Trinity*, pp. 476–7.
[51] *Ecrits techniques*, p. 291; *Papers*, p. 265.

sort of mere expressive value is extinguished. Here it is no longer any individual subject, but only the thing itself speaks.[52]

Homonymy is synonymous with voice insofar as tempo, rhythm and melody allow people to give the same words different subjective imports, and thus different meanings. In a similar manner, any specific language or discourse must necessarily designate its objects from a particular standpoint. Paradoxically, symbolization entails particularization even while it creates universals. The ideal of science, as the term objectivity so neatly articulates, is the annihilation of communal as well as individual subjectivity, the elimination of what Lacan would later term the 'enunciation'. For Cassirer as for Kant, this loss is a noble sacrifice worth making for the benefit of future knowledge. Lacan, however, constantly calls the value of this sacrifice into question, as MacCannell has so forcefully demonstrated. The problem in her critique stems from the failure to perceive that Lacan recognizes, as does Cassirer, that this sacrifice takes place by virtue of the iteration of the very process of metaphorization which made the subjectification of language possible in the first place. Without it the subject would have remained tied to the object, reified in an inescapable because too proximate meaning.

The foregoing analysis shows that Lacan's speech (*parole*) represents the truth of the subject insofar as it struggles to free itself from the shackles of objective truth by means of homophony. The status of this subjective truth in relation to the error of homophony still remains to be determined, however. Does voice simply convey a different kind of determinate meaning, as Cassirer implies, or a set of determinate but heterogeneous meanings like those of Aristotle's categories in Aubenque's interpretation? Or does speech imply a more radical dissolution of meaning in the crucible of the letter? Freud's explanation, which Lacan claims to be reading, maintains a certain ambiguity on this matter, but ultimately comes down on the side of meaning. In the concluding chapter of *The Psychopathology of Everyday Life* he asserts that the 'mechanism of the parapraxes' corresponds to that of the dream-work, which, as we recall, he considered to be a form of thinking rather than a content. Yet although he concedes that some slips are based purely on what he calls 'external', that

---

[52] Cassirer, *Philosophy of Symbolic Forms*, vol. III, p. 339.

is, meaning-less, associations, he nevertheless awards the leading role to meaning rather than form:

> We believe that in general we are free to choose what words we shall use for clothing our thoughts or what images for disguising them. Closer observation shows that other considerations determine this choice, and that behind the form in which the thought is expressed a glimpse may be had of a deeper meaning – often one that is not intended.[53]

For the Freud of *Psychopathology*, the truth that emerges from the mistake is a repressed meaning that can find no other path open to expression.

If Freud offers a reasonable explanation of the relation between slips and a certain kind of truth, and shows why the lapse might on some occasions borrow the primary processes as its path to expression, his theory does not demonstrate why the connection between the slip and homophony should be a necessary one. The solution to this problem depends upon finding answers to two additional questions: through what process does the specifically material, vocal or visual, dimension of language manage to combine with the semantic character of homonymy to produce a discourse in which truth and error are inextricably entwined? Why should the thoughts 'behind the form' have any greater claim to truth than those on the 'surface?'

As noted in chapter 3, at the time of his first seminar Lacan considered the aim of analysis to be the reconciliation of the subjective, contingency, with essence or being, universality. In this respect analysis was simply the continuation, or repair, of the process of retrospectively symbolizing one's history that continues throughout life. Lacan conceived this process as the integration of the 'subjective drama' into a social myth of extended or universal value,[54] and it is therefore in the realm of mythic discourse that we must seek the answer to our first question.

The eminent nineteenth-century proponent of 'comparative mythology', Max Müller, developed a theory of myth according to which language marries truth to error.[55] He contends that 'mythology is an inherent necessity of language', but an unfortu-

---

[53] Freud, *The Psychopathology of Everyday Life*, p. 216.
[54] *Ecrits techniques*, p. 215; *Papers*, p. 191.
[55] Delacroix mentions Müller's theories several times in *Langage et pensée*.

nate one: 'the dark shadow which language throws on thought'.[56]

Whenever any word, that was at first used metaphorically, is used without a clear conception of the steps that led from its original to its metaphorical meaning, there is danger of mythology; whenever those steps are forgotten and artificial steps put in their places, we have mythology, or, if I may say so, diseased language.[57]

The name Müller assigns to the bacillus that infects language, the obscure force that casts its shadow over the transparency of linguistic meaning, is the one he finds in Aristotle, homonymy. Homonymy has an equally deleterious partner, synonymy, or what the stoics called polyonymy (several words for the same thing). Each participates in the subversion of the one-to-one relation between words and objects, synonymy involving an excess of names over things, homonymy a surplus of objects over words.[58]

According to Müller, natural and supernatural beings and forces are named metaphorically in terms of their attributes, and since each one has many qualities, those beings which play an important enough role in the life and imagination of a group are capable of taking on a different name for each of their properties. At the same time, there are many objects which share the same attributes.

Synonyms, again, if used constantly, must naturally give rise to a number of homonyms. If we may call the sun by fifty names expressive of different qualities, some of these names will be applicable to other objects also which happen to possess the same quality. These different objects would then be called by the same name – they would become homonyms.[59]

In time, the metaphoric sense of some of these names having been forgotten, they would become 'mere sound', that is, simple labels or proper names without any other signification. *Zeus*, for

---

[56] Müller, 'Philosophy of Mythology', p. 65.
[57] Müller, 'Metaphor', pp. 375–6.
[58] Müller's polyonymy differs considerably from Aristotle's synonymy. For the philosopher, synonymy is a matter of things, and results from the legitimate overlapping of attributes, species and genera; thus one may designate the same individual as a man or an animal, as tall or wise. For the mythologist, polyonymy is a property of language that leads to confusion – the existence of several names to designate the same individual.
[59] Müller, *Comparative Mythology*, p. 92.

example, meant 'sky' at one time in Greek, but it later was reduced to a pure proper noun, the name of the god. In some cases, the phonetic make-up of the name facilitates the accumulation of new meanings. 'Thus, *Lykegenés*, the son of light – Apollo, was changed into a son of Lycia; *Délios*, the bright one, gave rise to the myth of the birth of Apollo in Delos.'[60]

A proper interpretation of a myth constructed on such a basis therefore requires that one ignore the coherence of the story-line and 'dissect' or 'decipher' it by 'reduc[ing] it to its constituent elements'.[61] Müller gives several impressive readings of mythological stories which arose through this process. He claims that the myth of Deukalion and Pyrrha, who create the human race by throwing stones behind them, originates from a pun, the mistaken identification of *láos*, Greek for people, and *laas*, stone. According to another well-known myth, Daphne is saved from Apollo's lustful advances when her mother, Earth, transforms her into a laurel tree. Daphne was the name of the laurel in Greek, but Müller endeavours to show that the word derives from the Sanskrit *Ahanâ* via the postulated *Dahanâ*, and means the redness of the dawn. The 'original' myth simply recounted the daily changes in the sky, as the sun chases the dawn into the earth. The metamorphosis into the laurel would then be a late alteration, once the metaphorical etymology of *Daphné* had been forgotten. Faded metaphor (the red dawn, the violent embrace), transliteration (rewriting the protoform Daphanâ in Greek letters), and homonymy (the goddess's name and the word for laurel tree) combine to render an originally intelligible story based on observation into a nonsensical myth.[62]

The most curious aspect of Müller's hypothesis, for the purposes of the present study, is that Cassirer formulated his theory of myth and language with the express purpose of refuting and replacing it.

---

[60] Ibid., pp. 93–4.   [61] Ibid., p. 112.

[62] I do not know whether Freud was familiar with Müller's theories before the gestation of his method of dream interpretation; the earliest mention of Müller I have found in Freud's works occurs in *Totem and Taboo* (1912–1913), and then only in the indirect form of a reference from Andrew Lang's *Secret of the Totem*. There is in any case an extraordinary similarity between the latter's system of myth interpretation and the former's method of interpreting dreams and other unconscious formations, due perhaps to their common intellectual heritage stemming from the German romantics' theory of *Witz*.

What we call myth is, for him [Müller], something conditioned and negotiated by the agency of language; it is, in fact, the product of a basic shortcoming, an inherent weakness of language. All linguistic denotation is essentially ambiguous – and in this ambiguity, this 'paronymia' of words lies the source of all myths.[63]

Cassirer rejects both the priority Müller attributes to language over myth and the claim that myth results from homonymy conceived as an essential defect of language. He asserts that the relation between myth and language is reciprocal rather than asymmetric, and, as we have seen, that both exemplify the creative power to produce a world. Ultimately Cassirer objects to Müller's thesis because he wants to impress both myth and language into the service of scientific truth. The irony is that the mythologist also wanted to demonstrate that the apparent sense-lessness (and immorality) with which critics from Pythagoras on have taxed myth is simply the residue of an intelligibility lost through forgetfulness and error. 'We deny in history an atomistic conglomerate of chances, or the despotic rule of a mute fate. We believe that there is nothing irrational in History and Nature . . .'[64]

Lacan agrees with Müller that, in order to qualify as a myth, a symbolization must contain a portion of unintelligibility, and that this opacity results from internal linguistic processes – attribution, obsolescence of verbal forms and meanings (repression), syno-nymy and homophony – rather than from some supposed funda-mental incommensurability between language and reality. But he rejects the contention that the shadow of senselessness can be illuminated by the discovery of a pre-existing meaning construed as the observation of an objective reality. No doubt it is just that presupposition which led Müller to the specious and monotonous conclusion that all world mythologies can be 'reduced' to solar myths. For Lacan, as for Cassirer, myth is a constructive process whereby the previously senseless is supplied with meaning. Yet he repudiates Cassirer's progressistic thesis that myth is simply one step along the way toward the ultimate triumph of science. Although rational in the sense that it can shrink the field of the unknown by integrating the particular into the social, myth is not controlled by an objective reason, whether conceived as origin – Müller's prototypical observation of nature – or end – Cassirer's

---

[63] Cassirer, *Language and Myth*, pp. 3–4.
[64] Müller, *Comparative Mythology*, p. 7.

dissolution of subjectivity in the concept. On the contrary, we have recourse to myth precisely when confronting some inexplicable aspect of the real. 'Nous voyons surgir des mythes au moment qu'il en est besoin pour suppléer à la béance de ce qui peut être assuré dialectiquement' [We see myths arise when they are needed to supplement the gap in what can be secured through dialectics].[65] Moreover, the ambiguity and potential meaninglessness inherent in the signifier as 'mere sound', highlighted by Müller and bemoaned by Cassirer, makes it impossible for any symbolization whatever to eliminate the zone of obscurity entirely.

Although Müller thinks of myth as an inevitable 'stage' in the progress of the human mind, his thesis actually furnishes a description of the mechanism of mythic distortion which makes error an ever-present, because intrinsic, moment of discourse, and this type of mistake is entirely conditioned by the specific structures and sounds of the particular language or languages involved. It will always be possible, therefore, for a truth alien to the socially accepted sense of a discourse, like the subjective meanings described by Freud and Lacan, to commandeer it in order to say something other. Why this other discourse should enjoy a special status in regard to truth Lacan endeavours to explain in chapter XXI of his first seminar, 'Truth Emerges from the Mistake', by bringing out the peculiar force of those German words beginning with the prefix *ver* by which Freud classifies unconscious processes – *Verdichtung* (condensation), *Verneinung* (denial), and *Verdrängung* (repression). Each one indicates a type of failure that is not a mere lack or negation but a positive action undertaken and thwarted. In Lacan's translation, condensation denotes the non-superposition of language with meanings (i.e. synonymy and homonymy), denial, the impossibility of fitting certain objects into discourse, and repression, the word that is lacking.

What Lacan calls the moment of speech (*parole*), the intervention of the subjective voice into language, thus has the status of an activity rather than of a static meaning either present or absent. The truth of speech is the act of speech itself. As a result, even though speech is in some sense beyond ordinary discourse, nevertheless both sorts of meaning, the discursive and the

---

[65] *Transfert*, p. 144.

subjective, are products of the same discourse. The truth of the mistake is not a second discourse like the first, but the vocal, 'phonematic', subjectivized moments of ordinary discourse marked by the primary processes of condensation, denegation and repression. In short, subjective truth necessarily emerges from error, because it can come into existence only where and because ordinary discourse fails. It is precisely that which escapes from the process of symbolization.

In order to appreciate the force of this argument we must bear in mind that for Lacan discourse begins with a primordial symbolization which is unavoidably defective from the standpoint of the ideal of objective truth, since in letting certain things be, it inevitably prevents others from being. There is always a share of lethe in the revelatory function of aletheia. In less metaphoric terms, no matter what set of categories one deploys, there will always be something radically Other which escapes from the former and therefore must remain unexpressible.

Lacan explains in chapter xvii of *Papers* that this unexpressible Other is not some ineffable reality but rather the hole dug into the real by speech. The notions of being and non-being, with their correlates of truth and falsehood, are inscribed into the real by language. The minus sign in the formula for metonymy, therefore, signifies not only the general loss of reference but also that which is temporarily or permanently inexpressible. Resistance to meaning becomes repression. Now, as we have seen, Lacan adopts a catachretic theory of metaphor and of transference in the first sense, in which the letter supplements the deficiency of symbolization. An unconscious desire is unconscious precisely because and to the extent that it is unexpressible without the non-sensical day-residues. But speech is a many-layered phenomenon in which one meaning emerges from behind another. Up to a certain point, then, the slip can reveal a second, a third, a fourth meaning and so on, which are in most respects no different in nature from the first.[66] But this process must necessarily come to an end at the point of the originary repression where there is

---

[66] The most significant difference is that their signifiers have been 'atomized' into what Lacan calls metonymic ruins, or remainders ('Formations de l'inconscient', *Bulletin de Psychologie*, 11.4–5, p. 295). More on this topic in our discussion of the role of free association in relation to transference in its customary sense.

nothing more behind speech than speech itself. Here is the place where sense encounters an ultimate non-sense, where the attempt to express particularity through the homonymic voice glides by the homonymic impossibility of capturing the particular being of the subject in a language constituted of universals.

In this regard, the process of lettrification resembles that of proper names. Although names generally evolve from common nouns which represent a meaning – place, profession, attribute, etc. – and although their use entails inserting the individual named into a system of social classification, nevertheless, the fact that they are usually not translated when transported from one language to another shows that they do not carry either meaning or class with them. The purpose of the proper name is to establish a direct identification between the name and the particular person or thing,[67] avoiding the violence of categorization by rejecting meaning. Common nouns are of course incapable of isolating the individuality of an object precisely because they indicate what is common to a class. When in his later writings Lacan strove to conceptualize this problem in terms of mathematical logic, he assimilated the function of the apperceptive unitary trait – unifying the disparate aspects of manifold experience – to the operation in set theory whereby absolutely heterogeneous things, taken only in their 'oneness' each, are collected into a set designated by a letter. Like Cassirer's metaphors, letters constitute sets rather than designating them.[68] As a result, although the 'little letters' of modern science are not identical to the letter that governs the unconscious, they arise and function in homologous ways. The letter picks out its set the way a proper name picks out an individual, not by virtue of some qualities that can be articulated, but as that which eludes expression.

The letter and the name point to a unicity that can only be evoked, a fundamental Otherness that can never be grasped within language yet would never be thought without it. This uniqueness must ever remain an exception to any rule. Now 'the exception to the rule' is the translation of the Greek word ciphered into the *instance* of the letter, *enstasis*. In Aristotle's logic, enstasis refers to the dialectic procedure of contradicting an opponent's universal assertion by adducing a counter-example, a

---

[67] Julien, 'Le nom propre et la lettre', pp. 34–5; Allouch, *Lettre pour lettre*, p. 134.
[68] *Encore*, p. 46.

particular exception which proves to be the obstacle to the rule.[69] Lacan, however, wants to use the exception to prove the rule of the letter, in a paradoxical fashion that does not quite conform to the old adage. In Russell's terms, which Lacan employs in *Encore* and other late texts, the negation of the universal changes the modality of the propositional function from the necessary – for all x f(x), always true – to the possible – for some x f(x), sometimes true – or to the impossible – for no x f(x), never true.[70] One way to prove a universal function, that is, that the predication is true for all possible values of the variable x, is to deny the existence of any counter-examples. Now 'the exception of the letter', as we might now translate the title of Lacan's text, is what I have termed its rejection of meaning, its exemption from the rule of the endless circulation of meaning which makes it impossible ever to give an answer to the question of the subject's being: 'What am "I"?' This exception would thus play the role of an element not subject to the play of differences of the symbolic system, like the centre described by Derrida in 'Structure, Sign, and Play'. In this sense, the letter is the phallus, the exception to the rule of castration which bars the subject from its being. As a single stroke, the phallic letter stands with one foot outside the symbolic system, functioning as the fulcrum for the lever with which Archimedes claimed he could lift the entire world. But that foundation is not a nameable absolute meaning; rather it designates an empty place and hence is utterly meaningless. In order to show that all subjects must pass through the phallic function of castration, one must first posit the exception – the non-castrated Father who can say 'I am that I am' – and then demonstrate its non-existence, its foreclosure from the symbolic order of castration – 'God is dead', in Nietzsche's words.

---

[69] Aristotle, 'Topica', 115b.

[70] Russell, *Logic and Knowledge*, p. 231. In *Encore* Lacan included the fourth modality, the contingent, which was the final member of the list of types of predication in traditional, Aristotelian logic, and which Russell had eliminated as an independent form (*Introduction to Mathematical Philosophy*, p. 165). Traditional logic admitted four types of propositions: those which are necessarily true and those contingently true; false assertions whose contradictories are necessary (the impossible) and those that just happen not to be true (the contingently false). The propositional function allegedly showed that the contingently true and the contingently false in fact form a single case, the possible. In chapter 6 we will examine the important role of Lacan's contingent propositional function in specifying the relation of the subject to the signifier.

But Lacan does not draw from this argument the straightforward conclusion that one should or could simply dispense with such a signifier. He maintains that its role as the only 'foundation' of the necessity of castration makes it necessary as well as impossible. In order for the 'brothers' of Freud's primal horde in *Totem and Taboo* to renounce their incestuous wishes, it is necessary that they institute the law, that is a prohibition, a limit, for each. And Lacan claims that they can do so only by giving a name to the impossible lack of limit which the law is designed to exclude. Only by including within the symbolic order a signifier for that which is impossible within that order can the set of signifiers which constitute the social world be given a provisional closure.[71] In Freud's myth this impossible is represented by the primal father of the horde, the male for whom all females are accessible. And even after foreclosure, it continues to be operative for the individual male subject, who continues to dream of incestuous *jouissance* and of occupying the position of the absolute Father.[72]

Although it is not possible to be the Father, one can nevertheless name the Father, and it is this necessary/impossible that Lacan seeks to capture in the compound proper name he adapts from Christian liturgy, the Name-of-the-Father.[73] Without the sense that language refers to something beyond itself, the whole symbolic order would collapse into itself, as occurs in the pandemonium of psychosis. Without the confidence that the proper name refers to a subject beyond language, so that I myself and the one who calls upon me are 'something more' than the sum of our attributes or the mere mechanical interplay of words or images, human society would be nothing more than the machine which forms the ideal of modern bureaucratic technocracy.[74]

The multiple senses of the term 'necessary' in the preceding

---

[71] See Copjec, *Read My Desire*, pp. 174–5, for an excellent discussion of the non-mathematical aspect of this process of 'suture'.

[72] Fink, 'Existence and the Formulas of Sexuation', pp. 71–2.

[73] In fact, Augustine comments upon the contradictory procedure of naming the ineffable (God) in *On Christian Doctrine*:

If what I said were ineffable, it would not be said. And for this reason God should not be said to be ineffable, for when this is said something is said. And a contradiction in terms is created, since if that is ineffable which cannot be spoken, then that is not ineffable which can be called ineffable.   (I, 6)

[74] See Lacan, *Concepts*, chapters 16 & 20.

arguments show that, for Lacan, the phallic letter does indeed form the joint between logic and ethics. When he points to what would happen if the limit were not named within the system, or when he specifies that in Freud's story of the origins of civilization, the limit (incest-taboo) is required if the brothers are to be equal, he thereby indicates that it is indeed possible not to have a subject, not to have civilization. The necessity in question is that of the means necessary to an (ethical) end. It is only once one has decided to work toward the one and the other that logical necessity then intervenes by demonstrating what must be done in order for the means to be operative. The only way to close off a potentially infinite set is to add to it the name of that which forms its border, the exception to its rule; in short, its limit.

The model for this suturing operation is what is called the 'Dedekind cut' in the theory of real numbers (decimals). The (infinitely) many real numbers which correspond to integers or fractions, the rational numbers, can be written completely as decimals with a finite number of digits, or as decimals with a finite series of digits that are repeated infinitely (e.g. .333 ... for 1/3). However, infinitely many reals fall in the cracks between the rationals, and these so-called irrationals cannot be represented completely by any finite sequence of digits. All one can do is give the latter a name, such as the square root of two, or pi, and then add this symbol, which designates the limit of the decimals that approach this hole, this cut in the rationals, from below and above, to the set of decimals.[75]

Like Lacan's other key terms, the phallus is fundamentally bivalent, indicating both the traumatic and the liberating qualities of Otherness. As the unitary trait, the phallus provides a representation of order and harmony; it projects an apparently unified meaning the subject can anticipate for itself in return for its sacrifice of its primary identification with the specular image of the object; namely, the sum of the unitary traits of the objects with which it identifies to form its ego-ideal.[76] In this sense, the phallus does indeed take on the function of guaranteeing the integrity of the subject and the unity of signifier to signified. But this unity, characteristic of the 'materiality of the letter', is

[75] See Porge, *Se compter trois* , pp. 133–5.
[76] *Transfert,* p. 458.

indestructible precisely because it is imposed onto objects through an act that is ultimately senseless. Once the phallus completes the transition from sign to signifier, it can no longer be, or guarantee, the unity it was introduced to protect; as signifier, it can operate only as opposed to other signifiers, as part of the incessant sliding of meaning of the signifying chain. The subject's unity, its meaning, its desire, therefore necessarily fall into the space, the gap, between the signifiers.

For the Lacan of the sixties, two paths branch out from this aporetic place. On the road of narcissism, the phallus becomes imaginarized: the subject strives to stop the sliding of his being, to fill the empty place of the guarantor of his 'real presence', by identifying with the emblem of the Father, the localized image of the phallic organ (see our chapter 3). On the route of castration, the subject is induced to give up this narcissistic identification, and to seek his completion in the object of desire, which, unlike the ego-ideal, always remains hidden behind its attributes. The subject projects his narcissistic investment into this void, that is, he fills the body of the Other with this symbolic phallus. At this point, then, the phallus 'is where it is not and is not where it is' in that the subject sees it within the other who does not have it, and sees himself as lacking it when, since it is his own investment, or being, in a sense he has it.[77]

In a similar way, before he had distinguished clearly between the letter and the signifier, Lacan had stated that 'la lettre volée ... sera *et* ne sera pas là où elle est, où qu'elle aille' ['the purloined letter ... will be *and* not be where it is, wherever it goes'],[78] because it exists simultaneously in both physical and symbolic space, the one organized in accordance with geometry, the other in terms of a signifying system of classification. This singular quality he attributes to the phallus is a transposition onto the realm of space of Hegel's description of time as 'the being which, insofar as it *is, is not*, and insofar as it *is not, is*'.[79] Aubenque adopts this language to highlight the fundamental ambiguity of being: 'L'être est et n'est pas ce qu'il est', [being is and is not what it is], because 'la prédication elle-même ... est aporétique, puisqu'elle consiste à dire que le même *est* autre [predication itself ...

---

[77] Ibid., chapter 27.
[78] *Ecrits*, p. 24; *The Purloined Poe*, p. 39.
[79] Hegel, *Encyclopedia*, vol. 1 para. 258.

is aporetic, since it consists in saying that the same is different].[80] The proposition, which is supposed to link subject and predicate together in the unity of being, at the same time and necessarily distinguishes between them. The assertion of unity therefore depends logically on the assertion of pure self-difference. Like the object of desire, and for the same reason, the 'true subject' of Poe's tale, the 'unit in its very uniqueness, being by nature symbol only of an absence', cannot but remain hidden behind its attributes.

The sense which the paternal metaphor guarantees thus always remains to some extent an illusion. The phallus hollows out that place where sense encounters non-sense, and which is therefore a no-place, a utopia, for 'Le S et le *s* de l'algorithme saussurien ne sont pas dans le même plan, et l'homme se leurrait à se croire placé dans leur commun axe qui n'est nulle part' ['the S[ignifier] and the s[ignified] of the Saussurian algorithm are not on the same level, and man only deludes himself when he believes his true place is at their axis, which is nowhere'].[81] This point is not a simple dead end, however; it is that umbilical place where the subject is knotted to the Other. And it is there that transference in the first sense joins with transference as the mainspring of the relation between subjects in analysis, for in both cases its action is needed to supplement ineffability.

80 Aubenque, *Le problème de l'être chez Aristote*, p. 448.
81 *Ecrits*, p. 518; *Ecrits* Eng., p. 166.

5

Desire and Culture: Transference and the Other

L'amour est une métaphore.   Lacan, *Le transfert*

[L'objet] fait de nous autre chose que le sujet de la parole, mais ce quelque chose d'unique, d'inappréciable, d'irremplaçable en fin de compte, qui est le véritable point où nous pouvons désigner ce que j'ai appelé la dignité du sujet.   Lacan, *Le transfert*

Freud states that the onset of transference in the psychoanalytic process – the formation of erotic and aggressive relations of the analysand to the analyst – regularly begins with a moment of silence, when associations are lacking and the subject stares out the window or at the carpet while forming unconscious thoughts about the analyst. Transference thus first appears as a resistance to the analytic process, an interruption in the flow of free associations without which there can be no analysis. It would seem that a precise description of the situation would avoid imputing the positive existence of unconscious thoughts to the subject at the time when the only observable phenomenon is the gap in her narration. He nevertheless infers that such a stoppage in the stream of associations does in fact betray transferential thoughts, for experience shows that when the subject has been informed that she is thinking of the analyst, her associations invariably resume.[1]

This inference leaves Freud with the problem of explaining why transference, whose effective establishment is the sine qua non of the psychoanalytic process, should emerge in the form of resistance, that is, as the most powerful hindrance to that very process. In 'The Dynamics of the Transference', he breaks this problem down into the following constituents: 1. Psychoanalysis consists in the investigation [*Forschung*], the bringing to light, of

[1] Freud, 'The Dynamics of the Transference', p. 101.

material ordinarily inaccessible to consciousness. 2. The analysand cooperates in this work because of her affection for the analyst. 3. That affection is a transference, a new or revised edition of past libidinal attachments, in which the analyst plays the role of love-object. 4. But transference always appears as the major obstacle to analytic investigation, as a resistance.

In short, without transference there would be no psychoanalysis; yet transference opposes the successful completion of the psychoanalytic process. Transference is thus both the driving force, the mainspring, of psychoanalysis, and 'le moyen par où ... l'inconscient se referme' ['the means by which ... the unconscious closes up again'], as Lacan put it in *Les Quatre Concepts Fondamentaux de la Psychanalyse*.[2] He sees this contradiction as the source of a permanent crisis in psychoanalysis, and repeatedly terms it a paradox.

Freud attempts to resolve this paradox by making two parallel sets of distinctions, each of which is sub-divided a second time. First, he separates libidinal investments into those that are capable of becoming conscious and are directed toward the real, and those directed away from reality onto childhood images, the non-real, which comprises both fantasies and entirely unconscious investments. The result is a tri-partite set of categories – the real, the fantasized, the unconscious (a set, by the way, which has obvious analogies to Lacan's real, imaginary and symbolic). Transference, according to Freud, involves the non-real types of libidinal investment, the fantasized and the unconscious, occurring whenever investigation awakens the forces which caused the regression to fantasy and the original repression. The 'mechanism' of the transference is a compromise between resistance and investigation, in which the repressed impulse attains expression, but only by attaching itself to the figure of the analyst.

The second set of distinctions apportions transference among three types: first it is classified according to its affective charge – positive (friendly), or negative (hostile). Then the positive transference is divided into two sub-categories, affectionate feelings, and attraction based on repressed erotic tendencies. Freud's solution to the paradox can now be stated: transference will appear as resistance if it is either negative or repressed erotic

---

[2] *Concepts*, p. 119; *Concepts* Eng., p. 130.

positive. The remaining positive, affectionate feelings, which are free from repression, aid the process of cure by inducing the analysand to do the work of analysis, to produce and interpret the free associations which bring to light hidden erotic impulses and thus fill in the gaps in her history.

As elegant as this solution is, it cannot account for several problems, the most serious of which is this: the existence of positive, affectionate, feelings, however necessary they may be, is neither specific to psychoanalysis, as Freud himself stated, nor is it sufficient to demarcate that engagement of the psychoanalytic process called the onset of the transference. It is only the 'repetition of the disease', namely, the repetition of precisely the repressed erotic impulses and hostile feelings, which can act as the mainspring of psychoanalysis, since it is only this repetition that constitutes that presence, that manifestation of the unconscious, without which the neurosis could only be attacked *in absentia* or in effigy, an impossibility, as he repeatedly affirms.[3] But this new edition of the disease is the very thing that makes transference a source of resistance! And resistance here means that which brings the investigation of the unconscious to a halt; for example, a total lack of associations, or even the termination of the analysis, as occurred with Dora.

Since this matter is both crucial and confusing, let me reiterate its essential coordinates. Freud claims that transference is necessary to the psychoanalytic process, that is, to the investigation of repressed eroticism by means of free associations and their interpretation. But he makes this claim for two different reasons. The first is that the positive, affectionate, transference is a necessary inducement for the analysand to accomplish the work of psychoanalysis – bringing forth associations, working through their interpretations and so on. The second is that the neurosis must be reproduced *in praesentia*, that is, in the relation of the patient to the doctor, in order for it to be attacked and destroyed. Moreover, it is only the second phenomenon, the production of the 'transference-neurosis', that is specific to psychoanalysis.[4] The first is common to all forms of suggestion, such as hypnosis or institutional authority. In short, the type of transference that characterizes the psychoanalytic process is not the friendly

[3] E.g. Freud, 'Remembering, Repeating, and Working Through', pp. 152–5.
[4] Ibid., p. 154.

attachment to the analyst which facilitates it but the very unconscious bondage which obstructs it. While analysis would be brought to a standstill without the analysand's positive conscious feelings, only the resistant form of transference is essential to it.

In light of this presentation of the problem, Freud's solution to the paradox could be restated as a recommendation to use the first type of transference – suggestion – as a means of combating the second type – repetition. And that is just what he seems to do at the end of 'Dynamics'; he portrays the major battle played out in transference as a 'struggle between the doctor and the patient, between intellect and instinctual life, between understanding and seeking to act'.[5] Once stated in these terms, it is easy to see where such a solution might lead. The alignment of doctor, intellect and understanding against patient, drive and acting-out can easily turn out in practice to justify the analyst in asserting that whenever the patient refuses to accept his interpretation, this refusal should be taken as a resistance; and if resistance must be the result of a negative, or positive repressed, transference, then it must itself be analysed, interpreted as such, in accordance with Freud's recommendation in 'Remembering', written two years after 'Dynamics'.

The main point of the essay on 'Remembering' is that analytic interpretation should be used to recognize resistances and make them conscious to the patient, so that he can then remember and fill in the gaps in memory in order to formulate a continuous, coherent, and complete, history. The secondary thesis of the article is that remembering does not necessarily follow interpretation immediately, but might require considerable repetition and working-through. Compared to the earlier practice of interpreting unconscious contents – naming repressed instinctual impulses – the analysis of resistances is a clear step away from the use of suggestion. But if the procedure is applied as an absolute, general, rule, that is, every single time that the analysand refuses an interpretation, then the implication arises that the analyst alone knows the truth about the subject. When taken this way, the so-called analysis of resistances becomes nothing other than a matter of pure suggestion in which the analyst pits his authority

---

[5] Freud, 'Dynamics', p. 108.

against the convictions of the subject. And that is just what the restatement of Freud's supposed solution to the paradox of transference implies: use suggestion as a means of overcoming repetition, use the authority of the doctor to overwhelm the resistance of the patient.

When the 'solution' is stated so baldly, it becomes apparent that something is seriously wrong. On the level of theory, the paradox has simply been displaced, for psychoanalysis, which purportedly arose precisely when it rejected suggestion (hypnosis) as its mode of operation, has now been redefined as the use of suggestion to combat that which constitutes the very specificity of psychoanalysis, transference as repetition. On the practical level, such analysis of resistance can lead to the interruption of the analytic process rather than to its successful completion. If in some cases Freud was more than willing to jettison interpretations rejected by the analysand (cf. 'Lucy R.' in *Studies on Hysteria*), in others his insistence on the correctness of his assessments resulted in the premature termination of the analysis. According to Lacan, one of the main reasons why Dora broke off her analysis was that Freud insisted on explaining away all her objections to his interpretation that her real love-object was the man who made advances to her, Herr K.[6]

Although Freud's statement of the resolution of the paradox of the transference is unobjectionable – use the analysand's good will and respect to induce her to continue the process of analytic investigation – the existence of a latent defect in his reasoning is betrayed by the ease with which he and some of his successors were able to transform this cooperation into coercion. The specific question that remains unanswered is how resistance can be overcome without the use of emotional constraint. Lacan's successive theories of transference are designed to conceptualize this 'paradox of the analyst's position', as he calls it, without falling into the trap of a completely alienating view of the analysis of resistances. In the 'Intervention on Transference' (1951), Lacan assimilates Freud's 'investigation' to the Hegelian concept of 'dialectic experience': a search for truth by means of a critical use of discourse, in which the opposition between theses about the same reality – generally supported by (at least) two

---

[6] 'Intervention on Transference', pp. 68–70.

different interlocutors – is resolved by the negation of the first negation.[7] Discourse in this context is not just any set of utterances, but is rather the attempt to answer a specific question by employing a specific procedure; in psychoanalysis the question is that of the analysand's desire, and the procedure is that governed by agreement to the basic rule of free association and free-floating attention. This definition emphasizes that both the mind doing the questioning – the subject – and the truth that might result from that process of interrogation, are constituted by and in the discourse itself. In other words, the process of questioning introduces both the subject and the object of knowledge into the world; it defines the real in a certain way by judging it according to certain expectations, and it is those expectations that form the subjectivity of the individual. In and through the analytic process, Dora acquired a particular subjectivity in accordance with a series of questions designed to fathom what Lacan calls the 'mystery of her femininity':[8] what am I? what do I desire? what am I as a woman? and especially as a (female) body, object of male desire?

In the same way, the formation of the subject's objects, including her love-objects, is itself the consequence of the discourse in so far as the progress toward the truth of the subject's being and desire has been facilitated or obstructed. Lacan does not hesitate to agree with Freud that if the latter had apprised Dora of her love for Frau K., that love would have become a reality and the analyst would have been experienced as the bestower of a precious gift. But Dora's so-called homosexual attachment to Frau K. was simply the expression of her desire to figure out what makes a woman attractive to men, just as her identifications with her father and Herr K. were designed to permit her to consider feminine desirability from the man's point of view. This is what would have become conscious and real, had Freud recognized and

---

[7] As usual, Lacan has adapted the idea to his own purposes. Hegel is above all concerned with the affirmation of the truth of living beings, the idea that subjectivity begins by a negation, differentiating itself from external objects which thus first appear to them as alien – nature – and then negates that negation in realizing that the latter is actually ruled by the same principle as themselves, rationality. See a typical summary in Hegel, *Aesthetics*, vol. i, pp. 96–7.

[8] 'Intervention', p. 67.

interpreted in time the sense of Dora's perplexity revealed by her identifications.

By clearly stating the goal of analysis to be the emergence of a truth, Lacan's formulation of analytic investigation also establishes a workable criterion for judging whether or not a particular statement, attitude, or behaviour, is or is not a resistance: anything that moves toward the goal is analysis (investigation), anything that hinders this movement is resistance. Furthermore, it places this truth where it belongs, in the discourse, that is, in the words, the associations and interpretations of analysand and analyst. Taken together, these two characteristics make it possible to isolate and reject the abusive practice of the analysis of resistances just described, for one can judge, as Freud eventually did in the Dora case, that the analyst's interpretation may be at fault, so that this interpretation has itself become the resistance. It was not Herr K. but Frau K. who had become Dora's love-object, and Freud's insistence that it was Herr K. constituted a resistance in exactly the same sense as an analysand's refusal to accept the existence of a repressed impulse. Moreover, since transference is often the source of the most powerful resistances, it is quite likely that Freud's resistance was the result of a (counter-) transference. Lacan concludes that the analyst and analysand are equally implicated in the process: there is no fundamental difference between the transference and the counter-transference, since both play the same role of hindering the movement toward the truth.

Now if discourse precedes object formation, and transference indicates that the analyst has become the analysand's object (or the reverse in the case of counter-transference), then it follows that the onset and each successive bit of transference, whether positive or negative, real or non-real, will be determined by what is occurring in the discourse, that is, in the subject's search for her truth. This precedence of discourse over subject–object relations is the thread of Ariadne that Lacan uses to find his way through the labyrinth of the paradox of the transference. As early as 'Function and Field', composed two years after 'Intervention', he contended that the general, positive, affectionate, transference whose establishment Freud considers necessary to beginning the analytic process – transference as suggestion – arises when the analysand comes under the sway of the illusion that 'sa vérité est en nous [l'analyste] déjà donnée, que nous la connaissons à l'avance ...'

['his truth is already given in us [the analyst] and that we know it in advance ...'].[9] To the extent that analytic investigation and interpretation succeed in producing changes in the subject by bringing him to successive apprehensions of his truth, he will perceive the analyst as one who is willing to give, and the positive transference will be maintained and reinforced. For the same reason, Lacan's thesis in 'Intervention' is that whatever the analyst may do to block that progress toward the subject's truth will be perceived as the withholding of that truth, and will thus provoke the so-called negative transference, the analysand's hostility toward the analyst. 'Par où nous allons tenter de *définir en termes de pure dialectique le transfert* qu'on dit négatif dans le sujet, comme l'opération de l'analyste qui l'interprète' ['I will be attempting *to define in terms of pure dialectics the transference,* which we call negative on the part of the subject as being the operation of the analyst who interprets it'].[10]

He therefore concludes that Freud drove Dora away by committing both the mistakes that he, Freud, later acknowledged: not recognizing and interpreting the onset of her transference onto him; and assuming that her love-object must be a man, not a woman. These errors were only compounded when Dora returned some fifteen months after breaking off the analysis, for, while Freud recognized her hostile intention, he still failed to understand its cause – his own misinterpretation – and thus he missed the opportunity to resume the analysis. According to Lacan, such errors arise from the 'passions of being' in the analyst – love, hate and ignorance – that is, from the counter-transference. But this counter-transference, like the subject's transference and other object-formations, emerges only when the search for truth has become bogged down. It is at that point that the one takes the other as object. When the analysand first poses his question authentically but cannot see its answer, then the transference of erotic impulses and the analysis *per se* has begun. Likewise, when the analyst is unable to interpret the material presented to her,

---

[9] *Ecrits*, p. 308; *Ecrits* Eng., p. 94.
[10] *Ecrits*, p. 218; *Feminine Sexuality*, pp. 64–5. Note that the comma has been displaced in the English translation (or perhaps a second comma was supposed to be inserted after 'subject?'): in the French version it appears after the word '*sujet*', whereas the English has it coming after 'transference'. This change tends to obscure Lacan's point, that it is the analyst's errors which provoke negative transference.

then she attempts to make the analysand conform to her passions and pre-determined ideas, so constituting the latter as her object.[11]

Thus transference acts as a sign to the analyst that something has gone amiss in the analytic process. That something is not always an error or omission by the analyst, however; the exemplary situation is the one Freud described as the stoppage of associations. It is here that the Lacanian conversion illuminates the paradox of the transference in a way that Freud's conceptualization does not. For Freud, these silences are caused by an already existing transference: the analysand is unconsciously thinking of the person of the analyst at the moment his associations fail, and they fail because the forces that repressed the impulse in the subject's past oppose its expression in the present of the analysis. For Lacan, on the contrary, the interruptions in the stream of associations are just that, moments of emptiness, and it is the stoppage that leads to the transference. The subject fills these moments of 'stagnation' or 'deadlock' of the psychoanalytic dialectic by constituting the analyst as object of his repressed impulses just as he always does with others in life outside of analysis.

Once the general positive transference has arisen, the analytic investigation progresses smoothly until the subject's discourse approaches a repressed erotic impulse. At that point he is unable to proceed because, according to Lacan, repression consists precisely in the lack of the needed word. The stoppage, the silence, is not caused by the suppression of unconscious thoughts about the analyst, but by this gap. The analysand literally has nothing to say. It is in and because of this state of distress, when the subject is unable to articulate the truth of his being, that he turns to the Other, the analyst in the present circumstance, in the hopes of receiving the missing word from her. Unable to reach expression directly for lack of the proper word, the impulse gets itself transferred onto the figure of the analyst, who, according to the basic rule of 'neutrality', has the obligation to hold in abeyance her actual character, thoughts and feelings in order to serve as a signifying material divested of its customary significance, like the letters of the manifest dream. Transference appears

---

[11] *Ecrits*, p. 225.

as both a resistance – an inability to articulate one's truth – and an appeal – to the Other for the means of doing so.

In Lacan's view, then, Freud's two uses of the word transference are totally consistent with each other. In both cases a desire remains unconscious because it cannot be expressed, and in both cases it strives to reach expression by attaching itself metaphorically to alternative signifying materials which have been emptied of their previous signification, that is, to letters. In dreams this parasitic relation gives rise to those strange mental phenomena Freud attributes to condensation, displacement and the other primary processes; in analysis and everyday life, to the organizational peculiarities we have examined under the name of voice or speech, whose influence on the subject's discourse may generate lapses in utterance or memory, failed actions, and even total silence.

It is in terms of this 'speech' that Lacan formulates his version of the paradox of the analyst's position in relation to the transference. Lacanian speech may be defined as those aspects of discourse which are differentiated from language as system. The one function of speech is, as we have seen, the revelation of the subject's truth as it struggles to disengage itself from the social doxa or the universal truth of discourse.[12] The second role is as mediator between the self and the Other as potential listener and responder. Lacan's rationale for including both these functions under the same heading of speech harks back to the age-old conjunction of action upon the listener and figures of speech codified in the tradition of western rhetoric. He argues that the presence of rhetorical tropes and figures even in the elaboration of what is ostensibly the most private text, that of the dream, bears witness to the fact that unconscious formations are governed by seductive, persuasive, deceptive or other 'intersubjective' aims. Transference dreams differ from others only in that the person of the analyst comes to fill the role ordinarily allotted to the non-personal Other, that *personne* who is both somebody and nobody in particular. The necessary presupposition of a third person as listener for the full enjoyment of a witticism likewise

---

[12] Lacan uses the word revelation in place of the word expression, since the unconscious is not something already existing internally that must be pushed out into the world (*Ecrits techniques*, pp. 59–60). No doubt revelation translates Heidegger's apophantic function of language.

points to the joke as demonstration for the benefit of a party alien to the self. This demonstrative quality is shared by the symptom which, although built up out of signifiers, operates on one level as a sign, that is, as representing something for someone, namely what the subject takes to be the desire of the other.[13]

Lacan takes these phenomena as proof that what I have called the second function actually has priority over the first. The revelatory function of speech is subordinate to its mediating function because repressed impulses strive to attach themselves to signifying materials in order to be recognized by an other. He thus complements the traditional rhetorical coupling of figure and action with the Hegelian notion of the struggle for recognition, as interpreted by Kojève. While revelation and mediation both have the same purpose of responding to the subject's 'want-to-be', the former would remain of no avail without the latter. 'La pure fonction du langage ... est de nous assurer que nous sommes, et rien de plus' ['The pure function of language ... is to assure us that we are, and nothing more'],[14] but that assurance can be confirmed only by the other who is implied as the potential receiver of a discourse. The early Lacan claims that any discourse whatsoever implies communication, even if it communicates nothing to anybody, for the mere fact of its utterance constitutes sufficient evidence of the attempt to reach an other.[15] As with the proposition, alterity is inscribed into speech from the start; the uniqueness of the individual manifested by the phenomena of voice can only arise on the basis of a prior relation to the other.

The ultimate source of the paradox from Lacan's standpoint is the fact that analytic practice seems to be designed purposely to fly in the face of this hierarchical order. Everything in the analytic situation, from the physical arrangement of the chair and couch to the basic rule which admonishes the analysand to ignore the rules of coherence and propriety meant to insure the speaker's bond to the listener in ordinary conversation, aims at reducing the presence of the Other – the analyst – to the absolute

---

[13] *Ecrits*, pp. 267–71; *Ecrits* Eng., pp. 58–61.

[14] *Ecrits techniques*, p. 180; *Papers*, p. 157.

[15] Later on, after distinguishing *lalangue* from language understood as the construct of a linguistic science, Lacan will deny that language is only communication, and he will insist on the solitude it produces (*Encore*, pp. 126–7, 109, 116).

minimum. The more 'full' the subject's speech, the more successful the investigation, the less he will find himself obliged to
'hook on' to the Other. The more easily the subject can articulate
his truth, the more the analyst will be excluded from the process.
Why then design a practice to eliminate the Other if the goal of
that practice – the realization of the subject's being – can be
reached only through recognition by that Other?

Lacan's answer to that question relies on the analyst's capacity
for interpretation, that is, to 'extraire, du langage, la parole'
['extracting speech from [the] language'] of the subject's associations.[16] The analyst's position is paradoxical because the analysand will be drawn to take cognizance of her presence precisely
in proportion to his inability to follow the basic rule of analysis.
But getting the subject to recognize the existence, or rather the
insistence, of this limit to the confession of his desire is a
necessary step in the analytic process. It is the ineffability of the
repressed which blocks the path of investigation, and the resulting deadlock focusses the attention of the analysand onto the
analyst. Speech, voice, rhetoric, are always catachretic, whether
as scriptural or intersubjective transference.

As a spontaneous process resulting from the break in the flow
of discourse, intersubjective transference effects the catachretic
displacement of the subject's impulses onto the other, responding
to his want-to-be by inserting the analyst as object into the gap
opened up by the stoppage of his discourse (associations). At this
point, the analysand generally considers himself cured and the
analysis at an end,[17] since, in Lacanian terms, his lack of being
has been covered over by the object. Any attempt to explain this
away as his need for love will simply trigger the aggressivity
latent in the imaginary relation between the subject and his alter
ego. But, as noted above, the moment of silence is also a mute
appeal to the imputed Other beyond language, and the analyst
can respond to that call by offering the analysand the word he
lacked, supplementing the gap on the level of the subject-to-
subject relation of speech rather than masking it behind that of
subject to object. The paradox of the transference is thus that the
only path to the 'fullest' speech – that which confers the greatest

[16] *Ecrits techniques*, p. 198; *Papers*, p. 175.
[17] Freud, 'Observations on Transference-Love', p. 162.

'presence' onto the other – goes through the 'emptiest' speech, the moment of stagnation.

Throughout his career, Lacan strove to explain this paradox at the heart of the analytic process by means of a dualistic conception of the relation of the subject to the other. In the early days of 'Function and Field' and *Papers*, he conceived of this tension as resulting from two types of interhuman relation, assigning repressed libidinal and aggressive impulses to the first, subject–object type, the imaginary relation in which the ego is formed as the mirror image of its counterpart other. The analyst could convert this situation into the subject–subject relation by giving the analysand the gift of speech, verbalizing her hitherto unexpressible imaginary fixations just when she became attuned to the presence of the analyst because of the stagnation of her own speech.

Starting from the second seminar (1954–5), Lacan began to formulate his theory of the Big Other as a place 'beyond intersubjectivity' in contrast to the little other and to develop his L-schema, a graphical representation of the two aspects of interhuman transference distinguished above. Aggressive and libidinal impulses were still attributed to the imaginary relation, but the role of the ineffable was now played by the symbolic rather than the imaginary. Whereas the ego could relate to the little other precisely because this other was in fact an image of the same, that is, it could be captured entirely in the categories of understanding of the ego, the Big Other became that which escaped the ego's system of categorization, that which was radically other. In his L-schema Lacan represented the unconscious as a four-sided relation in which the flow from the Other to the Subject, the revelatory speech of *Papers*, is modulated by the ego–other relation. He used the image of a triode vacuum tube to clarify this movement: the flow of electrons from cathode (o) to anode (s) is modulated by the third electrode (e–o, the imaginary relation) which can either interrupt the current or amplify it depending on its charge.[18] As with any electrical circuit, the current will flow only when the circuit is closed, and

---

[18] I am using the initials of the English words where Lacan of course uses those of the corresponding French terms – m (ego), a (other), A (Other) and S (subject).

in alternating current, a system of feedback is set up such that the flow in one direction reverses the charge and thus automatically opens the circuit, inducing it to flow in the opposite direction. Moreover, if the tube is filled with a gas such as neon, it will light up only when the flow of the electric current is interrupted and forced to move back onto itself. Like the famous sign in Baltimore that Lacan evoked in his speech at the 1966 symposium on 'The Languages of Criticism and the Sciences of Man' held at The Johns Hopkins University, the unconscious will thus blink on and off, the revelatory speech alternately flowing or subsiding depending on the state of the circuit.

The point of this little electronic parable, with its manifest similarity to the image of the lightning flash of Being, is that the interruption of the flow, transference as resistance, is necessary for the lighting up, transference as the relation to the Other. Normally, that is, according to the norms of the social system dominated by the categories of the ego, the o–s axis is obscured by the imaginary relation. Only slips, dreams, jokes and symptoms reveal the insistence of something that disturbs the total harmony of the totalitarian. Truth must emerge from the mistake because it does not actually exist, at least not before analysis. These disturbances can be confronted, however, only if the insistent can be made existent, if the latent signifiers can be made patent, if the subject's questioning of her desire can be metaphorized. It is this indispensable making-present, which Lacan later called the realization or actualization of the unconscious (*la mise en acte de la réalité de l'inconscient*), that is accomplished by the transference.[19] But this actualization can be effected only if the analyst becomes the analysand's object, occupying the place of the small other in the imaginary relation. To the extent that the analyst reacts in accordance with this relation, rejecting the alterity of the analysand and responding instead in terms of her own preconceived passions and categories of understanding, with her own love, hate or ignorance, the flow of speech will be temporarily or permanently interrupted. The current will have alternated, the unavoidable realization of the unconscious through the transference will have become resistance. In order to avoid this disastrous consequence the analyst must not respond

---

[19] *Concepts*, pp. 146, 149.

from the position of the small other but from that of the large Other, namely, by giving the proper analysis, or interpretation, of the transference. It is at this precise point that analysis becomes an ethical choice by virtue of the lekton. According to Freud, the analyst must remain in a state of *Überlegenheit*. While the Standard Edition translates this as 'aloofness', and the French gives *supériorité*, Lacan implies that it should be understood, at least in part, to indicate superposition (lying-over-ness).[20] The analyst's ego, the small other, must be removed from the circuit, superimposed onto the place of the big Other, in order for the repressed signifiers to emerge. In this position, the imaginary relation acts as an amplifier rather than as a resistance. The quadrilateral has been collapsed down into a triangle, whose base is the line e–(o)o; the e–o line no longer cuts through the a–s line at the middle of the square, but lies flat on top of the e–o line at the base. The analyst thereby allows the analysand to confront the shifting sands of difference which the latter had previously misrecognized in order to sustain the illusion of his autonomy.

In the article on 'The Mirror Stage', in which Lacan first defines the imaginary register, the main claim is that the ego of a child begins to take shape, is constituted by, its relation to an image of itself. This process, which is destined to be repeated throughout life in relation to the images of other people, is gratifying insofar as it seems to promise the eventual unity, completeness and autonomy of the self. But since the ego only comes into being by identifying with something outside the person, that autonomy could only come from the suppression of the very image upon which its existence depends. Otherness, mediation, precedes the selfness of the self. The desire for autonomy leads to a potentially murderous relation to the other. In so far as the identity of any member of a society is determined by a social reality defined by a congeries of sign systems, or cultural codes, this same tendency will cause the ego to imaginarize those codes, to reduce them to the level of pure signifieds.

The ego must rely on the seemingly stable units of the symbolic system, the categories in terms of which the subject represents herself and the world to herself, for it needs them in order to accumulate the knowledge of reality necessary for survival. Its

[20] *Le moi*, p. 373.

very life depends on the possibility of representation. The structure of this subject of the signified is thus identical to that of the traditional subject of knowledge. Now since they are composed of signifiers, all such cultural codes will in fact be subject to the law of the Other – pure differentiation. As a result, in order to sustain its autonomy, the ego must, in Weber's phrase, 'dissimulate the play of difference' which threatens to pull the rug out from under it.[21] Survival depends on establishing a ground for representation by misrepresenting difference as identity. It is not so much alienation that constitutes the ego as it is the denial of that very process of alienation. And whenever the solidity of that ground is shaken – be it religion, nationalism, ideology, or other systems of representation – people are ready to kill to shore it up.

The only ground of identity, of meaning, of representation, is in fact the non-ground of the play of difference which constitutes the signifier. At stake in the handling of the transference is the possibility of mitigating the tendency to maintain the illusion of autonomy, with its murderous misrecognition, by uncovering that senseless 'primordial signifier' on which the subject depends.[22]

Without abandoning the basic opposition between imaginary meaning (categorization) and symbolic meaninglessness, Lacan modified his explanation of the paradox of the transference substantially in his seminar, *Le transfert* (1960–1). The most important change involved splitting the repressed impulses off from the imaginary relation and situating them within the newly developed theory of the a-object. The subject–object relation was no longer the impediment but the facilitator of the subject's relation to the Other, and the affectionate transference-love was more clearly distinguished from erotic attachment, the former being characterized as a narcissistic phenomenon, the latter as the relation to the a-object. In order to elucidate the nature of the bridge connecting transference as resistance to transference as the mainspring of the analytic process, and thus redefine the relation between suggestion and analysis, Lacan adapted from Freud's *Group Psychology* a set of three distinct types of identification: direct, specular, narcissistic identification (the e–o axis of the

---

[21] Weber, *Return to Freud*, p. 105.   [22] *Psychoses*, p. 171.

L-schema; see page 82); identification with the ego-ideal via the *trait unaire* (the former o–s axis); and identification with the objects of desire. The crucial question then became: how can the object of love also become the object of desire? How, in other words, can the identification with the unitary trait function as an intermediary between narcissism and object love now conceived as the relation to the radically Other?

The seminar on transference started from an examination of the phenomenon of love rather than from speech and repetition, as had been the case until that point. The problem then was to find the connection between love and repetition in the transference. Along the way, Lacan encountered the same paradoxes he had dealt with before. If the analysand's discourse has to do with the past, to what end repeat it in the present? If the impression of being in love with the analyst is just an illusion, why is this mirage necessary to restoring the patient's memory? Most impor-tant, if the effect of the analyst's interpretation is partially due merely to her position as love-object, is that not tantamount to conceding that analysis must rely on the suggestive power of the presence of the analyst rather than on a pure process of reme-moration?[23] Lacan's answer to these questions is not substantially different from what he had been proposing since 'Function and Field'. Unconscious formations arise in order to be heard; they are directed toward an Other from the start, and in analysis the analyst comes to play the role of that Other, the person to whom one is speaking. It is impossible to separate the presence of the analyst entirely from the function of interpretation, precisely because transference occurs only when and to the extent that the former acts as addressee of the analysand's unconscious. For the same reason, transference is not simply identical to repetition: transferential repetition is a new creation, a sign which the subject constructs in order to indicate to the analyst that part of his desire which he cannot articulate directly. This desire is a present reality which the process of 'confession' to the analyst, and thus of transference onto the analyst, is allowing the subject to create. Lacan describes the analytic process as 'la mise au jour de la manifestation du désir du sujet' [bringing to light the manifestation of the subject's desire],[24] an early form of the

---

[23] *Transfert*, pp. 206–10.   [24] Ibid., p. 234.

famous formula for transference from *Concepts*. But just as the destiny and the destination of a material letter, a love-letter for instance, are distinguishable in principle from the one to whom the letter is sent (the *destinataire*), so the actual addressee of the message of desire may be someone other than the one to whom the words are spoken.[25] The ultimate paradox is that the desire of the analysand is in fact directed toward someone other than the analyst: thus the reality of the analysand's love for the analyst is itself a substitute, a transference.[26]

If transference-love is a reality, then it must have the same structure as any other love; and if it is the analytic situation itself that gives rise to the transference, then the theory of love in general should be able to pinpoint the specific aspect of that situation which constitutes its basis. The heart of the theory Lacan developed in the lengthy reading of Plato's *Symposium* he undertook in the autumn and winter of 1960–1 was that love is a metaphor. And a metaphor is of course a trans-fer. In a sense, then, transference-love is a reality because the reality of love is a transference. As we know, Lacan's metaphor is a signifying substitution which creates new meaning, specifically a catachretic supplement for something unknown. He is claiming, therefore, that love is a signifying process, a particular way of joining signifier to signified by means of substituting one signifier for another whose signified is unknown. In the situation of love, the two parties involved are of course the lover and the beloved. As signifiers, the first is the subject of desire, one who is lacking something, while the second, who has something hidden which constitutes his attraction to the lover, is thereby the object of love. In this case both signifiers have unknown signifieds in that the beloved does not know what he has that makes him attractive any more than the lover knows what it is she lacks. Lacan then can define the metaphor of love as the substitution of the one for the other:

C'est en tant que la fonction de l'*érastès*, de l'aimant, pour autant qu'il est le sujet du manque, vient à la place, se substitue à la fonction de l'*érôménos*, l'objet aimé, que se produit la signification de l'amour.

The meaning of love is produced when the function of the *érastès*, of the

---

[25] See Miller, 'Préface' to *Joyce avec Lacan*, p. 10.
[26] *Transfert*, pp. 210–11.

lover in so far as he is the subject of lack, comes to [fill] the place, substitutes for, the function of the *érôménos*, the beloved object.[27]

This metaphor of love is constructed on the model of the paternal metaphor described in chapter 3, in that each designates the process whereby the subject changes from being loved to loving, from desired object to desiring subject. The heart of this process, it will be recalled, is the formation of a lack in the subject, that is, castration, the loss of the symbol of one's being. This function makes it possible to distinguish between what Lacan calls demand and desire, a difference which corresponds more or less to that between narcissistic love and object love in the classical psychoanalysis of Freud's second topography of the psyche. According to Lacan, the interplay between Socrates and Alcibiades toward the end of *The Symposium* shows that love as desire involves the conviction that the loved one possesses a precious object, an *agalma* in the Greek term used in the text; whereas the demand for love that emerges in Diotima's myth tends to make the lover himself ever more lovable, leading to his perfection, his completion. In the one case love requires a movement outside the self toward the object one lacks; in the other it is an internal matter of transforming the self – the 'ideal ego' in Lacanian terminology – in such a way that it will no longer lack anything.[28]

This difference is, however, by no means an absolute opposition. On the contrary, the crux of Lacan's argument is that there is a reciprocal relation between the two aspects of love; as the one increases, the other decreases, and vice versa, precisely because all object love feeds upon the subject's store of narcissism.[29] The sense of the metaphor of love is that the one must emerge from and replace the other. Without narcissism there would be no object love, no desire as lack. That is because, as Diotima's myth demonstrates – and this is its positive contribution in Lacan's eyes – in both types of love it is the being of the subject that is at stake.

With Freud, Lacan rejects the sentimental notion that love is purely altruistic, or selfless in any absolute sense. Even though the subject over-values the love object and even disappears in the face of its overwhelming presence, what he seeks in this effort to

<hr />

[27] Ibid., p. 53.   [28] Ibid., p. 156.   [29] Ibid., pp. 442, 449–50.

know the being of the Other is the guarantee of his own. Never-theless, due to the intimate connection between love and lan-guage in human experience, this detour to the self around the object, which Lacan will interpret more and more literally in the theory of the drives he expounds in *Concepts*, is the only way out of the impasses of narcissism and the only path to full sexual functioning. Lacan's theory of the metaphor of love is designed to explain the interaction of narcissism and object love as the result of the operation of the signifier on the relation of the subject to the Other.

Human love takes the form of a metaphoric replacement because it develops only in the dimension of what Lacan calls demand. In order to have our needs met, we must express them in a language that, coming from outside ourselves, from the code of an Other, necessarily loses something of what we wanted to say in translation. Moreover, these requests may be granted or refused by an Other, who must be able to hear and understand me beyond what I actually say, to restore what was lost in translation. As a result, the process of requesting quickly becomes 'pure' in the formalist sense, that is, an end in itself, for the only way I can be sure that I am being understood is if I receive a response that is independent of the satisfaction of the need I express in my request. In his seminar on 'Les formations de l'inconscient', Lacan analyses a series of phenomena which betray pure demand, the earliest of which is the one described by Spitz, in which the baby smiles at others, usually its mother first of all, in order to arouse a smile in response to its own.[30] Lacan points out that this interplay forms part of that primitive symbo-lization which precedes language; he calls it symbolic because it invokes the presence of the Other beyond the satisfaction of any need, even though this Other only appears in the form of the mask (the human face or figure). In this way smiling comes to act as the acknowledgement of receipt which first marks the signifier as separate from meaning; it can henceforth symbolize the pleasure experienced when one feels assured that one's demand has been received.[31]

Lacan explains the much more complex case of laughter produced by successful jokes along similar lines. Although the

---

[30] René A. Spitz, *The First Year of Life*, pp. 86–107.
[31] 'Formations de l'inconscient', p. 251.

momentary lifting of an inhibition on an erotic or aggressive impulse plays its part in what Freud calls tendentious jokes, the characteristic common to all witticisms, tendentious or not, is their temporary exemption from the obligation to use language for rational, conceptual, meaning-ful, discourse. The materiality of the signifier comes into play insofar as the success of the joke depends on the specific form of its wording, such as the use of puns or combination words like Heine's 'famillionaire', which manifests a kind of 'stumbling' of the signifier. The teller of the joke obtains the satisfaction of seeing that the listener can hear him beyond the words he utters and so recognizes that words are always insufficient to make himself understood. In short, in laughing at the stumbling signifier, the listener acknowledges, at least for a few instants, that the speaker is a subject beyond language. Yet there is something illusory in this phenomenon, for the presence of the Other can never be experienced as such; it can only be indicated in and through the very language whose mediation it seeks to surmount. The Other can appear only as the seat of the very linguistic code whose violation produces the joke as manifestation of the Other.[32] The mark of the relation to the Other is therefore the presence of something that disrupts the code, whether it be the 'primal lie' whereby the subject first manifests itself as symptom, or something non-conceptual, non-sensical, non-rational, useless (unrelated to any need), in short, gratuitous.[33]

No longer concerned to obtain this or that object of need, pure demand thus loses its specificity. Its aim is to assure the subject of the presence of the Other as a subject beyond language, and thus of her own ultra-linguistic being.[34] In this way, demand becomes unconditional, a request for nothing in particular. But this 'nothing' is precisely the metonymic remainder of demand, the place it opens up for sheer desire. At this place, unconditional demand has become what, with some modifications, Lacan will dub a few years later the 'invocatory drive' – the desire to ensure that one's demand is received, to make oneself heard.[35]

In establishing the connection between the nothing and the place of desire, Lacan follows the logic of Hegel's notion of distinctively human desire, as interpreted by Kojève. The tradi-

---

[32] Ibid., p. 184.   [33] *Ethique*, p. 90.   [34] 'Formations', p. 184.
[35] See *Concepts*, p. 164.

tional philosophic definition of 'man' as the rational animal is insufficient because cognitive activity focusses on the object of thought or contemplation; only desire reveals the subject, by giving one a sense of self, as when one experiences hunger. Desire stimulates action upon the object, which, even if it does not lead to its destruction, always involves 'negation' insofar as it brings about a change in the object and thus causes some aspect of it to cease existing. The 'truth' of the desire, its objective verification, can be seen only in its effects on something external to itself. Actualization thus makes desire stand outside itself, 'ex-sist'.

Now, in order to demonstrate to myself that my desire is truly human, as opposed to being a natural condition, I must act on a non-natural object; but the only such object is desire itself. Thus I must act on another desire, the desire of another person. Ultimately then, I can fulfil my desire to assure myself of my human being only if I can get this other to recognize that my value is autonomous, outside the given order (whether of nature, as in Hegel, Kojève and the early Lacan, or of the social code, the symbolic order, as in the later Lacan). Desire is thus the desire to be the desire of the other's desire, the desire that the other should recognize my desire.[36] The object of this desire for recognition is therefore not something of use to me in the struggle for survival, nor in fact any kind of 'thing' in the customary sense of the word, but something whose value derives precisely from its uselessness – 'the desire of the Other' as Lacan often phrases it – because only such an object can assure me of the presence of the Other, necessary to the assertion ('certitude') of my own being.

A desire which focusses on another desire, as opposed to a real object, is related to nothing (real), a 'being that is a nothingness' in Hegel's phrase. To act with the aim of achieving recognition is to act in relation to something that does not yet exist, and may never do so, for the desire of the Other is not a reality but a hole in the space of what is empirically there, and in the time of the given present. At best, a future of desire may come to inhabit this void.[37] The place of desire is therefore a nothing.

Now in *Transfert*, Lacan argues that this desire for the desire of the Other entailed by the nothing of unconditional demand

---

[36] Kojève, *Introduction to the Reading of Hegel*, pp. 10–15.
[37] Ibid., pp. 367–8.

shows that love necessarily involves the metaphoric superposition of the function of desiring onto that of being desired. Indeed, since the object of my desire is the desire of the Other, I can attain it only by myself becoming the object of the Other's desire. In other words, as desirer I must strive to make myself desirable in order to occupy the position of the desired. In short, the demand for love is the demand to be loved; object love necessarily involves narcissistic love.

This dialectic of demand and desire can lead in two directions, either towards a beyond along the slope of narcissism or towards a before, along that of object love. The problem in the first case is to appear lovable to the Other, or better, to see oneself as desirable in the eyes of the Other. The crucial factor in this process is thus the gaze of the Other. Now if each of us were nothing more nor less than the desire of the Other, that is, a pure reflection of the other subject, then love could not accomplish its goal of conferring being onto the nullity, the want-to-be, of the subject, for the Other's view of me would have no greater claim to validity than, indeed it would be conditioned by, my view of him. The purely specular image projected by the Other, therefore, cannot realize the goal of eternalizing the object with which I identify in the imaginary field by transcending all movement and change. That is the substance of Lacan's argument against Sartre: the truth of the Other cannot be based on his reflection in my eyes, since I merely reflect the Other himself, so that he would be the basis of his own truth. To ensure that the subject may find her truth, the status of the Other must be independent of this play of mirrors; there must be a non-reciprocal relation in which the Other must occupy a third position *vis-à-vis* the two players of specularity, that of the ego-ideal (I).[38]

Since the subject is in fact a nullity, she cannot see herself anywhere. In order to reach some kind of solidity, to see herself as something, she must see herself from the place of the ego-ideal insofar as it is outside the circle of specularity, and she must identify herself with the image produced there. Only in this way can she begin to emerge from the 'shadow' cast on the narcissistic field by the specular image of the lost object, the mother as unfathomable 'Thing'. This, then, is the second type of identifica-

---

[38] *Transfert*, pp. 435–7. See chapter 19 of *Le moi*, where Lacan introduces the concept of the Other as third.

tion, which satisfies a certain narcissism by effecting a change in the subject, but which at the same time establishes a connection between the narcissistic field and that of the Other. Through this identification the subject embarks on that metaphoric process of changing viewpoints described by Cassirer.

The new element Lacan added in the seminar on transference was that this identification at the level of the ego-ideal is with a unitary trait (*trait unaire*), whether that be the gaze or some other attribute. In his later teachings, he will write this unitary trait as s1, and he will call this the 'master signifier', or the fundamental identification of the subject. The primary goal of psychoanalysis could then be conceptualized as bringing forth this basic identification with one or more master signifiers (such as 'woman', 'American', 'leader', etc.). The unitary trait acts as a fixed point to which can be attached the other signifiers in the chain that makes up the identity of the subject (e.g. what it means to be an 'American' or a 'woman'), just as the identification with the ego-ideal involves imagining the Other as a point of reference from which everything is seen. It is thus precisely what Lacan had earlier designated as the *point de capiton*, the illusion of a place beyond language, representation, phenomena.[39] We saw in chapter 4 that the metaphoric process at work in identification via the unitary trait reduces the diversity of objects to the one trait it affixes to all of them. As Lacan's oft-repeated pun indicates, the s1, pronounced in French as 'ess-un', thus equates in one set the homonymic swarm – *essaim* – brought together under each master signifier.[40] To the extent that these objects are equated to each other on the basis of an attribute, they can be counted up and exchanged for each other.

In *Identification* and *Concepts*, Lacan literalizes the term 'stroke' by tracing the origins of writing to the use of notches or lines in the paleolithic age to count up the number of animals killed or goods to be exchanged, although he certainly does not want to restrict the meaning of the unitary trait to this usage. His explanation of the 'goods' of utilitarianism or of the capitalistic system of exchange derives from this theory of the metaphoric

[39] See *Envers*, p. 219.
[40] This pun is apparently an allusion to the phrase '*essaim d'essences*' of the ancient philosopher referred to as 'Pseudo-Alexander' (see Aubenque, *Le problème de l'être chez Aristote*, p. 149).

substitutability of narcissistic objects, whose common denominator is their participation in the pleasure principle; that is, they are judged solely according to their capacity to be of benefit or harm to the ego.[41] Indeed, some ten years later in *Encore*, Lacan would state ironically that the universe[al] and the ego are flowers of rhetoric, alluding both to the analogy between the collecting function of the anthology and that of the mathematical set, and to the diagram of flowers in a vase (*pot*) with which he had often visualized the creationist identification of the ego in relation to the pleasure principle.[42]

It is worth noting that Lacan differs significantly from Freud in his conception of the relation between needs, the pleasure principle and sexuality. While they are in agreement that sexual desire arises in a beyond of need, their views of the exact locus of the gratuitous aspect of sexuality diverge considerably. Freud follows the theological and naturalistic traditions in locating the gratuitous in the realm of pure pleasure which 'leans on' (is 'anaclitic') the functions of needs that ensure the survival of the individual or the species. Lacan, on the other hand, situates the gratuitous beyond the pleasure principle, in that fundamental otherness of the 'Thing' he delimits in the seminar on ethics. Lacan's gratuitous is that unsymbolizable real which, independent of the goal of reproduction as well as of the good of the individual, forms the originary lack, or hole, of the subject's internal object.

Now one of the main benefits of the identification with the image of the ideal ego regulated by the ego-ideal is that it serves to maintain a safe distance between the subject and its internal object. On one level this dangerous object is the mother from whom the subject is ostensibly barred by the incest-taboo; on another it is the Thing as 'lost object', the void opened up simultaneously within the subject and the world by the introduction of the signifier, which entails the failure of reference. It is this Thing which forms the nucleus of what Lacan will eventually define as the impossible Real, which escapes direct symbolization and whose place can only be indicated by a 'letter' while it is kept in abeyance [*en souffrance*].[43] The subject seeks to keep the traumatic Thing at a distance by obeying the pleasure principle,

---

[41] *Ethique*, pp. 43–4; *Transfert*, pp. 285–6, 458.
[42] E.g. *Ecrits*, p. 674; *Transfert*, p. 402.   [43] *Concepts*, pp. 55–6.

that is, by regulating the quantity of pleasure and pain admitted into the system, binding excitations into representations, master-able meanings, which determine the specifiable goals necessary to survival, to the good of the subject. From this perspective, it can be seen that metaphoric universalization, the equation of objects via the unitary trait has a defensive as well as a libidinous aim, in that it blocks that fusion which threatens the subject with dissolution. Not only an attempt to attain narcissistic pleasure, this second type of identification also acts, as in Duras's novel, as a 'barrage contre le Pacifique de l'amour maternel' [dam against the Pacific of maternal love].[44]

In sharp contrast to the exchangeable goods of the utilitarian pleasure principle stands the gratuitous object that beckons beyond the pleasure principle, at the horizon of the slope of love as desire. This *agalma*, this precious jewel contained within the subject one loves has nothing to do with goods in general; on the contrary, the lover's relation to it is unique, purely personal. As such, this object of desire forms the heart of Lacan's theory of love and hence of his ethical teaching. It is often supposed in modern humanist thought, whether within psychoanalytic circles or without, that the only basis for ethical action is to treat the Other as a subject, not as an object; that is, as an unique being who is thereby endowed with a special value which constitutes his dignity and entitles him to the 'Rights of Man' (as they are called in French). This particular way of conceiving human dignity arose in reaction against the implications of the modern dilemma usually referred to as the 'subject/object split', ac-cording to which treating other people as objects is tantamount to devaluing them, to lowering them to the level of interchangeable, inanimate, things which I observe and utilize for my own ends from my vantage point as sole subject. (Lacan is no doubt thinking of Kant, Heidegger and the existentialist Sartre among others, in addition to the French psychoanalytic tendencies he mentions explicitly.) To this Lacan objects that while one object (in the sense of goods) is *worth* another, one subject *is* another. By which he means that, when we suppose the Other to be a subject, we can only mean that this Other is identical to ourself in that she too is the subject of the signifier, of speech, and therefore we can

[44] *Transfert*, p. 456.

have her enter our calculations as someone who combines signifiers just the way we do. In short, as Lacan would later put it, as subject she becomes countable, both predictable and universalized; that is, not a 'subject' at all.

Paradoxically, then, the proponents of humanist intersubjectivity have in fact played into the hands of those they claim to oppose, the proponents of the various ethics which place the value of the community above that of the subject. Whether it be the conformity of 'adjustment' preached by the American culture of the melting-pot, subordination to the 'objective truth' of History and the communist state, subservience to the Truth of God or to that of Science, or service to the good of the greatest number, all these value systems share the Hegelian view, which of course was also that of Lacan in the early fifties, that the individual is nothing more than what the community makes of her. To paraphrase Silesius, the particular must 'fall away' whereas the universal 'stands fast'. Having eliminated both the object and the subject, both the individualistic narcissism of capitalism and the altruism of humanism, from consideration as viable bases for an ethics of the dignity of the individual, it would seem that Lacan has reached a dead end.

It is here that, in order to extricate himself from this impasse, Lacan has recourse to the theory of another kind of object, the one that psychoanalysis calls the 'partial object', and which Lacan will henceforth term the 'a-object'. Already in the seminar on unconscious formations (1957–8) and in 'Signification of the Phallus' (1958), he had put forth the notion that the particularity lost in unconditional demand returns as the 'absolute condition' of the desire that runs along beneath or beyond demand, in the form of the metonymic difference between signifiers, the incessant sliding of the meaning of the subject's being. In this way demand is transformed into desire.[45] Then, in the seminar on ethics, Lacan introduced the notion of the Thing, or internal object (later to be dubbed the 'extime'), in order to emphasize that the field of the (lost) object is there from the start, prior to and independent from the play of identifications, but not without important effects on the latter. The special value of the partial object derives from the fact that the lover sees it as the repository

[45] 'Formations', p. 253; *Ecrits*, p. 691; *Transfert*, p. 235.

of his individual being; it alone can serve to recover the 'lost object'. As a result, such an object becomes capable of stopping the metonymic slippage of meaning, of fixing the subject's being, of covering over the gap opened by the loss of the originary maternal object.

The development of the theory of the a-object goes hand in hand with that of the concept of *jouissance*, enjoyment, introduced as a technical term for the goal of desire in the ethics seminar and elaborated throughout the sixties. As Lacan began to conceive of the metaphoric substitutability of narcissistic objects as a function of the symbolic order, when the swarm of objects united by the master signifiers s1 had become exchangeable one for another, then the signifier could no longer designate the uniqueness, the particularity/alterity, of the individual subject.[46] Now in the modern world of political economy, this exchangeability of subjects has been realized in the marketplace in which each person is valued according to his or her usefulness, as Marx demonstrated so decisively. As a result, the unique value of the subject could be embodied only in something entirely gratuitous, of no use beyond itself. And in order to maintain the alterity of the subject to himself as well as to the social order, this gratuitousness had to be embodied in an object that was external as well as internal to the subject, the a-object.

It is this combination of gratuitousness and uniqueness/alterity which a long tradition, starting from Augustine, had associated with the term *jouir*, enjoying, as opposed to *user*, using:

Some things are to be enjoyed, others to be used ... Those things which are to be enjoyed make us blessed ...
To enjoy something is to cling to it with love for its own sake. To use something, however, is to employ it in obtaining that which you love ...[47]

For Augustine, of course, the only thing worthy of enjoyment as an end in itself is God, the plural ('things') indicating only the multiple personages of the trinity. The nearer source for Lacan was no doubt the German idealists of the late eighteenth and early nineteenth centuries who secularized this principle to include individual human beings. Kant, for instance, made the

---

[46] Miller, 'Extimité', p. 79.
[47] Augustine of Hippo, *On Christian Doctrine*, 1, 3 & 4.

rule of treating people as ends in themselves rather than as means to another end one of the two expressions of the basis of pure practical reason, i.e. of ethics. F. Schlegel, Goethe and many other thinkers vaunted a similar autonomy and self-sufficiency of poetry as the object of such *jouissance* and thus the realization of human freedom, equality and creativity.[48]

In *Transfert*, Lacan concludes that it is only by becoming the subject of desire for the a-object that the subject of speech can find his dignity as something unique and irreplaceable; this is the only true individuality. Several controversial corollaries follow from this stance. On the one hand, although the object of desire is overvalued, the Other who embodies it must nevertheless be lowered to the level of object (an allusion to Freud's article on the most common form of degradation in modern love life). On the other, paradoxically the subject can find his individuality in that object only by 'fading', by disappearing as subject. That is because the partial object is the separable part of the body – breast, faeces or phallus – with which I identify, and which can serve to unite our two bodies. Alternatively, the partial object can be considered to be the Other minus the missing body part, especially the genitals. Now the quintessential partial object is the phallus, which, it will be recalled, is also the signifier of the subject. Desire involves the dialectic of castration, described in chapter 4, in which there is a fateful conflict between fear of castration, the tendency to renounce desire in order to preserve one's status as full subject and the willingness to achieve one's lack by renouncing self-sufficiency and self-consciousness, *aphanisis*. I must relinquish the phallus in which I identify my being in order to re-find it within the object. At the same time, I can locate it within the Other only if I have accepted the latter's incompleteness, that is, only if I have lowered the Other to the status of partial object.

This catachretic superposition of the phallus onto lack, then, is the other aspect of the metaphor of love: in order to answer the Other's demand to be loved, in order to react to the Other as desirable, I have to be able to take up the position of the lover, to

---

[48] See Todorov, *Theories of the Symbol*, chapter 6. Unlike these predecessors, however, Lacan also emphasizes the relation of *jouissance* to the death drive and its inherent tendency toward violence and destruction, as we will see in the next chapter.

learn to accept my lack, and thus to become a subject of desire, a desir*er* as Lacan phrases it. But I can find my being in the Other only if the metonymic remainder of demand is preserved; that is, only if something is left unspoken and unknown. The subject must be 'eclipsed' in that a chain of signifiers must be kept outside the field of knowledge and consciousness, for the moment I try to explain myself, to articulate my desire, I thereby lose my status as pure desirer and fall back into that of one who is asking for something, who demands. The construction of desire thus necessarily entails the closing off from consciousness of a chain of signifiers; that is, the constitution of the unconscious.

We are now in a position to explain how the very situation of analysis gives rise automatically, so to speak, to the reality of love as metaphor. From the start, the analysand is in the position of the beloved, in that the analyst is there for the patient's good, to worry about and care for him. This manifest effect, as Lacan calls it, results from the relation of demand established by the patient's conscious request to be relieved of his suffering, to be cured. Not basically different from the relation of any patient to doctor, it is that of suggestion, which Freud and Lacan interpret as identification via the ego ideal. But in analysis there is also a latent effect, which derives from the operation of the unconscious, namely, the fact that the analysand does not know the structure of his desire, but imputes such knowledge to the analyst. In supposing that his *agalma*, the unknown object of his desire, is in the analyst, the analysand spontaneously assumes the position of the lover. Due to the specific combination of the analysand's non-knowing and the analyst's imputed knowledge of desire, the analysand's object is already located in the Other, and the former is virtually constituted as desirer. Hence the metaphor of substituting the position of the lover for that of the beloved is fulfilled by the conditions which preside over any psychoanalysis.

As Freud demonstrated in *Group Psychology*, the condensation of the love object with the ego-ideal is precisely the condition of being in love (*Verliebtheit*). The transference that love thus built into the psychoanalytic situation consists of two elements super-imposed the one upon the other, and it is this bi-polarity which explains its paradoxical action. Identification with the ego-ideal represents the resistant aspect of transference, the side of narcissism and demand, while identification with the a-object is the driving force of analytic revelation, transference as desire. Insofar as the primary goal of psychoanalysis is to bring to light the unconscious signifiers which constitute the subject, and ultimately her fundamental identification, the task of the analyst must be to keep the gap between demand and desire open. In order to encourage the analysand to accept himself as lacking, the analyst should first strive to separate the two elements of the metaphor of love by avoiding the position of ego-ideal, trying instead to occupy that of the object. The role of the analyst is not to work for the analysand's good, but for his desire. This means that she must maintain a margin of the non-known even while interpreting the meaning of the subject's unconscious formations.

The analyst must walk a kind of tightrope between the two poles of the transference, responding to the letters the subject addresses to her, yet not imagining, still less insisting, that this comprehension be accepted as complete. Interpretation, which puts the analyst into the position of ego-ideal as one who knows, is necessary in order to bring out the chain of signifiers that form the patient's unconscious, but it is always also insufficient. The analyst should therefore abstain from trying to 'understand', expecting rather that every interpretation will elicit some resistance, because all interpretations are metaphors which therefore to some extent cover over the lack inherent in what the subject needs above all to safeguard – the metonymic signification that constitutes his desire. Lacan has thus reversed the stance he had taken in the early days of 'Intervention', according to which the object arose from an impasse in the analytic dialectic, that is, from a lack of comprehension by the analyst. Now, since *Ethique*, the hole left by the lost object is there from the start, and an excess of understanding leads to the closing off of this place reserved for the partial object, which is also the place of the unconscious.

Because desire is the desire of the Other, during the transference the desires of analysand and analyst will be interlocked. Lacan rejects the notion of the analyst's 'neutrality', insisting that she will inevitably have human reactions to the patient's words and deeds.[49] As the addressee of the analysand's letters, she is inevitably implicated in the transference as the latter's love-object. For neutrality Lacan substitutes the requirement that the

---

[49] In this he is following Reik, *Listening with the Third Ear*, p. 468. See our chapter 6 for the relevant citation.

analyst know something about her desire, and has formed a desire that outweighs those inherent in her reactions, one which allows her to give direction to the analytic interaction. As object of the analysand's love, the desire of the analyst becomes the fulcrum which gives her leverage over the mindless repetition which otherwise governs neurosis. She must have learned that no object is worth more than another, and thus have mourned her own desire, her own being. This knowledge allows her to forestall identification with the ego-ideal by evacuating the place of the beloved in favour of that of the lover. Renouncing any attempt to appear desirable, she must occupy the place of pure desirer. It is for this reason that the analyst should 'act as a mirror', as analytic jargon has it, although not that of specular identification; only by saying nothing about herself can she avoid falling into the role of demander. Thus she can only give the other a sign of her desire. Ultimately, as pure desirer the analyst helps the analysand to recognize that what the latter says about her is in fact a transference; that is, it applies to the analysand himself.

When Lacan discussed transference as one of the four fundamental concepts of psychoanalysis some four years after *Transfert*, he explained its resistant function as a matter of deception. Since transference love begins once the analysand has fallen prey to the illusion that the analyst knows the meaning of his desire, at that point he finds himself in the situation of dependency already described above. Thinking the analyst possesses the object of his desire, he imagines he must win the latter's love in order to have that object at his disposal. He therefore tries to make use of this very subjection by making the analyst love him, offering him the ultimate deception of narcissistic love. By convincing the analyst that he (the analyst) has that which can complete the subject, the latter can all the more easily avoid recognizing what he himself lacks. Deception of the Other is thus a means toward self-deception; and it is in order to fulfil that function of pure deception *vis-à-vis* the analysis that transference love must be a present reality.

Lacan's analysis of the paradoxical aspect of the onset of the transference does not differ substantially from that in *Transfert*, but he replaces the terminology of the metaphor of love with that of the *Sujet supposé Savoir*, the subject supposed to know. As before, the key factor is the analysand's willingness to impute knowledge of his desire, and even a certain infallibility, to the analyst, which in turn leads to the conviction that the latter contains his *agalma*. As before, the appearance of love, however narcissistic and deceptive, thus signals at the same time the bond between the desire of the analysand and that of the analyst. In *Concepts*, however, Lacan takes greater pains to explain why the desire of the analyst cannot fail to be hooked onto that of the analysand. As stated in *Transfert*, desire has a defensive function as well as one of direct libidinal investment. As a consequence, desiring and avoiding desire are the same. Even if the analyst makes every effort not to respond to the desire of the analysand, even if the former attempts not to desire, that avoidance is still a desire, a wish: 'Ne pas vouloir désirer, c'est vouloir ne pas désirer' ['not wanting to desire is wanting not to desire'].[50] Since desire is the desire of the Other, the analyst cannot help but respond, as desire, in some way to that of the analysand. Including the desire of the analysand from the start, the sss necessarily makes the desire of the analyst the lever, the point where force can be applied through the transference to open up the unconscious.

In *Transfert*, Lacan had hesitated among various formulæ to express what it is the analyst was supposed to know. By the time of *Concepts* he had worked out an expression that was pithy and yet able to capture the various aspects of that knowledge formerly implied by the concept of love as metaphor: 'Il est supposé savoir ce à quoi nul ne saurait échapper, dès lors qu'il la formule – purement et simplement, la signification' ['he is supposed to know that from which no one can escape, as soon as he formulates it – quite simply, signification'].[51] By signification he means those catachretic processes whereby sense and non-sense are combined to form the subjects of speech and desire. As sss, the analyst is supposed to guarantee that what the analysand tells her will have a meaning, and that she can use the latter's very deceptions to find it out.[52] He calls this an 'absolute point' because it is autonomous, involving no prior positive knowledge about the analysand (or about sex, or life, or anything else), and because it links the analyst's desire, which he cannot withhold, to

---

[50] *Concepts*, p. 213; *Concepts* Eng., p. 235.
[51] Ibid., p. 228; ibid., p. 253.   [52] Zizek, *Looking Awry*, p. 57.

the effort to penetrate all deception and pinpoint the meaning of the analysand's unconscious formations. That effort becomes the object of the analyst's desire, his a-object.

As in *Transfert*, the focus of that effort is to shift the analysand from the identification with the ego ideal that stands in both the field of narcissism and that of the Other to the position of subject of desire via identification with the a-object. In order to articulate the complex relations between sense and non-sense which structure human sexuality, desire, society and language, Lacan recasts his description of the various a-objects as a full-fledged theory of the drives (*pulsions*), and he introduces the processes of 'alienation' and 'separation'. Adopted from Hegel, Marx and their interpreters, Lacan's alienation designates the birth of the subject of language, an occurrence that is more like a stillbirth. The subject comes into existence through the discourse of the Other, when the Other (the mother first, but later on any authority or social institution) imposes a signification upon the individual, calling her to take up a particular function, investing her with a certain position in the human family or society at large.[53] The subject is the effect of the signifier whereby '[le] sujet [est] appelé à l'Autre' ['the subject [is] called to the Other'].[54] At this point the subject is confronted with the forced choice of the Lacanian *vel* (Latin for 'either', 'or'), which results from the interplay of subject and meaning (attributes) in the functioning of language as predication: either he chooses being, thus losing out on meaning entirely, or he chooses the meaning imposed on him, and thereby forfeits that meaning-less aspect of signification which constitutes the unconscious.

In linguistic terms, the choice of being over meaning implies the refusal of all predication; the subject of the verb to be becomes

---

[53] *Ecrits techniques*, pp. 307–8; *Papers*, pp. 278–9. In a work to which Lacan often refers, especially in *Ethique*, Bentham developed a theory of symbols which sought to explain, among other things, 'the respect and awe with which otherwise worthless individuals can be invested, *qua* dignitaries' (*An Introduction to the Principles of Morals and Legislation*, p. xv). This notion evolved into his general *Theory of Fictions*, in which, while considering various types of symbolism, he centres his attention on the capacity of language to create non-existent entities. Although they escape the bounds of reason, like the badges and accoutrements of a judge, some of them, such as the hypotheses of the scientist or the postulates of the mathematician, are necessary to reason.

[54] *Concepts*, p. 188; *Concepts* Eng., p. 207.

so purified that it is completely empty, a nothingness. On the social level, if you choose being, then you refuse the social mandate contained in the meaning imposed upon you, exclude yourself from social life and, since subjectivity can only exist in society (through recognition, the desire of the Other), you renounce subjecthood. The ultimate phase of this process is the complete alienation of psychosis, the loss of belief in the Other. When you opt for meaning, on the other hand, you become 'petrified', reified in the function laid out for you by the Other. Joining society, acceding blindly to the demand of the Other, turns you into something like an inanimate object, a pure universal rather than a subject. Like the waiter Sartre describes in *Being and Nothingness*, the subject becomes so completely identified with her social role that she loses the distance from herself that constitutes subjecthood. She rushes to embrace the apparent solidity of what Sartre calls the 'in-itself' in order to escape the anxiety of confronting her nothingness. Lacan claims that signification alone can produce this effect: the loss of the subject as such results only when, as subject of the verb, it is included in its entirety within its predicates, so that nothing whatever escapes predication. Once again, the subject, whose existence depends on the maintenance of a margin of senselessness, disappears; the unconscious closes up.

The advantage of defining alienation in terms of the *vel* is that it allows Lacan to present the birth of the subject as the result of a mathematical and logical operation, union. In elementary mathematics, the union of two sets is defined as the set of all the elements in the two sets. Lacan's interest in this operation is twofold: on the one hand, the number of elements in the union may be less than the total of the one added to the other, usually because there is an overlap: some elements are contained in both sets but are not counted twice, e.g. $\{3,4,5\} \cup \{4,5,6\}$ is $\{3,4,5,6\}$. On the other, in elementary symbolic logic, union corresponds to the logical operation of joining two sets of propositions by the connective 'either/or'. Indeed, when the elements of each set are taken to be the values for which the particular proposition is true, then the union will contain all and only those elements which make their conjunction true. For example, if the first proposition is: x is an integer greater than 2 and less than 6, and the second is: x is an integer greater than 3 and less than 7, then the union

{3,4,5,6,} includes all the values for which either the first or the second is true, and no others.

Now Lacan's *vel* is an operator similar, but not identical, to union, in that it involves joining two sets together in such a way that the new set contains fewer elements than the total of each taken separately. Unlike union, however, this *vel* entails the complete disappearance, rather than the simple overlap, of the elements in question. When forced to choose between 'your money or your life', you lose your money in either case. This 'example' is of course a parable for the choice between your *jouissance* – the satisfaction of the 'want-to-be' – and your existence as subject, or that between your freedom and your life. Using truth tables and Venn diagrams to visualize the general solution set of Lacan's *vel*, Fink cogently demonstrates that the combination of the two propositions joined by the *vel* is true only when the first is false.[55] In the particular case in question, both being and meaning exclude the existence of the subject. The effect of the Other's call is to map out a place for the subject, but to prevent it from being occupied. Before the social mandate, the subject does not exist at all, but after it the alienated subject is nothing more than a potentiality. It can as yet have no being.[56]

As an empty place within the Other, the subject renders the signifying system incomplete. In the language of *Transfert*, the Big Phi that stands for impossible real presence, that of the subject as well as of any object, is the meaningless signifier that is excluded from the system from the start. In *Concepts*, Lacan tends to align this signifier with the unitary trait, and to call it the unitary signifier (s1). As we saw in chapter 3, the subject tries to localize the missing presence within the space left by this fall by invoking the representation of the penis, the imaginary signifier, or little phi, that is lacking in the Other, and which represents first of all the enigma of the mother's desire. This latter becomes the 'binary signifier' (s2) of *Concepts* and later writings, whose rise and fall, as Weber humorously puts it, determines the outcome of the formation of desire.

The new term, separation, now designates the process formerly referred to as the constitution of the subject of desire. Playing on the etymological and homophonic resonances of the French

---

[55] Fink, 'Alienation and Separation', p. 85.   [56] Ibid., p. 86.

'*séparer*', Lacan parses it variously as giving birth to oneself, defending oneself, and adorning oneself. In fact, the term picks up many of the ideas we have reviewed in conjunction with metaphor: the violent separation and individuation mentioned by Cassirer; predicative articulation, which separates the subject from its attributes; the pure being which the proper name alone makes it possible to separate from one's accomplishments and sufferings; and, of course, the physical separability of the a-objects, especially of the phallus, which makes the latter the privileged means of attaining that union of bodies which constitutes the heart of sexual desire. The advantage of the new usage of the term is once again the possibility of expressing the process in the precise form of a logical operation, and thus of pinpointing its exact relation to the alienation that precedes it and makes it possible.

Lacan defines separation as a matter involving the superposition of two sets. In mathematics, the set resulting from such a superposition, which includes only the elements the two have in common, is called their 'intersection', and is equivalent to the 'both/and' of symbolic logic in that it is true only when both individual propositions are true. As with the *vel* and union, here too Lacan has isolated an operator that both resembles and differs from intersection, but this time it is one that is well recognized in logic – neither/nor, or disjunction.[57] Like intersection, disjunction is true only when both propositions have the same value, but whereas both must be true in the former, in the latter both must be false. Separation consists in the superposition of two lacks – the lack of being of the subject and the lack of a signifier for the desire of the Other. As such, it corresponds to the second metaphoric process described in *Transfert*, in which the phallus that represents my unique being is considered to be contained within an Other, in the place where the Other is lacking.

Separation is thus a kind of return to the point of departure which preceded alienation, but a return with a 'twist'. It allows the subject to regain a measure of the 'natural' being, or *jouissance*, which supposedly preceded language – the imposition of the alienating 'union' of signification – but in an imperfect, and ultimately deceptive way, for this fixing of the subject's being is

[57] Ibid., p. 90.

186

only evanescent and punctual. In order to see the relation between the two operations, we must recall that the *vel* of alienation presents an all or nothing situation. Either the subject refuses language (meaning) entirely, in which case the non-subject of psychosis results. From this point nothing further can result. Or she accepts meaning, in which case her individual being is crushed by the universalizing function of the signifier. From this 'all' there is a possible way out, provided the totality of meaning can be disrupted. And that is just what separation involves: opening up a space of non-meaning within language; that is, forming an unconscious.

Separation begins to become possible when a non-known exists in the Other; a gap in the otherwise apparently seamless signification of the Other. In order for meaning to 'leak', or 'limp', or 'stumble', as Lacan variously puts it, there must be an interval between at least two signifiers which provides the space for the subject. That is the force of Lacan's dictum that a signifier represents a subject for another signifier. It is this fissure that allows the subject to call into question the desire of the Other, rather than accept it blindly as law. Transference as the motive force of analysis begins in the field of separation, then, when desire is attached to a signifying system whose minimal element is the binary signifier, in which the presence of one side is experienced as the absence of the other, and vice versa.

But in order to capitalize on this opening, the subject must be willing to accept her own mortality and the resulting implication of her fundamental nothingness. If the Other is incomplete, and I put my want-to-be in play there, then I can come to be there. *Wo es war, soll ich werden*, in the Freudian formula Lacan so often reinterpreted. In other words, only if neither the Other nor the subject has full being, if neither proposition is true, can the subject escape from the alienating oscillation between nothingness and petrification in the signifier.

Like Hegel's master, the subject must first choose death rather than life, in order to find a new life. That is because the sole way to be absolutely sure that the Other will recognize my desire as lying beyond any concern for my mere welfare is to demonstrate my willingness to renounce that very value, life itself.[58] The

---

[58] Kojève, *Introduction to the Reading of Hegel*, p. 14.

gratuitous a-object which lies beyond the narcissistic demand for happiness and love must therefore start from the offer of my death. The subject must be willing to accept death (castration) in order to begin creating a new life *ex nihilo*.[59]

The successful completion of separation thus depends on the institution of the a-object. In the theory of the drive Lacan elaborates in *Concepts*, he begins to call the latter the 'cause of desire', both to indicate that it serves the cause of desire, and to specify that it does so by preventing the subject from simply coinciding with the pure alienation of demand, with self-identical, finished meanings. Following Russell's argument in *Mysticism and Logic*, Lacan opposes the notion of cause to that of law, in that cause implies discontinuity, whereas law implies continuity and regularity. The place of the individual as barred subject opened up by alienation is in this sense that of the cause.[60] In so far as the object keeps this place of individuation open, it therefore acts as cause of desire.

One might expect that there would be a signifier, a general expression or law, for the sexual union that forms the goal of desire. If the search for a sexual partner were coordinated on the basis of a general image, the individual would be nothing more than an instance of the type, and thus would be annihilated as individual in relation to that type. But in fact there is no typical representation of human reproduction or of the sexual difference necessary to it. Moreover, such a relation cannot even be written, formalized, as the notorious statement from *Encore* has it: 'There is no sexual relation.' The only general significance of sexuality is the necessity of death, for each subject is thereby rendered dispensable, a mere carrier of the life of the species from one generation to the next. The field of sexuality is therefore covered over by the dialectic of life and death played out in terms of the experience of the individual in relation to his parents and their culture(s). The a-objects are merely representatives, figures, catachretic metaphors, rather than representations, of the pure life-instinct, of immortal life that is subtracted from the living being due to sexual reproduction. Each of these 'objects' is a part of himself lost to the Other, and thus an intimation of his, and the Other's, mortality. The drive makes present the necessity of death

[59] *Ethique*, p. 251.   [60] Miller, 'To Interpret the Cause', pp. 32–3.

implied by sex as well as the pure life of the libido. It represents the attempt to recuperate the missing parts of one's life by joining with the Other.

Lacan now conceives of the drive as a circular movement which links the subject to herself via a detour around the Other. The gratuitous a-object supports this movement by acting as a kind of darning egg, or solid post, that fills the void left by the lost object, and around which the subject can weave the strands of the text that will constitute her new being. As in *Transfert*, these a-objects correspond to the dialectic of demand and desire linked to the erogenous zones of Freud's pre-genital sexual drives. To the breast of the oral stage and the faeces of the anal, Lacan added the voice of the invocatory drive and the gaze Freud analysed as voyeurism and exhibitionism. Each involves the more or less hidden activity of 'making oneself be [seen, heard, eaten, shat]' by the Other.[61] He thus acknowledged that although the pre-genital drives have a narcissistic goal, they are not the purely narcissistic relations he had previously thought, for they supplement the lack of a 'genital' drive that would represent the sexual relation.

It is by occupying the place of the a-object instead of that of the ego-ideal that the analyst can intervene to help the subject attain separation. Due to the alienation of desire, when transference begins, the analysand puts the analyst into the position of master in the Hegelian struggle for recognition, while the subject occupies that of the slave. The ethics of psychoanalysis requires the analyst to reverse this situation, constantly moving into the place of the slave, keeping the a-object separate from the ego-ideal, in order to bring out her own incompleteness, her own need for the Other, in short, the impossibility for any subject to know and control his desire the way the subject imagines the ego-ideal can. By keeping his desire an unknown, an x, the analyst reproduces the condition for separation in which the subject had first confronted the enigma of his mother's desire. When the analyst

[61] *Concepts*, pp. 177–8; *Concepts* Eng., pp. 194–6. One might think here of Benveniste's article on the middle voice, to which Lacan refers in *Psychoses*. The linguist states that such verbs designate precisely those aspects of life with which psychoanalytic experience deals because they all indicate that 'le sujet se constitue comme tel dans le procès ou l'état que le verbe exprime' [the subject is constituted as such in the process or state that the verb expresses] (*Problèmes de linguistique générale*, p. 317).

refuses to act as the authority for a universal set of standards of behaviour to which the subject need only conform in order to please and thus to be loved, the latter is forced to call upon her own repressed signifiers in the attempt to construct her own, individual, desire.[62]

The analyst thus strives to make it impossible for the subject to engage in the narcissistic deception which constitutes hypnotic suggestion. This conception of the analytic process unequivocally contradicts the notion of the analysis of resistance according to which the analyst must use suggestion to controvert repetition. In a sense, the analyst must use repetition, the repetition of the encounter with the traumatic Other or real which cannot be symbolized, to counteract suggestion. Psychoanalysis becomes a kind of inverted hypnotism in which the analyst must strive to occupy the 'slave' position of the hypnotized subject.

Lacan returned to the problem of transference in 1967, when he devised the system of the *'passe'* for the new Freudian School of Paris he had founded in 1964 after being 'excommunicated' from the International Psychoanalytic Association.[63] Since the object of the *passe* was to determine when analysts in training were ready to be sanctioned by the school as analysts, Lacan concentrated on the transition from the position of analysand to that of analyst that marks the end of analysis: how judge that the 'desire of the analyst' had been formed in the process classical psychoanalysis calls the dissolution of the transference? The answer he provides depends on his new analysis of the pivot of the transference, the Subject supposed to Know.

In his earlier theories he had stated unequivocally that the sss was the analyst.[64] Now he nuances that assertion. The onset of transference still results from the analysand putting the analyst (or anyone) into the position of sss, and the task of the analyst is still to acknowledge her ignorance and therefore to remove herself from that place; but now he emphasizes that the only subject in analysis is the analysand, and that, in fact, it is the analysand who is the *Sujet supposé Savoir*. This contention follows in part from the definition of the subject as that which is represented by a signifier for another signifier, for it is the

---

[62] Fink, 'Alienation and Separation', p. 96.
[63] 'Proposition du 9 octobre 1967'.   [64] E.g., *Concepts*, p. 204.

analysand whose signifiers, whose speech, constitutes the substance of analysis. The other part of the justification derives from a theoretical modification introduced in the mid-sixties, the idea that the unconscious is a kind of knowledge. He now argues that the unconscious is a secondary phenomenon whose raw material is the pure spoken language of signifiers he henceforth dubs *'lalangue'*. The homophonies essential to the various operations of the unconscious, such as metaphor and metonymy, slips and jokes, depend on the prior codification of a certain knowledge about the signifier into the linguistic rules of a grammar, and this codification (*linguisterie*) requires writing.[65]

At first sight this claim seems to be a direct contradiction of the stance in *Transfert*, where he repeatedly stresses that the construction of the unconscious requires a space for non-knowledge. But in fact he qualifies the assertion that the unconscious is a form of knowledge with the complementary claim that this knowledge nevertheless remains outside the realm of consciousness. That is to say, it is sup-posed, both imputed and supra-posed under the signifier;[66] it is the signified of a catachresis. In this respect it is like the subject, which Lacan now designates by the Greek term for both subject and supra-posed, *hypokeimenon*. The subject of the transference is thus supposed to know a chain of signifiers; it is a matter of textual rather than referential knowledge. And since in fact the analyst knows nothing about this text, she must still, as in *Transfert*, choose non-knowledge in order to mark out a space for the desire of the analysand.

The end result of analysis is still the completion of the process of separation, but this is now understood in somewhat different terms. Reviving Freud's notion that the id is all that which is not 'I', Lacan assimilates the former to the 'battery' of already existing signifiers, the grammar or knowledge of the Other which he designates as s2, and the latter as the signified produced when

---

[65] Miller, 'A Reading of Some Details in *Television*', p. 19. It is for this reason that, in his later teachings, Lacan stresses the difference between the letter and the signifier. The roots of this conception can be found in the seminar on 'Le désir et son interprétation' (1958–9), where Lacan argues that, in a certain way, desire is interpretation (whence the play on the homophones *et* and *est* in the French title of that seminar). One effect of the need to express demand in language is that the id (*ça*) becomes 'atomized' into a cluster of metonymic elements, which correspond to the individual attributes that one tries in vain to add up into the totality of the subject's being in predication ('Désir', p. 329).

[66] 'Proposition', pp. 10–11.

the s1 that represents the subject intrudes into the s2.[67] The subject is thereby split into an 'it', or object appreciated by the Other, and an 'I' or desire that is depreciated. The goal of analysis can now be stated as allowing the analysand to become the cause of his own splitting. Becoming the subject of desire entails becoming the cause of the Other's desire. In Freud's terms, the id (one sense of Lacan's Other) must learn to take the ego as its object the way the ego was taken as object by the mother (another sense of the Other), so that he can then love someone else (a third sense of the Other). 'Il est devenu ce signifiant qui suppose le sujet du savoir' ['he has become the signifier which supposes the subject of knowledge'].[68] In other words, he has learned to identify with the summation of the a-objects that make up his history, with the *agalma* (phallus) which is the *Sujet supposé Savoir* of the unconscious.

The result of this acquisition of the *agalma* by the analysand is that the analyst loses her *agalma*, becoming nothing more than a waste product. Lacan now proposes to call this effect on the analyst the 'dissolution' (*liquidation*) of the transference, instead of imputing that to the patient, as he himself had done in *Concepts* when he described it as the analysand's renunciation of the use of love as deception in order to close off the unconscious.[69] But this '*désêtre*' (loss of being and desire) may result in the development of that desire of the analyst already described above, if it leads to the capacity to articulate the subject of the incomplete Other (S(𝐀)). Since each of the partners in analysis alternates between the role of subject and that of object, the analyst who has long since 'passed' from the role of analysand to that of analyst is less well placed to judge his training analysand than are the latter's own analysands. The *passe* is therefore based on the testimony of three analysands, who are presently going through the process of separation and thus in the best position to judge whether the analyst is able to accept her *désêtre*. This ability is radically opposed to anything that depends on recognition by others, such as the qualities defined by the bylaws of psychoanalytic societies. For the S(𝐀), as we know, indicates the lack of any guarantee of the Other, the absence of foundation that serves as the only possible genuine foundation of transitory being.

---

[67] *Envers*, pp. 11–12.   [68] 'Proposition', p. 16.   [69] *Concepts*, p. 241.

At the end of 'Proposition' as of *Concepts*, Lacan highlights his solution to the paradox of the transference by contrasting it to its opposite, the Nazi genocide. The alternative to articulating the signifier of the barred Other is to imagine that the Other is complete and somehow present behind the veil of appearances, a personified image of the law. The goal then is to look for a sign of the desire of the Other by offering it the sacrifice of the object of our desire, an object that represents the transgression of the law.[70] Lacan argues that the Kantian ethic, which responds to the modern scientific conception of the universe, requires the sacrifice, the murder, of the human warmth of the love-object because the a-object is necessarily non-universalizable, 'pathological' in Kant's jargon, and thus outside the 'moral' law.[71] In the terms used to describe transference, Kant wants to eliminate the alternation of subject and object, to isolate the pure being of an autonomous subject in the field of the signifier alone. That is why Lacan calls the universalist notion of the moral law 'désir à l'état pur' ['desire in its pure state'].[72] Nazism, then, was the actualization of this renewal of the monstrous allure of the ancient power of sacrifice.[73]

[70] Lacan states that Spinoza's intellectual love of God, the conviction that everything real is rational, and vice versa, was at one time a possible solution to the problem of desire and thus of sacrifice, but that in our world, Kant, unfortunately, is truer (*Concepts*, p. 247). With this statement Lacan is grudgingly backing away from the ideal which underlay his own teachings up until *Ethique*.

[71] *Concepts*, p. 247; *Ecrits*, pp. 780–2.

[72] *Concepts*, p. 247; *Concepts* Eng., p. 275.

[73] See Roudinesco, *Esquisse d'une vie*, p. 408 and note 12, for a discussion of the similarity between Lacan's view and that of Arendt on the relation of Kant's ethic to Nazism, a parallel first pointed out by Marini. Without deciding whether Lacan had read Arendt's book on Eichmann, Roudinesco accepts the idea that Lacan's comparison of Kant to Sade stems from Adorno and Horkheimer via Foucault's *Histoire de la folie* (pp. 407–8, and Adorno and Horkheimer, notes 9–11). See 'Excursus II: Juliet, or Enlightenment and Morals', in *Dialectic of Enlightenment*, for the Frankfurt School authors' comparison of Sade to Kant.

My sense is that Lacan's whole analysis of Kant's 'purified' practical reason is a psychoanalytic explanation of Horkheimer's remark in 'The End of Reason', that 'Sacrifice can be rational when it becomes necessary to defend the state's power which is alone capable of guaranteeing the existence of those whose sacrifice it demands. The idea of reason, even in its nominalistic and purified form, has always justified sacrifice' (pp. 32–3).

Likewise, the connection he establishes between Nazism and transference seems to follow closely Adorno's analyses, summarized in his essay, 'Freudian Theory and the Pattern of Fascist Propaganda'. It is perhaps not without interest to note that Adorno called the culture industry and fascist propaganda

This presentation of a Kantian revival of holocaust is a revision of Lacan's earlier analysis of the relation between the imaginary and the symbolic. What he previously called the primordial signifier is now the binary signifier that must fall under the bar in order to serve as the nucleus of the process of repression that gives rise to the unconscious. The desire of the analyst that acts as the mainspring of analysis is therefore not pure, but works to effect the separation of the paternal metaphor by bringing out the signifier that covers the subject's lack, so that the subject can then 's'y assujétir' ['subject himself to it'];[74] that is, so the subject can acknowledge his difference in both senses of the word – his lack of autonomy, but also his individuality. That is the place beyond the universal moral law where a love without limits can live. In short, the ethical force of psychoanalysis is to prepare the subject to 'combat the desire of the tyrant' when the latter claims for himself the power to subjugate the desire of the Other, to resist the 'command' introduced into the world by the signifier.

The only concrete means at the disposal of the analyst in this battle to play the role of the hypnotized subject is interpretation. From all that has been said thus far, however, it should be apparent that interpretation in this context is not restricted to finding meanings, whether hidden or otherwise. As a transferential action, it must somehow realize the analyst's desire 'd'obtenir la différence absolue' ['to obtain absolute difference'].[75] As it turns out, reading the letter of the subject's desire involves tracing the subject of repetition. The key to this process is the poetics of historical contingency.

'psychoanalysis in reverse', a notion to which Lacan most likely alluded in calling his 'discourse of the master' *l'envers de la psychanalyse* in the seminar of the same name he gave in 1969–1970 (*Envers*, p. 99). (Lacan himself refers to the phrase he used in 'De nos antécédents' (*Ecrits*, p. 68) to characterize his own discourse as a reprise of Freud's project in reverse (*Envers*, pp. 10–11). This reference does not contradict my hypothesis, since he later states that analytic practice is initiated by the discourse of the master, i.e. by identification with the single trait of the ego-ideal (*Envers*, p. 177).

74 *Concepts*, p. 248; *Concepts* Eng., p. 276.
75 Ibid., p. 248; ibid., p. 276.

6

$\diamond$

The Subject and the Symbolic Order: Historicity, Mathematics, Poetry

$\diamond$

Une langue entre autres n'est rien de plus que l'intégrale des équivoques que son histoire y a laissé persister. C'est la veine dont le réel qu'il n'y a pas de rapport sexuel, y a fait dépôt au cours des âges.

Lacan, 'L'Etourdit'

The textual material toward which the analyst's interpretation is directed is provided by that peculiar form of discourse somewhat misleadingly called 'free association'. Lacan repeatedly insisted that this technique is not merely one means among many possibilities for reaching the same end; rather it derives necessarily from the very structure of the object of analytic enquiry. There is an 'absolute coherence' between the process of free association and the functioning of the unconscious.[1] Negatively, the effect of the basic rule is to free the analysand from the constraints imposed on ordinary discourse by consideration for the addressee (see chapter 5). In the early fifties, Lacan's assumption was that this liberation would somehow permit the subject to complete her understanding of herself by filling in the gaps in her history which have been caused by repression.[2] Underlying this assumption was the notion that the subject is nothing other than a historical process. But even in his latest theories, in which the psychoanalytic subject became that of the *cogito*, the universal 'I think' of the Enlightenment, a certain kind of historicity remained an ineluctable mark of the Lacanian subject. Some 500 years ago Pico della Mirandola declared that 'man' is 'that creature to whom [God] had been able to give nothing proper to

---

[1] *Ecrits*, p. 514.
[2] *Ecrits techniques*, pp. 205, 213–15; *Papers*, pp. 181–2, 189–91.

himself ... a creature of indeterminate nature'.[3] With a little help from Hegel, Marx, Heidegger and Freud, Lacan transformed Pico's notion into the indeterminacy of the subject, whose essence is the lack of essence.

But how does loosening the ties between speaker and addressee liberate the unconscious? How does free association supply what is lacking from the subject's history? Why should it be just this mode of discourse and not any other which has this power? In sum, what specific interrelations link free association to transference, repression and historicity? Ignoring the rules of propriety and morality, overcoming the inhibitions imposed by shame, guilt and disgust, would seem to encourage the analysand to achieve a degree of sincerity unreachable in social discourse. The object of the basic rule would thus be to promote the most direct confession possible of the truth of the self. Free association would then be a kind of verbal striptease, or even the response to a psychological inquisition in which the subject would exchange her customary right to privacy for the possibility of deliverance from her symptoms and inhibitions.

As we have seen, confession, understood as the revelation of the self in discourse, does indeed play the preponderant role in free association. Liberation from social fears, however, cannot account for the requirement to ignore those constraints that are also imposed by consideration for the listener but are independent of standards of propriety and morality – the principles of logical and spatio-temporal consistency and of contextual unity and clarity. It is not at all apparent that the violation of these latter norms should contribute to increased sincerity. Moreover, the very fact of repression indicates that there is an internal limit placed on confession, no matter how 'sincere'. Free association must therefore owe its special efficacy to some additional factor which is consonant with the structure of the unconscious phenomena at issue in analysis – slips, dreams and symptoms.

The coherence which Lacan discerns between Freud's practice and his theory pertains to the interaction of the two distinct modes of expression operative in the formation of unconscious phenomena – the primary and secondary processes. Lacan con-

---

[3] Pico della Mirandola, 'Oration on the Dignity of Man', p. 224.

tends that the condensation and displacement which characterize the primary process of the dream-work are in no way distinguishable from the metaphor and metonymy operative in discourse, except insofar as the former must also fulfil the condition of being representable in visual images.[4] In other words, there is a certain unconscious component in ordinary discourse as in all mental productions, which carries the ineradicable expression of the subject's voice. Just as in dreams the dream-thoughts are first articulated in the form of the signifying elements produced through the primary processes, before these signifiers are then woven into a text that appears more or less coherent when judged by the standards of consciousness, so discourse is organized according to the same two principles but with their relative weights reversed. For Lacan, then, by cutting discourse loose from its moorings to the other (the listener) – the very factor which gives it its character of speech – free association paradoxically makes it possible to distill out from discourse the element of speech as voice, that is, the unconscious component of metaphor and metonymy whose function is homologous to the condensation and displacement of dreams and symptoms.

Free association can accomplish the task of liberating the unconscious constituent contained in an utterance, because it isolates the signifiers which constitute the discourse by setting them free from the context of conscious meaning. If the basic rule requires the analysand to ignore the rules of logic and spatio-temporal consistency along with those of propriety and morality, it is because both sets of standards contribute to the formation of meaning. In ordinary speech as in the recounting of a dream, that meaning is supplied by the 'quilting' process of the *point de capiton* whereby the text is closed off retrospectively. The string of signifiers is formed into a unity, a whole, through the retroactive action that gives the sentence a meaning at all times. Free association breaks up this retrospective unity, opening up 'une chaîne signifiante morcelée avec ses éléments interprétables' ['a fragmented signifying chain with its interpretable elements'], each of which may be attached to another signifying chain that intersects the first one.[5]

The elements so isolated are none other than those letters

---

[4] *Ecrits*, pp. 511–12.
[5] 'Désir', p. 329.

which come together in rebuses to form the other signifying chain, that of the unconscious. Although the basic rule leaves the subject free to speak of whatever pops into her head, in fact her associations, like her dreams, constantly gravitate toward the articulation of her most significant experiences. 'Significant' in this context means not only those events which are loaded with meaning but especially those which, precisely because the subject can assign them no meaning, are felt as traumatic. The chain of signifiers which constitutes the unconscious consists, then, of the results of the subject's repeated attempts to symbolize her experience. And the most visible sign of these only partially successful efforts are the analysand's symptoms. In the last analysis, the congruence between Freud's practice and his theory stems from the structure of the symptom as a catachretic record of failed attempts at symbolization.

If there were no repression, if symbolization were perfect, then there would be no unconscious, for everything could be contained within conscious meaning. If repression were perfect, however, the unconscious would be totally inaccessible, for the repressed would then leave no traces whatsoever behind to mark the spot of its disappearance. The process of free association is predicated upon the assumption of what psychoanalysis designates as 'the return of the repressed': repression exists but is generally incomplete, so that the missing word can still make itself felt by sending up what Freud calls 'offspring' (*Abkömm-linge*). Thus he concludes his study of parapraxes (slips) in *The Psychopathology of Everyday Life*, for example, by remarking that *'the phenomena can be traced back to incompletely suppressed psychical material, which, although pushed away by consciousness, has nevertheless not been robbed of all capacity for expressing itself'*.[6] In the famous case of Freud's forgetting the name of the painter Signorelli, for example, upon which Lacan commented many times, the names of Botticelli and Boltraffio came to mind as substitutes for the lost signifier.

Lacan points out that these substitutes are related to the repressed term only by virtue of the combination of signifiers – the syllables 'elli' common to Signorelli and Botticelli, and 'bo', 'traf' and 'her' which connect the painter's name to the idea of

---

[6] Freud, *The Psychopathology of Everyday Life*, p. 279.

death – the absolute master, or lord, *'Herr'* – via the intermediary links Bosnia, Herzegovina and Trafoi.[7] These syllables are just such interpretable fragments as are isolated from discourse by free association. Because they are related to the missing name by homonymic combination, and because the 'object' which leaves them behind (death) remains absent from the signifying chain, Lacan calls these bits and pieces 'metonymic ruins' or 'remainders'.[8] In the 'Seminar on "The Purloined Letter"' Lacan recreates this process of fragmentation by comparing the stolen letter, which Baudelaire translated as *la lettre volée,* to the movable pages of a loose-leaf notebook, *des feuilles volantes.* This play on the title enacts the meaning of the transposition implicit in the comparison by detaching the three letters v-o-l from their first binder and inserting them into a second; stolen (*volés*) from the one signifier, they can fly (*voler*) over to the other.

These metonymic ruins mark the place of an absence the way extraordinarily strong blasts of energy radiate out from the spot where a black hole is swallowing up matter and energy from the universe. In the case of symptoms, including those produced by the transference-neurosis, the black hole is that of the unique being of the subject. One of the first signifiers that is supposed to represent the subject, thereby bringing the latter into being, is the proper name. As the representative of the subject's particularity, her name can serve as the 'unitary trait' of the ego-ideal with which she wants to identify herself in order to preserve the integrity of that particularity. As such, the name cannot be metaphorized; no substitute can take the place of the proper name, for any such replacement would contradict the uniqueness it purports to represent. As long as that identification can be maintained, the subject knows what and who she is. But whenever it is undermined, whenever the subject's mastery and unity are called into question by some traumatic event, the name becomes subject to the processes of suppression and fragmentation into its constituent letters. Thus, in one of his later analyses of the Signorelli episode, Lacan rejects the explanation that the

---

[7] For the purposes of this discussion, I've reproduced only the bare essentials of these connections. See chapter 1 of *Psychopathology* for Freud's subtle and detailed analysis, in which he traces the many chains of associations leading to the ideas of sex and death, and ultimately to the name Signorelli.

[8] 'Formations', p. 295.

basis of the lapse was the semantic connection between the German *Herr* and the Italian *Signor*, the first syllables of the painter's name, for that would entail a relation of translation, and thus a metaphoric substitution. He emphasizes instead the literal transfer of the three letters S-i-g from Freud's first name, Sigmund, to the painter's last name, Signorelli, which marks the loss, the failure of Freud's identification with the painter as one who has mastered death through his art (since Freud was unable to recall the latter's name). These three letters do not return to the surface in the substitute names that occurred to Freud (Botticelli, Boltraffio); removed from the name like the sheets of a loose-leaf notebook, they remain in abeyance (*en souffrance*), waiting to fly onto some other signifying chain.[9]

By opening up a specific hole in the proper name from which some letters are stolen, the mistake succeeds in creating a space in which to locate the desire of the subject. Freud can no longer be satisfied with himself as originator and master of psychoanalysis and the unconscious; his identification with the ostensible unity represented by his name, Sigmund, can no longer suture, or cover over, the inadequacies, the lack of plenitude which constitutes him as subject. If the letter 'est unité d'être unique, n'étant de par sa nature symbole que d'une absence' ['is a unit in its very uniqueness, being by nature symbol only of an absence'],[10] in this late version of his theory Lacan makes it clear that the absence in question is the unity the subject wishes to preserve through the proper name. Once the name has been fragmented into its letters, it becomes a signifier like any other and as such a part of the signifying system in which one member can always substitute for another by means of homophony, like the *pot* of *po-lice* (see chapter 4). The alternative to suturing the hole over is, therefore, as we have seen in our discussion of metaphor, to reattach the flying letters to another signifying chain, as in the more complete unconscious formations of jokes, dreams, symptoms or sublimations. Thus Freud's response to his trauma was his act, the historical actualization that consisted of writing and publishing his treatise on the psychopathology of everyday life.

---

[9] Julien cites the seminar lesson of 6 January 1965, p. 41. I am indebted to Julien's excellent presentation in 'Le nom propre et la lettre' for my entire discussion of this point.

[10] *Ecrits*, p. 24; *Purloined Poe*, p. 39.

Before and beyond the proper name, the being of the subject is tied to those signifiers which mark her first experiences of satisfaction, of *jouissance*. Freud claims that the subject strives to fulfil its wishes through hallucination because the desired object is the 'identity of perception' with the lost object. Shifting the emphasis commentators generally place upon this phrase, Lacan construes it to mean that what the subject seeks in life is the 'identically identical' of the object; that is, some mark which will identify the uniqueness of what was perceived at that particular time.[11] It is only this sense of the unifying entity of the lost object behind the collection of attributes, or qualities perceived which confers reality on perception for the subject. Repetition, whether hallucinated or not, always has as its goal, or rather as its hope, the reappearance of the unitary signifier in its singularity. But that mark of the particular time, the unicity of that originary fulfilment, will always be lacking in the symbolic order of phenomena, for the universality of the signifier, even if it be in the form of an image, precludes recording the uniqueness of a perception. Moreover, as with the detached letters of the name, once the subject has to link together the objects of the outside world in a signifying form, once there are at least two elements in the field – the binary signifier – *'il ne peut que les recevoir dans leur différence'* ['he can only receive them in their difference']; as a result, the search for perceptual identity, whose success would constitute absolute meaning, can never be satisfied.[12] The particularity of the real to which the letter points can never be made the object of perception or knowledge; it must always remain in sufferance.

But if meaning always ultimately fails, analytic discourse nevertheless has the capacity to follow the signs by which it indicates the direction of its failure. As explained in chapter 5, sexual desire is the metonymic remainder that runs underneath the discourse of the demand for narcissistic love and happiness, which constitutes most of what is said in psychoanalysis. By disengaging the subject's signifiers from the coherence of the secondary process and thus effectively randomizing them, free association allows the metonymic remainders of the repressed to surface and fly over to the figure of the analyst in their habitual

---

[11] *Identification*, p. 136, cited in Andrès, *Lacan et la question du métalangage*, p. 134.
[12] Ibid., p. 136; in Andrès, pp. 134–5.

forms of repetition, i.e., to produce the transference-neurosis. Even though the identity of perception remains a mythical entity, these remainders do point to the symbolization of actual perceptions and events of the subject's life. In fact, it is the very impossibility of ever refinding the object, the necessity of the missed encounter, or *distuchia*, which institutes repetition.

Although repetition 'begins' as the attempt to reproduce the signs of a situation in which a need was satisfied – the identity of perception – because of the structure of the signifier, that is, due to the fact that the presence of one signifier functions as the absence of another independently of any reality, the repetition of the need changes into the need of repetition. Lacan interprets Freud's discussion of 'facilitations' (*Bahnungen* in German, *frayages* in French) in his *Project* as a kind of formalist manoeuvre: because it is easier to retraverse a path that has already been broached (*gebahnt*), pleasure is experienced in so doing; then, in a second step, repeating that trajectory becomes a pleasure in itself, without reference to any utilitarian or external goal involving the satisfaction of a need. The pleasure of the satisfaction aimed at in the attempt to refind the lost object is replaced by the pleasure experienced in what had been the search – repeating the sequence of signifiers that constitute the pathway opened up by that first experience. Consequently, the path of desire that leads to satisfaction can never be laid out in advance of the symbolization of experience nor established as a universal goal; desire is historized through and through. The heart of Freud's thought, according to Lacan, is that the function of memory, '*la remémoration*', is the rival and even the enemy of the satisfactions it is supposed to ensure.[13]

In a sense, its goal is the failure to satisfy the need, for it is only thus, as we have seen, that a space for desire can be maintained. Through rememoration, the pleasure principle turns into its

---

[13] *Ethique*, p. 262. In *Transfert*, Lacan mentions that he adapted this notion from Lagache. Perhaps so, but once again it is an Augustinian model that seems to guide this interpretation. Figuring the approach to blessedness as a voyage, and the enjoyment of God as our homeland, the latter cautions:

> But if the amenities of the journey and the motion of the vehicle itself delighted us, and we were led to enjoy those things which we should use, we should not wish to end our journey quickly, and, entangled in a perverse sweetness, we should be alienated from our country ...
>
> (*On Christian Doctrine*, I, 4)

ostensible opposite, the death drive, which impels the subject to repeat her failures masochistically, as in Kierkegaardian repetition.[14] Now since fusion with the Other at the centre of the object threatens the resurgence of the imaginary body torn to bits,[15] and ultimately the annihilation of the subject, both sides of the pleasure principle are operative simultaneously; repetition serves to preserve the subject by regulating her distance from the object, even while it appears as a demonic force that governs her destiny according to incomprehensible rules. The subject's behaviour will thus be directed by the repetition of these signifiers, a process that functions independently of any concern for her well-being and thus appears as senseless, as traumatic to the ego.

Detached from the ego, these letters, these lost (repressed) constituents of the self, float freely until they seize the opportunity to attach themselves to other signifying chains through the process of transference. One such chain is furnished by the subject's bodily parts, functions and her thoughts and behaviour, that is, the component parts of hysterical and obsessional symptoms. If one follows the direction in which meaning fails, therefore, before arriving at the pure otherness of the Other which constitutes its ultimate point of failure, one is first led to a metaphoric realm in which the history of the subject – her traumatic approaches to satisfaction – has already been recorded (see chapter 4).

In the early fifties, Lacan modelled his theory of historicity fairly closely on Heidegger's analysis of temporality in *Being and Time*.[16] When he insists that there is no fundamental difference between a neurosis and analysis, or between the subjectivity of the analyst and that of the child living through the anal 'stage', he is transporting Heidegger's claim that historicality forms an essential constitutive component of subjectivity into the domain of psychoanalytic experience. Psychoanalysis can hope to remake the history of the analysand precisely because the latter's experience has always already taken shape within a 'primary

---

[14] *Ecrits*, p. 519; *Envers*, p. 51.
[15] *Ethique*, p. 219.
[16] For an analogous discussion of temporality in Husserl, Heidegger's teacher, see Derrida, *Speech and Phenomena*. Like Heidegger, Derrida is concerned to show that the notion of time as a sequence of discrete points, or presents, is secondary, derived from a pre-phenomenal time based on the combination of the future and the past.

historization' that precedes and conditions the cognitive relations of 'subject' to 'object' in understanding historical events (Heidegger's 'historiology'). In short, '[Dasein] exists historically and can so exist only because it is temporal in the very basis of its being'.[17]

Heidegger argues that symbolization and interpretation form the basis of human historical existence, because they allow people to become aware of their own finitude.[18] Since the human subject has no fixed nature, it is nothing more than a set of possibilities; that is, it defines itself only in terms of a future. Interpretation involves awareness of the future insofar as the latter is constituted as the realm of projected possibilities. Anticipation, the attempt to take cognizance of those future possibilities, is thus the fundamental attribute of subjectivity, its 'being'. But anticipation involves something more than the mere imagining of possibilities; it involves projecting the actualization, the real occurrence, of the anticipated event. Now, death has the peculiar characteristic that it can never be actualized, can never be given as a concrete content that could occupy thought. As a result, awareness of death forces the mind to concentrate on its own existence rather than on that of external (conceptual) objects, and to recognize that what distinguishes that existence from other sorts of beings is precisely the pure anticipation of possibility prior to and independent of any particular content.

This heightened awareness and the action which flows from it, which Heidegger calls 'being-towards-death', is therefore a kind of anticipation of anticipation; anticipating death brings about the anticipatory understanding that it is just the possibility that there will be an end to my possibilities. And since death is a phenomenon in which, unlike most other occurrences in life, no one can take my place, this anticipation brings home to me what Heidegger calls my 'ownmost potentiality-for-being'; that is, the awareness that my possibilities are at some level independent of other people or circumstances. Having possibilities, however, means having choices. Recognizing both that my life consists of

---

[17] Heidegger, *Being and Time*, p. 428.
[18] Heidegger has of course good theoretical reasons for using the term '*Dasein*' in place of 'human', 'people' and so on, but I think that if I were to follow his lead here, it would only obfuscate my explanation without adding to its intellectual rigour.

having possibilities and that the latter are finite, I will understand that I am responsible for choosing among them. Thus I will be moved to 'choose to choose'. If human being is conditioned by the anticipation of the implication of death as the end of my possibilities, then it would be just as correct to say that human being is determined by not-being. This negativity indeed carries over into the specific choices I make, for every such choice necessarily excludes other possibilities. In a sense I kill myself, or at least I kill off certain possible selves, whenever I choose to follow any particular course of action. The 'second death' which Lacan posits as the object of the death drive starting from *Ethique* involves just such a killing of the self with the aim of starting over again, of recreating oneself from nothing.

The actual possibilities of existence with which I project my future upon becoming aware of the implications of death are themselves limited by the heritage of the cultural world into which I was born. Whether I choose to accept or reject them, my choices are conditioned by the modes of living and thinking, themselves the result of historization, which exist prior to my entry into the world. And these modes are transmitted to me in the form of discourse, of that which has been interpreted in that primordial symbolization ('disclosedness', aletheia) discussed in chapter 4. Making this heritage one's own, 'taking it over' as the English translation terms it, or 'assuming' it as in the French translation, is what Heidegger calls *repetition*: '*Repeating is handing down explicitly*' to oneself a possibility of existence.[19] This repetition is neither a simple reproduction of the past in the present nor a reversion of the present to what is past, but an active response to the possibilities (as opposed to past realities) provided by one's cultural heritage in light of one's choice for the future, that is, in light of a being which does not yet exist as a reality and could only do so as a completed totality in death. As a moment concentrated on the past as a function of the future, it is, therefore, as much a disavowal (or a 'destruction') as an embrace of the past.[20]

[19] *Being and Time*, p. 437.
[20] As with 'human' and 'people', so here too, for theoretical reasons, Heidegger uses the words 'past' and 'present' only very sparingly, in order to avoid the connotation of a linear conception of time consisting of a succession of points. Since it would take too long to introduce and explain here the jargon he substitutes for the customary terms, I have tried, as with his '*Dasein*', to convey the sense of his thought within the more easily accessible vocabulary.

In sum, although historization may take more or less 'authentic' forms according to Heidegger, it is always the case that 'Dasein temporalizes itself in the way the future and having been are united in the Present'.[21] It is to this temporalization, fundamental to all human experience, that Lacan refers under the name of 'primary historization'. He claims that the symptoms which bring a person into analysis are themselves products of this process of historization dominated by the futural, and he therefore calls them documents, monuments, traditions and texts. If these symptoms inevitably concern the subject's relation to sexuality, as all psychoanalytic experience shows, that is because in every human society it is in the realm of sexual desire that the subject is first subjected to a law, and that law could not be formulated without a process of symbolization. Resulting from the necessary imperfection of repression known as the return of the repressed, symptoms come not from the past but from the future. Heidegger's temporalization thus supplies the conceptual framework for Lacan's famous explanation of the unconscious (the repressed) as that which *'will have been'.*[22]

Lacan starts from the concept of retrospective interpretation (*Nachträglichkeit*) Freud developed especially in his analysis of the so-called Wolf Man. As a child of 6 months or 1 and a half years, the latter allegedly witnessed his parents having sexual intercourse with entry from the rear. This primal scene accrued its traumatic, and hence symptom-producing, power only several years later. The infantile neurosis which appeared at the age of 4 resulted from what Lacan calls a 'symbolic integration', in terms of which the stored memory took on a shocking value and hence led to its repression, that is, to its detachment from the more or less coherent history of the self the child's mind was constructing in its symbolization.[23] The meaning that is attributed to the traumatic element, or rather, the lack of meaning which constitutes it as traumatic, emerges only from the retrospective attempt to construct a history of the self that would offer an all-inclusive answer to the question, 'What am I?' Repression (*Verdrängung*) is thus an 'after-(re)pression' (*Nachdrängung*), and the return of the

---

[21] *Being and Time*, p. 449.
[22] *Ecrits techniques*, pp. 181–2. See both Weber, *Return to Freud* and Zizek, *Sublime Object*, for excellent clarifications of Lacan's 'future perfect'.
[23] Ibid., p. 215.

repressed – the neurotic symptom – brings 'back' something which never did exist in the past – the trauma – but which came from that future symbolization. It is for this reason that the unconscious is a pulsation in which the movement of closing up precedes, and must precede, its opening. The symptom is thus a trace, but a trace of nothing. In the terms of an image Lacan found in the writings of the cyberneticist Norbert Wiener, historization brings you to observe the disappearance of the object – the exclusion of the repressed from the symbolized – before you perceive the thing that is about to disappear – the repressed that will have been if and when it finds adequate symbolization.[24]

However paradoxical the role of the future in this explanation, the mere fact that interpretation is retrospective does not yet justify calling primordial symbolization 'primary historization'. The question still remains as to what comprises the specifically historical character of symbolization. It is here that Heidegger's temporalization adds an important clarification. Not only does retrospective interpretation rearrange the impressions of the past in such a way as to invert the customary temporal order where repression is concerned; it does so, and is able to do so, only because it operates as a function of the future. Subtending the repression and eventual reintegration of specific impressions is the prospect of completing the process of symbolic integration – establishing a continuous history of the self, in Freud's termi-nology – in the future. Lacan stresses that the analytic concern for restoring the continuity of the subject's memory does not stem from the fear of omitting some occurrence in her life nor from the belief that the subject's history is an unbroken, linear, progres-sion, but from the importance of establishing the chronological sequence of what are in fact the subject's discrete, discontinuous, acts of historization. For Freud, '[la] remémoration ... [fait] reposer sur le seul couteau des certitudes de date la balance où les conjectures sur le passé font osciller les promesses du futur' ['recollection [is a matter of] balancing the scales, in which conjectures about the past are balanced against promises of the future, upon the single knife-edge or fulcrum of chronological certainties'].[25] That is why he was so careful to determine the

[24] *Ibid., pp. 181–2.*
[25] *Ecrits*, p. 256; *Ecrits* Eng., p. 48.

objective dates of the traumatic events in the childhood of the Wolf Man.

Heidegger considers datability (Lacan's *datation*) – the relational structure of the 'now', the 'then' [of the future], and the 'on that former occasion' – as one of the key indicators of the fundamental temporality of subjectivity. When we arrange the objects that matter to us according to such a relational sequence, we reveal our own temporality in making those objects present, that is, in symbolizing them. In other words, we express our own mode of determination in relation to possibilities – future, past and present – that are always outside ourselves, 'ecstatic'. Lacan can thus read Freud's excessive concern with finding absolutely accurate, objective, dates for the occurrence of the Wolf Man's primal scene and its subsequent traumatic interpretation as an expression of Freud's own desire to establish the truth of psychoanalysis in order to symbolize himself. What was Freud's act as subject, however, was reification, alienation for the Wolf Man, and Lacan suggests that Freud's feverish attempt to reach this piece of the real may have provoked the patient's ensuing psychotic episode.[26]

Before any participation in the process of analysis, the subject repeatedly attempts to symbolize her life as a unique totality. She projects the unity of her future being, that which Lacan would later translate as the unitary trait, in relation to which alone repression can occur. Without this desiring relation to a purely ideal future, gaps, omissions and mistakes would be impossible. The infantile neurosis is the equivalent of analysis, therefore, because both are governed by the same anticipation. The institution of desire as split off from demand in the castration complex, the search for a lost but now anticipated *jouissance*, marks the beginning of history, for the individual as for specific societies.[27]

Outside of analysis, the anticipation of Being motivates that repetition which, according to Freud, characterizes symptoms (see chapter 4). In Lacan's reading, Freudian repetition resembles that of Heidegger, as well as that of Kierkegaard, in that, although not subject to conscious control, it is not a purely passive state but an act. The subject keeps repeating the same sequences in an active attempt to hand the past down to herself

[26] *Concepts*, p. 54.
[27] *Transfert*, pp. 268–9.

in view of future possibilities; that is, to (re-)capture the ostensibly 'lost object' of her 'signifying unicity' 'dans le but de faire resurgir l'unaire primitif d'un de ses tours' [with the goal of making the original unitary emerge from one of those sequences].[28] Within analysis, the motivation for the transference is the subject's same hope of 'hauling' her potential unity forth from her past, as the etymology of the German *Wiederholen* seems to indicate in Heidegger's and Lacan's meditations:

L'attente de l'avènement de cet être dans son rapport avec ce que nous désignons comme le désir de l'analyste ... voilà le ressort vrai et dernier de ce qui constitue le transfert.

The expectation [anticipation] of this being in relation with what we designate as the desire of the analyst ... that is the true and ultimate mainspring of what constitutes the transference.[29]

As a mode of repetition and thus historization, the symptom is a metaphor, a catachresis, in that it is necessarily constituted around a lack, or rather by the traumatic lacks which, as the subject's attempt at symbolization, it itself institutes. Like the artisan's vase upon which Heidegger meditates, the signifier introduces the nothingness of the Thing (the internal object) into the world. As the return of the repressed, the metonymic remainders which compose the symptom mark the place of the disappearance of those possibilities which were inevitably thrust away when the subject made the choices inscribed in her symbolizations of her life. By providing the subject with the opportunity to isolate the metonymic remainders of her past symbolizations through free association, Freud has made it possible to subject those modes of historization to rigorous study. Psychoanalysis thus brought repetition, which remains outside the field of principled enquiry in Heidegger, into the realm of scientific metaphorization, thereby allowing the subject to make her history her own.

The apparent inertia of the symptom derives from the traumatic (senseless) character of that which it has excluded, for instead of capturing the particularity of the moment of satisfaction, in fact it memorializes the impossibility of so doing. In the fifties Lacan interpreted the symptom as an unsuccessful repeti-

---

[28] *Identification*, p. 253, cited in Andrès, *Lacan et la question du métalangage*, p. 129.
[29] 'Position de l'inconscient', in *Ecrits*, p. 844.

tion in Heidegger's sense; the subject lacks that which stands in the place of his tradition, the investiture by the (paternal or social) Other. Insofar as this traumatic discourse of the Other remains uncomprehended by the subject, her symptom acts as a question about herself she asks of the Other. Because that Other remains indefinite outside of analysis, the unconscious question inevitably remains without a response. The missing word does not come forth, no matter through how many turns the wheel of repetition revolves. Within analysis the subject's symptoms and other unconscious formations become focussed more and more directly onto the figure of the analyst in the process of transference. The task of psychoanalytic interpretation, therefore, will be first of all to respond to the subject's question about her being by uncovering the discourse of the Other within the successive layers of the subject's historizations; that is, by piecing together the missing word(s).

Before reaching the ultimate level of sheer ineffable particularity, interpretation will first encounter all the specific possibilities that the subject has thrust away, but which insist in her discourse in the form of metonymic remainders. In the transference, the discourse containing the subject's question will produce an effect on the analyst. In the words of Theodor Reik, who was one of Freud's early pupils and whom Lacan often praised despite their obvious theoretical differences, the analysand's talk will give rise to the 'analytic response'.[30] This response is first of all the analyst's transference onto the analysand, which forms the necessary basis for any analytic interpretation of the subject's unconscious impulses.

We have ... seen that it is not the other person's impulse as such, but *its unconscious echo in the ego*, that is the determining factor in psychological

---

[30] Reik, *Listening with the Third Ear*, pp. 269–70. No doubt Reik's sensitivity to language and his talent for coining images and expressions made Lacan recognize in him a kindred spirit; one, moreover, who fought the same battle for the same reasons against the American reification of psychoanalysis in the fifties by Fenichel and the proponents of the 'autonomous ego'. In fact, Reik was a student of French literature before being analysed and becoming a psychoanalyst in his turn. It is therefore not surprising that some of Lacan's most striking phrases seem to derive from his reading of Reik. Reik speaks, for instance, of the heightening of the uncanny effect produced when one's unconscious thoughts seem to materialize 'from the atmosphere of radio and radar, telephone and television' (p. 238), a remark Lacan imitates in a mysterious-seeming way in his article on 'Kant avec Sade' in *Ecrits*).

conjecture. Thus our own mental reaction is a signpost pointing to the unconscious motives and secret purposes of the other person ... The assertion of the unfeeling attitude, of the impassibility of the analyst, is a fairy tale.[31]

Reik illustrates this unconscious echo with examples of analysands whose discourse aroused in him a vague sense of uneasiness or irritation, which he was later able to trace to his picking up the strains of irony in the subject's 'voice' – the choice of words, intonations, or the gestures accompanying speech – an irony of whose hostile intent, indeed of whose very existence, the speaker remained totally unaware. The analyst's pain, however mild and fleeting, thus formed an inverted image of the antagonistic impulse at the core of the patient's unconscious message. Reik recounts a telling example of this process in a non-transferential situation. A young woman who had recently moved from a southern town to New York was afraid that no man in the city would marry her because she had allowed a married man at home to caress her. Since there was no one in New York who knew her or anything about her past, it seemed preposterous for her to be so worried (even if the men of that era would have placed so high a price on 'purity'). Her fear of being found out, and thus ruining her chances for marriage, was genuine enough to reduce her to a paroxysm of uncontrollable sobbing, yet the unconscious message it conveyed was in fact the reverse of that fear, namely the wish to let everyone know that at least one man had found her desirable, for, as it turned out, in her teens she had been unattractive.[32]

The unconscious message takes this inverted form only because it began as a response to the Other in the first place; not necessarily to a particular person, however, nor even to something actually said or done, but to the anticipated reaction of the Other. Others are always 'present, so to speak, in that I unconsciously anticipate what their attitude would be to my thoughts and to the actions that concern them'.[33] Reik describes this unconscious anticipation purely in terms of the subject's fear of

[31] Reik, *Listening*, p. 468.   [32] Ibid., pp. 216–17.
[33] Ibid., p. 483. I suspect it would be possible to trace this conception of the presence of the Other back via Goethe, not to Hegel as in Lacan's case, but to the philosopher's master in this area, the Rousseau of the *Discourse on Inequality* and of the *Confessions*.

criticism and desire for approval by the ego-ideal (which he calls the 'superego'). For him, self-observation can occur only through identification with, and then introjection of, the observing Other.[34] But since the satisfaction of all human needs involves the maternal or social Other, that is, the relation to the 'internal object', for Lacan observation and satisfaction are tied together in the anticipation of the Other. He therefore extends the notion to include all historizations, in which the subject aims to find out what he is by defining himself through his choices in relation to the Other. The self that is sending the message is as 'other' to itself, as much an anticipation of the future, as is the projected reaction of the Other. Consequently, Lacan often spoke of the 'fundamental discourse' whereby I attempt to satisfy my desire by declaring that 'you are my master', or 'you are my wife'.[35] Within the framework of such an open-ended, and thus necessarily ambiguous, commitment, what I am will only emerge from the basically unpredictable way in which you and I relate to each other in the future. Thus it would be possible to read the report of Reik's patient not merely as a demand for sympathy and reassurance that she was in fact (referentially) attractive, but as an attempt to ascertain through his awaited response in what her desirability (will have) consisted.

Even when Lacan had abandoned the Hegelian idea that symbolization (naming) leads to mastery over that which is symbolized (see our discussion of his various interpretations of the *fort/da* in chapter 3), and therefore also the Heideggerian notion that being-toward-death makes possible the attainment of the freedom to choose one's historization, he still maintained that interpretation is meaningful because the subject's relation to the unconscious signifiers has a determinate, not an arbitrary, value.[36] The analyst is able to read his own reaction to the

---

[34] Ibid., pp. 7–8. The optical system Lacan charts in *Ecrits techniques* and 'Remarque sur le rapport de Daniel Lagache' (in *Ecrits*) is designed to demonstrate that self-observation is a process that involves the unconscious subject beyond the narcissistic relation between the ego-ideal and the ideal ego.

[35] *Psychoses*, pp. 335–42; *Ecrits*, p. 351.

[36] *Concepts*, pp. 226–7; *Concepts*, Eng., pp. 250–2. The translation gives 'particular value' (p. 252) for '*valeur déterminée*' (p. 227), which I have rendered as 'determinate value' in order to play up its opposition to the expressions 'just any signification' and 'open to all meanings' (p. 226; p. 250, Eng.) that Lacan had used in the preceding paragraphs.

symptom as an inverted form of the message it sends, because something within that symptom – Lacan's metonymic remainders – marks a rejected impulse which anticipated satisfaction, as well as judgement, by the other from the start. The process of symbolic castration which leads to the institution of the subject produces two simultaneous effects, which Lacan likens to the two numbers in a fraction. Beneath the bar, in the place of the denominator, is the repressed signifier shorn of meaning and therefore traumatic, a kind of zero in that it abolishes all meaning. In the numerator, however, one finds the various meanings that have been attached to that signifier in the course of the subject's successive historizations, 'significations dialectisées dans le rapport du désir de l'Autre' ['the dialectized significations in the relation of the desire of the Other'].[37] With a zero term in the denominator the fraction which represents the subject takes on an infinite value, but the terms which appear in the numerator are specific and determinate. Consequently, although the long-term purpose of analysis is to bring out the meaningless signifying chain which forms the core of the subject, this result can be attained only by first calling forth the various stages of symbolization built up around this core.

It is the 'infinitization' of the subject to which Lacan now attributes the function of freedom. In other words, it is no longer the power to name which confers the freedom that derives from mastery, but the ability to escape the power of meanings imposed by the Other, which opens up the subject's meagre margin of freedom. While the subject no longer has the Heideggerian power to choose to choose – that is the sense of the Lacanian *vel* discussed in chapter 5 – once the initial forced choice has been made, she can strive to map out an area of indeterminacy where the leeway required to elude reification can be preserved. The

Unfortunately, the translation of another important phrase in this passage is badly botched. Where the French has 'Cela n'empêche pas que ce n'est pas cette signification qui est, pour l'avènement du sujet, essentielle' (p. 226), which, in a translation simplified for the sake of clarity, means: 'Nevertheless, this meaning is not essential for the advent of the subject', the English reads: 'This does **not** mean that it is **not** this signification that is essential to the advent of the subject' (p. 250), reversing the sense by the inclusion of one negative too many, and thus making incomprehensible the contrast to the following sentence which stresses that the essential thing is just the opposite to meaning, namely, the lack of sense, or non-meaning (pp. 250–1).

[37] *Concepts*, p. 227; *Concepts* Eng., p. 252.

goal of analysis thus becomes a double 'destitution' of the subject: on the one hand, self-'assumption', reconciliation with oneself insofar as one is subject for one's particular historical existence to the specific forms of the Other into which one has been born; on the other, the preservation of an unknown, non-universalized, unconscious core that escapes that subjection.

During the later stages of his career, Lacan reformulated his conception of the relations we have been describing between the signifier, the subject and repetition in the light of set theory. At stake in this theory of the subject is that 'ownmost being', the unity of one's most intimate identity which constitutes the dignity of the individual. No longer restricted to identification with the ego-ideal, in the late sixties the single trait, s_1, comes to indicate that unity of the subject. Lacan's theory is an attempt to integrate two major aspects of Freud's observations: the unconscious manifests itself in the form of slips, dreams and symptoms, which Lacan designates as signifiers; and Freud's contention that 'the ... ego is a precipitate of abandoned object-cathexes ... [the ego] contains the history of those object choices'.[38] Lacan sees the subject of the unconscious as a kind of point which is capable of forming identifications,[39] and the separated subject as one who has integrated the history of those identifications.

The subject of Lacan's theory is not a matter of subjectivity in the usual, psychological, sense, but a quasi-mathematical function which relates a single signifier taken separately, s_1, to a set of letters, the collection of other signifiers that mark the subject's history, s_2.[40] This formulation is an expansion of Lacan's definition of the signifier as that which represents the subject for another signifier. The sup-position of the subject is the assumption that each member of this 'swarm' of marks has something in common with the others, beyond their differences; that is, that the repetition of the *jouissance* which the subject seeks in each love-object in fact constitutes a unity. As a pure potentiality, however, as something that can only be anticipated, this unitary trait never actually appears: it always remains outside the set of signifiers. Lacan dubs it therefore the '*un-en-moins*', the 'one less'.

---

[38] Freud, 'The Ego and the Id', p. 29.
[39] Miller, 'To Interpret the Cause', p. 41.
[40] Nasio, *L'enseignement de sept concepts cruciaux de la psychanalyse*, p. 170.

'*Le sujet de l'inconscient est un trait absent de mon histoire et pourtant la marquant à jamais*' [The subject of the unconscious is a trait which remains absent from my history and yet marks it forever.][41]

In the late sixties, Lacan designates this *jouissance* anticipated from the a-object as surplus enjoyment (*le plus-de-jouir*), in analogy with Marx's surplus value. As we saw in our discussion of the 'Proposition du 9 octobre 1967', at that time he considered the unconscious to be a kind of unknown knowledge, whose object is the surplus enjoyment to which the repetition of the series of signifiers is supposed to lead. Unconscious knowledge is the 'riddle' (*énigme*) of the signifier, because what is articulated in *lalangue* leaves open an infinity of readings. In other words, the signifiers (the *énoncé*) are known, but the subject (*énonciation*) of that statement, or thought, is not. Lacan can then explain historization, or symbolization, as knowledge working (*le savoir travaillant*) to make up for the loss of *jouissance* in the hopes of reaching a *plus-de-jouir*.

This new version of the limiting function of the paternal metaphor brings out the relation between the constitution of the subject and the economy. Lacan remarked that, in a sense, the unconscious is the perfect capitalist slave, for the slave is slave of nothing other than the *jouissance* he awaits.[42] It works ostensibly to reach *jouissance* while in fact the a-object is a means of avoiding the latter. In the consumer society, advertisements operate on a-objects, which hold out the promise of a gratification which in fact is never achievable. This surplus enjoyment prevents people from going toward *jouissance* outside the commodity system. Once the surplus enjoyment had become entirely countable in capitalism, there was no longer any barrier to the command of the superego to 'Enjoy', that is, to produce and consume. Beyond its function of providing the means for survival, the economy plays the same role as the fantasy, approaching and avoiding a *jouissance* that is beyond the pleasure principle.[43]

The fact that the single trait is excluded from the set of objects that constitute the subject indicates that complete *jouissance* is

---

[41] Ibid., p. 172.
[42] Miller, 'A Reading of Some Details in *Television*', p. 25; Pommier, *L'exception féminine*, p. 86.
[43] Braunstein, *La jouissance*, pp. 104–6.

impossible. Such an impossibility, created by the imposition of writing insofar as the letter is homologous to the formation of a set, is precisely what in the later Lacan belongs to the register of the real. Previously, he had used the term 'impossible' to designate the (non-existent) point where the rails of metonymy converge, the goal of desire, *jouissance*. The real, on the other hand, was that plenum into which the signifier introduced gaps, places and elements. Lacan arrived at the equation of the real with the impossible at first by the roundabout route of comparing two different negations of the same term. If the impossible were understood as a negative term, then its opposite would be the possible. But since the opposite of the possible is the real, that would make the real the equivalent of the impossible, a conclusion he at first rejected as preposterous because based on an obvious change of meaning of the term 'possible' in mid-argument. Nevertheless, he acknowledged that, for Freud, the real is akin to an impossibility in that it appears as the obstacle to the pleasure principle.[44]

It would seem that this conjunction of the impossible and the real began to take on a significance beyond pure word-play as Lacan connected it to two further conceptions linking the real and the impossible in modern thought, Kant's notion of the 'thing-in-itself', and Koyré's explanation of the revolutionary element in Galileo's theory of motion. The former argues that only the pure concept of a transcendental object, that is, one which it is impossible to experience, can confer objective reality on our empirical concepts. And this 'x' that must be regarded as 'necessary *a priori*' to what Freud calls 'reality testing' is the unity of consciousness, and, more generally, 'our subjective constitution', without which 'the represented object ... is nowhere to be found'.[45] Koyré, for his part, claims that the notion of inertia which underlies modern science requires us to ignore the evidence of our senses in order to accept the theory which best explains that very evidence. For Galileo, an object moving in a straight line will persist in its state of motion forever (if there is no external intervention), yet such uniform motion is 'absolutely impossible' in the real world, and, according to the theory, could only occur in a total vacuum.

[44] *Concepts*, p. 152.
[45] Kant, *Critique of Pure Reason*, pp. 56, 86.

This amazing attempt to explain the real by the impossible ... these bodies moving in straight lines in infinite empty space are not *real* bodies moving in *real* space, but *mathematical* bodies moving in *mathematical* space.[46]

From Koyré Lacan seems to have taken the notion that it is the mathematical formalization of modern science which conjoins the impossible and the real, and from Kant the idea that the impossible Real behind appearances is nothing other than our own subjectivity.

As Lacan developed his set-theoretical definition of the subject, this conjunction began to resonate in many areas of his teaching. You will recall that the word '*instance*' conceals within itself the term '*enstasis*' drawn from Aristotelian dialectics. In chapter 4 we described Lacan's use of this term to justify the necessity of that 'impossible' exception to the law of castration, which paradoxically acts as the 'foundation' of that law. In various places, Lacan had glossed this impossible obstacle as the 'Real presence' which has no signifier, and the 'Real father' of the primitive horde whose murder Freud placed at the origin of civilization in *Totem and Taboo*. For Lacan this figure of the absence of limits, of the male who has all females at his disposal, is Freud's dream, a defensive manoeuvre designed to hide the fact that such a notion only arises within the very language that imposes the limit of castration.

The dead father is thus the sign of the impossibility of total *jouissance* once you are in language, in that it points to the inevitable loss of the real.

Le réel, c'est l'impossible. Non pas au titre de simple butée contre quoi nous nous cognons le front, mais de la butée logique de ce qui, du symbolique, s'énonce comme impossible. C'est de là que le réel surgit.

The real is the impossible. Not as a simple obstacle against which we bump our heads, but as the logical obstacle of that which, in the symbolic, is stated as impossible. It is from there that the real arises.[47]

When Lacan objected in *Concepts* that it is an oversimplification

---

[46] Koyré, 'Galileo and Plato', p. 419.
[47] *Envers*, p. 143. It is this logical necessity which distinguishes Lacan's impossible real from Barthes's 'reality effect'. The latter also indicates that which escapes symbolization, such as the now famous barometer in Flaubert's *Un cœur simple* which remains outside the literary code of verisimilitude in force in that period, but in Barthes there is no sense that this object must be so excluded.

of Freud's thought to say that for the latter the real appears as an obstacle to satisfaction, it was because he wanted to emphasize the logical necessity of this impossibility beyond any impediments that happen to arise in the life of a given individual.

In the thermodynamic terms in which psychoanalysis generally describes the operation of the pleasure principle, this Real father of *jouissance* without loss would embody the total conservation of energy. The s1 that represents the energy before the operation would be identical to that afterwards. Thus, you'd have s1 both above and below the bar of signification; s1 would be identical to itself. But the second law of thermodynamics expresses the rule of entropy according to which some usable energy is lost in any transformation. Lacan draws a parallel between this entropic loss and the inevitable loss that occurs when one attempts to formalize knowledge, to transfer it from implicit 'knowing how' to explicit 'knowing that' by the process of writing, i.e. by using language on itself to form those symbols of symbols called letters.[48] Now the rule which founds the logical deduction of mathematics states that no set can represent (include) itself. This means that the set which functions as the number one, as unity, is not primordial; it must be defined in terms of another, the empty set. Alternatively, this precept implies that no signifier can signify itself. As a result no 'master-signifier' (s1) can in fact stand alone and close off the chain of meaning. While it appears as though the single trait precedes its attachment to the other signifiers (s2), in fact it can be defined only in relation to them. Hence they must precede it. Thus the allegedly self-identical *signifiant-maître* (master-signifier), which is also the signifier of my being (*signifiant-m'être*), is secondary to the differential symbolic context. In the beginning must have been the word rather than the act (or deed): not murder but knowledge. To illustrate this contention, Lacan points out that Descartes could use doubt to assert his individuality only by calling into question a body of knowledge that had been developed over the centuries before him.[49]

This impossibility of the discourse of the master is not the only

---

[48] *Envers*, p. 91. Although Lacan refers explicitly to Hegel alone in this context, it is difficult not to see Ryle's famous distinction in *The Concept of Mind* in Lacan's theoretical opposition between *le savoir-faire* and *le savoir*. To be sure, he had discussed Wittgenstein in a previous section of *Envers* (pp. 66–73), but only in reference to the *Tractatus*.

[49] *Envers*, p. 178.

impasse that arises from formalization. The strict meaning of the term impossible depends on the formalization of truth. Goedel's theorem states that it is impossible to close off the field of a purely formalized set of propositions in a true/false logic. There will always be at least one well-formed proposition in such a field which can be proven neither true nor false. Moreover, there are some propositions which can be proven true in a higher level system, but which cannot be demonstrated in the original field. The field of truth must therefore remain incomplete, and it is this impossibility of saying everything which Lacan symbolizes in his notation by $S(\cancel{A})$, and which he calls the *mi-dire* (half-say, half-truth, malign (*médire*)) in his later teaching. As a result, the truth of knowledge, the Truth that says, 'I speak', is not the coherent transcendental ego of the university, but a non-denumerable (*innombrable*) set.[50] This non-universalizable 'I' is the no-one-in-particular of the unconscious subject which constitutes the impossibility of the discourse of the university.

The most coherent effort to explain the relations among the various terms we have been discussing, the impossible real, the master-signifier, the non-denumerable subject and its repetition, is found in Miller's article on the theory of 'suture'. Designed to articulate the paradoxical logic of the signifier, this theory attempts to show precisely why the master-signifier, such as Freud's dream of the primal father, is necessary as well as impossible. The signifiers in question in Miller's article are the set of whole numbers, whose existence the mathematician Frege attempted to justify without any recourse either to real things or to the thinking activity of a subject, but on the basis of logic alone. As it will turn out, the numbers in general starting from one correspond to the s2 or symbolic order defined as the field of truth; the class 'zero' to the master-signifier; the objects in the set designated by the zero to the subject; the place of the latter set to the impossible real; and the function of the 'successor' which leads to the endless series of whole numbers instituted by the zero to the repetition compulsion with its unappeasable search for the unicity of the subject.

Frege sets out to show that the three terms necessary for the construction of the set – zero, one and successor (meaning the

[50] Ibid., p. 73.

number resulting when one is added to a member of the set, a previous number) – can be derived from pure logic alone. Although Frege does not give it that name, it is clear from his description that his 'concept' is in fact a set, a class of objects defined by its properties; as a result, his notion of number arises as a propositional function, which assigns certain numbers to certain sets. Specifically, it is the concept 'identical to itself', derived from Leibniz's definition of identity as that which can be substituted in a proposition without affecting its truth, which serves as this basis, since the number 1 is assigned to each object that can be subsumed under this category. Now Miller shows that the entire construction is made possible only by the introduction of an element which is excluded from the domain of truth thus defined in terms of identity; namely, the number zero, which Frege assigns to the members of the set of things not identical to themselves, the empty set. The closure of the set of truth can be achieved only by including in it the name, or signifier, of something that is excluded from the set of objects on which it operates (those which are self-identical). That is because Frege's logical definition of successor, of the term which allows you to progress from one to all the succeeding numbers, requires the inclusion of this zero: the successor of a number is the number of numerals in the series ending with that number. In Miller's example, the number 3 designates three objects, but, because of the presence of the zero, it is the fourth in the series, 0,1,2,3.[51]

Only by introducing something non-real into thought and counting it as one – the concept of absence that names, represents, lack pure and simple – can the metonymic chain of numbers be held together. It should now be easy to recognize that the use of the zero as suture in this way is none other than the process of catachretic metaphor described in chapter 3. It is for this reason that one can rightly claim that for Lacan metaphor must precede metonymy. But at the same time, it would have been impossible to articulate this metaphor of the zero without having first defined the field of truth, of the Other, as that of the self-identical. In that sense, metonymy understood as the linguistic structure must precede metaphor. As Miller points out, the secret to this paradox is that the procedure, which is equivalent to that of the

---

[51] Miller, 'Suture', pp. 30–1.

subject and the signifier, is circular but non-symmetrical, so that each can precede the other, depending on where you enter the circle, or rather the Möbius strip.

'The central paradox', Miller concludes, 'is that the trait of the identical represents the non-identical.'[52] The impossible object, the one that cannot exist in the field of objects designated by concepts because not self-identical, this excessive element which must be added on to the series in order to complete it – the 'one more' – is precisely what Lacan names the subject. The identity of the unique, the unitary trait as Lacan calls it, is used to represent within the field of the Other that which is excluded from it, the non-self-identical subject. Whence the $, the barred subject now conceived as the 'one less'. Nasio's formula can now be made more precise: the s1 is a member of the set of signifiers, the s2, but the object it designates can by definition never be so. For if the subject were to become identical to itself, it would no longer be a subject, but some object in the customary sense of objectivity. But this same bar which divides the subject from itself also thereby decompletes the field of the Other (the A), since it indicates that there is always 'one more' that can be added to the field. The very thing that indicates its completeness also points to its incompleteness, symbolized by Å. Because it necessarily refers to and depends upon something outside itself – the excluded non-self-identical – the field of signifiers is not a fully autonomous realm, nor can it serve as the ultimate ground. That role is paradoxically reserved for the impossible real, the excluded non-self-identical which takes the place of the noumenal subject or thing-in-itself.

In sum, Lacan's hypothesis, as he calls it in *Encore*, is that the subject is a pure sup-position to the signifier; it exists only as the pure difference – comparable to the zero term as successor – which enables the symbolic system to function.[53] The most important conclusion to be drawn from this discussion of these relations among the real, the subject and the symbolic order, therefore, is that there would be no subject if the symbolic order were complete and autonomous. The place reserved for the subject can only be that of the incompleteness of the system of signifiers, and the subject is a metaphoric covering over of that place. As the flaw in the system, the subject is therefore defined

[52] Ibid., p. 32.
[53] *Encore*, pp. 129–30.

by that system which, as a cultural order, is historical through and through. Yet as flaw the subject also escapes from the historical confines of the culture. As we shall see in our concluding chapter, it is this double contention and its implications which distinguish Lacanian cultural critique from that of other schools of thought.

Lacan strives to explain human sexuation – sexual identity, sexual enjoyment, sexual relations – by means of the set-theoretical considerations described above. His starting-point in *Encore* is that there is no sexual relation: the relation between the sexes cannot be written, in that there is no logical expression of the form 'xʀy' assigning specific values to the y term for every possible value of x. There is, and can be, no universal formula for sexual attraction among human beings in the field of the signifier (chapter 5), for the simple reason that sexual difference is not a concept. It has no inherent content. Rather it corresponds to difference itself, the very function which makes signification possible and which, in Lacan's hypothesis, coincides with the place of the subject.[54] Sex is thus another name for the failure of meaning, the gap in the Other which renders it incomplete.

Since the subject is, in the sense defined, the gap in the system of signifiers, reaching one's enjoyment becomes the problem of covering over that space. The process Lacan had previously articulated as a kind of struggle between the infinite and the finite in which one had to find the metaphor to stop the process of endless metonymy (comparable to the infinite procession of whole numbers), he now describes in terms of two different orders of the infinite. Whereas the class of signifiers is a countable, or denumerable, infinity like the integers or fractions, the set of the subject is of a higher order; it is non-denumerable. The most familiar example of the latter is the set of real numbers, which cannot be fully expressed by any finite, or infinitely

[54] Ibid., p. 129. Lacan goes on to say that the only proof that the subject does in fact coincide with this hypothesis is that the signifier becomes a sign of the subject. Since Lacan accepts the Peircean definition of the sign as something which represents something for another person (*Concepts*, p. 188), I would suggest that this 'hypothesis' is based on Kant's presentation of the noumenal subject as purely intelligible cause. In *The Critique of Pure Reason*, he remarks that the latter is just an 'assumption' which may simply be a fiction, for it is 'completely unknown' except that empirical effects are its 'sensible sign' (258–9).

repeating, series of decimals, for the irrationals form a set of cuts or gaps in the rationals (see chapter 4). This impossibility, the fundamental incommensurability between the set of signifiers and the subject, characterizes the real of *jouissance*.[55] The function previously reserved for metaphor is now assigned to suture, the addition of the limit in the sense that, for those who accept Dedekind's view, a real number is defined in modern mathematics as the limit of such an infinite (convergent) series, or better, as the set which includes the series and its limit.

Such a collection is called a 'closed' set in mathematical topology, and Lacan invokes the definition of the property of 'compactness' from that discipline in order to represent the space of *jouissance*. He states that, since this space includes a place for absolute difference or Otherness, it is a 'geometry'. Presumably he means that it is not autonomous, just as Frege concurs with Kant that the propositions of geometry are not purely logical but depend necessarily on something heterogeneous, something outside of logic, namely intuition.[56] Now the question Lacan asks is whether it is possible to make the closed sets of sutured male subjects cover completely (overlap) this place of gap of the Other sex. Although Lacan's language in *Encore* is extremely confusing, he seems to be referring to a definition of compactness according to which a topological space that includes infinite subsets (such as the irrationals in the set of reals) can be covered only by the intersection of an infinite number of closed subsets.

Because of its infinitude, this covering prevents the man from ever reaching the absolute Other (sex), from closing the gap completely. It forms an obstacle to enjoyment. Zeno's paradox of Achilles and the tortoise serves as a parable of the man's attempt to catch up with the woman in the sexual relation, to close the

[55] For some of Lacan's other mathematical illustrations of the incommensurability of the one of the unitary trait and the a-object that stands in for the *jouissance* of the subject, see Porge's discussion of the anharmonic division, or golden number, in relation to Lacan's mathematized notion of sublimation (*Se compter trois*, pp. 129–42).

 As the term 'sublimation' suggests, Lacan's notion of the a-object and its incommensurability derives from Kant's definition of the sublime in his *Critique of the Power of Judgment*, in which he notes that an essential aspect of a situation that arouses in us the feeling of the sublime is that it must appear 'incommensurate with our power of exhibition' (p. 99). (See Zizek, *Sublime Object*, pp. 194–204, for a lucid explanation of the relation between Kant's idea of the sublime and Lacan's a-object.)

[56] Frege, *The Foundations of Arithmetic*, pp. 101–2.

gap between himself and her so that he can enjoy her body. Each time he runs to the point where the tortoise was at a given moment, she will have moved forward from that spot, and thus he will not have reached her. The point of the paradox for Lacan is not that motion is actually impossible, but that it cannot be represented in the symbolic. And the solution is furnished by the modern definition of real numbers: although, as the paradox implies, there are an infinite number of numbers between any two real numbers, nevertheless a given series never exceeds a certain limit. (See Russell's simplified account of this phenomenon in chapter 5 of *Mysticism and Logic*, 'Mathematics and the Metaphysicians'). As a result, although the number of steps (as represented in the number system) is infinite, the actual distance covered is finite. Moreover, the series that designates the tortoise's motion also has a limit, although a different one from that of Achilles. Lacan takes this to signify that in the real they can never coincide; he can only pass her. To put it another way, they can meet only in infinity, at the (non-)place of the limit.

The man has recourse to the phallic a-object in order to parry (one of Lacan's plays on the French *séparation*) this infinitude of *jouissance*. The detour through the a-object is necessary to masculinity precisely so that he need not attempt to reach the otherness of the Other (sex). Those who stand on the masculine side of the division of the sexes (regardless of their biological sex) seek to construct their phallic letter, the single trait (s1) that endows them with a limited identity. In this late version of alienation, the problem is not that the being of the subject is crushed by meaning, as in *Concepts*, but that the only being available to the subject is the hollowness of the shifter, I (or of some other pure mark). 'Either I am nothing but this mark or I am not this mark'; in which case 'I am not at all.' I can thus 'be' a mark, or not be.[57]

Phallicism is a (catachretic) supplement to the impossible real of the sexual relation. It takes the place of that difference, which is to say that what Lacan calls *La femme*, the idea of woman or the notion of an essence of the feminine, is the result of the fantasy which stands in for the absence of the sexual relation. Lacan now calls the a-object a *semblant*, a semblance of being, which makes the basically solipsistic phallic *jouissance* possible. Enjoyment of

[57] *Seminar XV*, 10 January 1968, cited in Fink, 'Alienation and Separation', p. 103.

the woman's body *per se* is blocked by that of the phallic organ itself.

Up until this point, Lacan's theory deals with a single type of subject corresponding to the flaw in the symbolic. In principle it starts out as the 'I think' of Descartes and Kant which accompanies all experience of an object and makes it possible. To be sure, Lacan immediately qualifies this notion of the subject by pointing out that this consciousness is a result of the symbolic order rather than its cause, and that the positions left open for this subject are historized. Nevertheless, his mathematized subject does seem to be a kind of universal function, all the more so because the phallic order operates to cover over gender difference. Indeed, since the early fifties Lacan had remained steadfast in his contention that women could get a sense of their own sexuality only by looking at themselves from the point of view of men precisely because there is no representation of the feminine sex in the symbolic, and that she could define herself only in terms of being or receiving the phallus ('Intervention', *Psychoses*, 'Signification of the Phallus', and elsewhere). Nor did he rule out this kind of enjoyment for woman in his later teaching. As for the man, the enjoyment of the organ still acts as an intermediary, indeed an obstacle, between the (feminine) subject and the Other (the man in this case). The woman relates to the phallus rather than to the man as man. The fundamental dissymmetry of the phallus results from the fact that, in heterosexual intercourse, sexual enjoyment by both the woman and the man depends on the erection of the male organ.[58] And like the man, she can substitute other a-objects for this phallus, especially a child.

The innovation in *Encore* is the claim that there is not one flaw in the symbolic, but two different flaws, and, consequently, two different ways of turning around the lack of a sexual relation, which are the equivalent of two different 'letters', or types of sets.[59] The one we have already discussed is that of incompleteness and its cover, universalization through suturing, which can now be seen to define the male subject. The other imperfection in the system is that of inconsistency, and this it is which opens up the possibility of a specifically feminine subjectivity. Lacan first

[58] Braunstein, *La jouissance*, p. 143.
[59] *Encore*, p. 53.

introduces this other possibility by referring to a second definition of compactness in topology. In the first definition, it was the
fact that the individual sets are closed, in that each is a whole
(*tout*) that includes its limit, which resulted in the infinitude of the
intersection and thus the impossibility of true coincidence of the
male and the female. The second definition states that if there
exists an infinite number of open subsets whose union covers a
topological space, then there is necessarily a finite number of
open subsets whose union also covers the same space. This finite
covering of the space of pure Otherness by open sets is the
feminine mode of making up for the lack of inscription of the
sexual relation and thus represents a feminine enjoyment different from phallic libido.

The key term here is the open set, which designates a collection
that does not contain its own limit. It is this lack of limit that
characterizes the woman's *jouissance* which makes women 'not-
all' (*pas-toute*) in Lacan's terminology. Because the sets in question
are finite in number, it becomes possible to count them provided
they be arranged in an order, such as that furnished by the
system of proper names in the symbolic. Once such an ordering
has been established the sets can be counted one by one. That is
why Lacan considers that the Don Juan myth is actually presented from the feminine side, portraying the woman's notion of
the man as one who takes each woman individually. Feminine
sexuation thus results neither from the body nor from the meanings assigned by culture but from the logic of language. It is this
logic of the Other em-bodied (*en corps* homonymic for *encore*)
which requires that women be considered individually, one by
one.

While describing the 'one-by-one' of the woman in this first
section of *Encore*, Lacan slides almost imperceptibly from the
verb of possibility, 'can be taken' (*peuvent être pris*) to that of
necessity, 'requires' (*exige*). But there is nothing in the topological
notion of a covering by open sets to require such counting. It is
merely an option, and one that would rarely be exercised with a
finite collection of sets. Countability and ordering become much
more important in the case of infinite but denumerable sets such
as the integers or fractions. Lacan's justification for this shift must
therefore be sought elsewhere. Now the possibility of two distinct
kinds of enjoyment, of two different types of coverings of the

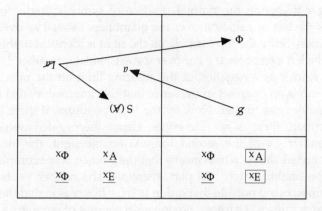

flaw in the Other, derives from the existence of two different kinds of sets, the one closed and the other open. These he defines in a subsequent section in a set of four formulae, or propositional functions, two for the woman and two for the man. (These formulae appear in the upper portion of the diagram.)[60]

The formulae for the man, on the left side of the vertical line, are straightforward enough; they express the sutured subject already described. The function marked as phi is of course the phallic function of castration/establishment of the symbolic order. The first formula, 'there exists an x such that not phi of x', defines the real father who escapes/is foreclosed from symbolic, phenomenal, existence, but which ex-ists as an ideal limit for the man. The second, which if taken on the same level would contradict the first, asserts that 'for all x, phi of x'; that all men are phallic. This formula has a supplementary reading as well, however: given the sense of the phallic order as that of signifiers, it also means that, since men are completely in the symbolic order, there is a universal concept of man. *L'homme*, man in general, exists. The contradiction is thus avoided because the one is on the level of the real (ex-ists), the other on that of the symbolic (exists).

With the formulae for the woman it is clear that Lacan is no

---

60 Ibid., p. 73. In a brilliant essay, Copjec has demonstrated the general congruence of Lacan's two sets of formulae to Kant's two pairs of antinomies of pure reason in *The Critique of Pure Reason* and has thereby clarified the specific nature of this inconsistency (*Read My Desire*, pp. 201–36). I have found several of her analyses helpful in presenting my understanding of Lacan's explanations of the significance of his formulae in *Encore*.

longer following the normal practice of symbolic logic, for he puts the bar of negation over the quantifiers as well as over the function. Since the top formula on the right is identical to the one on the left except for the bar over the existential quantifier $\overline{\exists}x$, we can read it as a negation of the suturing limit on the man. The woman is an open set in the sense that this impossible/real limit does not exist for her. Now by the logic of suture, if there is no exception, there is no rule either. Hence the negated universal quantifier $\overline{\forall}x$ of the second formula on the right, the 'not-all' mentioned above, which means that the woman is not completely in the phallic order.[61] In part, therefore, she neither exists nor signifies, being outside that order. It is for this reason that there is no such thing as *La femme*, no universal concept of woman.

Here then is the reason that one must take women one by one: since there is no universal concept of woman that could be grasped all at once, it is only by coming to know each one separately that one could hope to acquire such knowledge, and the perfect enjoyment that it would bring. This argument seems to be flawed, however, by the assertion that a woman is 'not-all' in the phallic order, for in classical Aristotelian logic the fact that an element escapes from the general rule makes of it an exception, a counter-example, and an argument based on a counter-example simply converts a universal truth into a particular truth. Instead of asserting that something is true for all x, you are reduced to asserting that something is true only of some x. In the terms of Russell's modalities for propositional functions, a necessary function (always true) is changed into a possible one (sometimes true), which is still just as determinate as its predecessor. The not-all would thus entail the actual existence of the One exception: the second formula for woman, $\forall x\, \Phi x$, would be the strict logical equivalent of the first formula on the man's side $\exists x\, \overline{\Phi} x$. In other words, if the necessity of the phallic function was based on the foreclosure of the exception to castration, on the impossible real, then the not-all would seem to imply the actual existence (and not 'ex-istence') of the real within the symbolic, a contradiction in terms.

Lacan counters this argument by claiming that, under certain circumstances, propositional functions may take on the fourth

---

[61] Fink, 'Existence and the Formulas of Sexuation', p. 73.

logical modality that Russell had eliminated: in addition to Russell's three categories of the necessary, the possible and the impossible, Lacan reinstates that of the contingent, which, he claims, is not simply equivalent to the assertion of the quantifier of existence when the range of values of the variable, x, is an infinite set. Since he is in fact talking about an infinite enjoyment – symbolized, you will recall, by the gap of the irrationals within the rationals – it follows that one cannot determine existence unless one can specify a procedure for constructing the element in question, but that is impossible in this case since the point of departure for the whole argument, the not-all, was that one cannot formulate a set of properties that would define a concept 'woman'. This contingent modality for infinite sets thus maintains a certain indeterminacy in that it precludes both the determination of the existence of a specific counterexample and the affirmation of its nonexistence (which would be tantamount to the reassertion of the general rule). The indeterminacy of the not-all, then, is that of not being able to ascertain whether the exception exists or does not exist.[62]

This indeterminacy is therefore the ultimate reason for the one-by-one. The latter is thus the product of a process which resembles the loss of the originary (maternal) object through primary repression, and the consequent impossibility of 're-finding' that object. Freud explains the situation in a way which recalls Lacan's notion of the metonymy of desire that must be covered over by the catachretic metaphor:

Psychoanalysis has shown us that when the original object of wishful impulses has been lost as a result of repression, it is frequently represented by an endless series of substitute objects none of which, however, bring full satisfaction.[63]

Lacan's idea in *Encore* differs from this one in two respects: the originary object has been split into two, the maternal and the feminine, and only the first, the concept of 'mother', exists in the symbolic; and the feminine position is characterized by the non-necessity of any such unifying metaphoric cover. In his diagram

---

[62] Compare Hintikka's analysis of the distinction between the possible and the contingent in Aristotle's logic; Hintikka uses the latter term to designate that which may be or may not be (*Time and Necessity*, pp. 30–5). Lacan refers to this work in *Les non-dupes errent* (cited by Porge, *Se compter trois*, p. 159).

[63] Freud, 'Contributions to the Psychology of Love', pp. 188–9.

of sexuation he therefore symbolizes the contingency of feminine enjoyment by a line which connects the barred *La* both to the phallus and to the S($\mathbb{A}$), the symbol for the incompleteness of the Other, indicating by the latter an enjoyment independent of the phallus.

The distinction between the two flaws of language can now be specified: the incompleteness of the masculine is the lack of the referent, of a Real Presence that would act as the foundation beneath the system; the inconsistency of the feminine is the impossibility of totalizing the terms within the system due to the pure differentiality of the signifier. Each flaw designates a specific type of ineffable. For the man it is the being he tries to capture through the a-object. For, as Russell explains, the logic of propositional functions shows that universalization – Lacan's phallic function for the man – does not include existence. A proposition of the form, 'All S is P' is true whenever there are no S's whatsoever. Thus, 'all S is P' does not imply 'some S is P', because 'some' does imply existence, and is the equivalent of 'there exists an S'.[64] For the woman it is the sheer Otherness of the unconscious, the pure differentiality of the signifier which makes it necessary to seek meaning in an endless movement from signifier to signifier, one by one, and which Lacan formerly described as the rails of metonymy. Since the male (phallic) domain is that of the universalizing tendency of language, insofar as the woman is not male, she is, by definition so to speak, Other. There can be no term for woman in general precisely because woman is the Other of language, of universalization.

Now this Other cannot be added on to the One, the universal of the phallic order as another category alongside the One, for in that case it would simply be absorbed back into that order. Lacan concludes that difference as such cannot be posited, but must always appear, or rather fail to appear, as something subtracted from it; hence the designation, the 'one-less'.[65] As a result, she cannot be localized in a specific place in the system; she is always between any pair of signifiers that might be marshalled in order to capture her. In short, her set cannot be limited. At some level her *jouissance* comes from what cannot appear in the symbolic system of representation and must

[64] Russell, *Introduction to Mathematical Philosophy*, pp. 163–4.
[65] *Encore*, p. 116.

remain, therefore, outside the field of self-consciousness. If Lacan claims that it is not possible to say whether the woman can say what she knows about this *jouissance*,[66] it is because his idea is that it arises from a relation to the inexpressible, the unknowable as such.

By introducing this Other enjoyment, Lacan is forced to qualify his previous contention that the phallic function was necessary: for all x phi of x. As we've stated, the 'instance' of 'Agency' was the phallic obstacle which protects the subject from the limitless *jouissance* that threatens its dissolution. In *Identification* the argument of the negated exception, the impossible Real father, purported to demonstrate the necessity of the phallic function. Now, however, Lacan argues that this necessity is only apparent: 'l'apparente nécessité de la fonction phallique se découvre n'être que contingence' [the apparent necessity of the phallic function turns out to be nothing other than contingency].[67] The logical reason for this lack of necessity is, to be sure, the impossibility of writing the sexual relation, and the resulting not-all which opens up the space for the modality of contingency. As such, it corresponds to the impossibility of full knowledge of the Other, of the pure difference of the signifier. But at the same time, the Other cannot know the unconscious subject completely, either. Indeed, 'il y a corrélation entre ce *ne pas savoir* chez l'Autre, et la constitution de l'inconscient. L'un est en quelque sorte l'envers de l'autre' [there is a correlation between this *not knowing* in the Other and the constitution of the unconscious. They form, so to speak, opposite sides of the same coin.][68]

The result of this contingency is not only to make the existence of the woman within the phallic order indeterminate; it also re-emphasizes the importance of the particular. Analytic experience shows that desire is inscribed by contingencies of the body, and first of all by the particular experiences of satisfaction resulting from the ways the infant's body is handled by the mother, nurse or other caretaker.[69] Lacan now calls the s1 the signifier of the most 'idiotic' *jouissance*, taking '*la plus idiote*' to mean both emptiest – the pure mark – and most singular – differing from individual to individual. Because there is no universal (necessary)

---

[66] Ibid., p. 82.   [67] Ibid., p. 87.

[68] 'Hamlet, par Lacan', *Ornicar?*, 24, p. 12.

[69] See also Silverman, *The Subject of Semiotics*, pp. 155–6.

formula for the relation between the sexes, individual societies will inevitably strive to institute a Law that supplements that lack by proclaiming a general definition of that relation, whether it be the subjection of women to men in traditional reactionary patriarchies, the full equality between the sexes that constitutes the ideal of certain Marxist and democratic societies or the subordination of men to women favoured by proponents of a mothergoddess. Lacan's claim is that the contingency of the phallic function makes any such established distribution of roles precarious at best, and in the last analysis, quite impossible to sustain. As the flaw within any system, the feminine style exception will tend to break out of any phallic conceptualization or regulation. And if men are so interested in causing women to enjoy orgasm, it is because to them the woman's cry signals a momentary victory over the phallic limit, the death of the father who presided over their splitting.[70]

Love, the supplement to the impossibility of the sexual relation, will likewise inevitably depend on contingent factors resulting from the subjects' particular historizations. It arises as the result of a chance encounter in the partner of the latter's symptoms and affects, 'de tout ce qui chez chacun marque la trace de son exil, non comme sujet mais comme parlant, de son exil du rapport sexuel' [of everything which, in each one, marks the trace of his exile, not as subject but as speaker, from the sexual relation].[71] Insofar as the feminine is the relation to a non-knowable knowledge – Freud states that the subject knows his unconscious, but he does not know that he knows – it represents the possibility of a non-objectifying relation of subject to subject predicated on resistance to the determination of either meaning or non-meaning. In specifying a feminine *jouissance*, Lacan thus returned to a notion of love similar in some respects to that of the early fifties, before he had rejected the idea of intersubjectivity. This new version of the subject-to-subject relation, which plays the role of the metaphor of love in *Transfert*, arises when each of two persons imputes unconscious knowledge to the Other. Such a coincidence gives the illusion that something is thereby inscribed into the destiny of each one, and that the sexual relation thus has gone from contingency to necessity. Of course, once the lovers

[70] Pommier, *L'exception féminine*, p. 98.
[71] *Encore*, p. 132.

attempt to articulate their love, by universalizing each other they may quickly transform love into hate.[72]

Since transference is just a special case of this general rule according to which love is based on the recognition of the way the other is affected as the subject of unconscious knowledge,[73] analytic interpretation must somehow preserve the subject's contingency even as it brings to light the successive layers of her symbolizations. The trick of the analyst's response is first, in the words of the seminar on psychosis, simply to 'note down' her reaction, to inscribe it without acting upon it. Ignoring that reaction, explaining it away, or acting upon the corresponding impulse even if only in the form of a retort, would all constitute modes of that (counter-) transferential resistance discussed in chapter 5 under the heading of the imaginary relation of the ego-object axis of the L-schema (see p. 162). Although the attitude of 'aloofness' Freud recommends to the analyst consists in avoiding the kind of specular action one might find in everyday life, absolute impassiveness – the absence of any unconscious reaction on the part of the analyst, and hence any possibility of genuine recognition of the analysand's desire – would be just as damaging.

Instead of supplying the analysand with the reaction anticipated, the analyst must strive to articulate both it and the impulse it would satisfy, sending the message back to the speaker in verbal form. In order to do so, the analyst must first succeed in finding, or inventing, words that will fill the space of repression in his own response. Indeed, repression consisting of the absence of language, all analytic discovery must involve catachretic invention. Once again Reik provides the starting-point for Lacan's theory.

A new insight into the dynamics of unconscious processes is bound to the creation of new expressions or to a new meaning of old words already used in another sense ... It is not accidental that the great psychologists, those who reach the remotest recesses of the human mind, are at the same time great stylists, creators in the realm of wording.[74]

In a successful analysis, the Lacan of the seventies says, the analysand will have learned 'l'art de bien dire'.

---

[72] Ibid., pp. 131–2.   [73] Ibid., p. 131.
[74] Reik, *Listening with the Third Ear*, p. 453.

Reik's major argument in *Listening with the Third Ear* is that interpretations based on abstract knowledge gleaned from lectures and textbooks and couched in the terms of complexes and phases will have no effect on the analysand's unconscious, and therefore will lead to the deleterious effect of terminating the analysis without any resolution of the latter's symptoms and inhibitions. Only interpretations based on translation of the analyst's unconscious response, ones which therefore manifest her particular style, will manage to 'awaken the Sleeping Beauty of unconscious events, emotions, and ideas'.[75] As in a witticism, the specific wording of an analytic communication is of paramount importance to the production of the desired effect on the unconscious. For Reik, 'there is an inner likeness between analytic explanations and jokes',[76] which starts from, but does not end with, their dependence on that linguistic form which we recall distinguishes unconscious productions according to Freud. Reik is thus at pains to refute the objection that 'there must be some notion attached to the word':

> In truth, in the truth that logicians and psychologists do not like to hear, the conscious notion often follows upon the inwardly spoken word ... *It is not at all difficult to find words for what we think. It is much more difficult to find out what we think.*[77]

He attempts to support his argument by emphasizing that a genuine interpretation must cause surprise in the patient the way a joke must initially catch its listener unawares in order to be successful.[78] 'Surprise is an expression of our opposition to the demand that we recognize something long known to us of which we have become unconscious'.[79] Such an interpretation causes a shock in the analysand because in it she suddenly confronts her hitherto ghostly thoughts embodied in the material reality of the analyst's utterance. In this form, they are doubly alienated in that the mental ('psychical reality') appears within the physical, and

---

[75] Ibid., p. 453. This characterization of the unconscious as Sleeping Beauty is one of those Reikian metaphors Lacan repeats, in *Concepts*, p. 131.

[76] Reik, *Listening with the Third Ear*, p. 250.

[77] Ibid., p. 209.

[78] In fact, Reik's evaluation of the importance of surprise is one of the observations to which Lacan refers approvingly in *Concepts*, although he immediately claims that Freud had noted its significance before Reik (p. 25).

[79] Reik, *Listening with the Third Ear*, p. 236.

what is presumed to be inside comes to the analysand from the outside.

When the analytic patient laughs, as frequently happens after an effective interpretation, she plays two parts in the joke scenario simultaneously: that of the listener – Freud's 'third person', and that of the butt of the joke – the so-called 'second person'. But this second person is in fact an alien part of herself – the repressed – to which she has been, so to speak, reintroduced, in the return of the repressed. Laughter in the analytic situation thus signals the beginning of the analysand's reconciliation with herself. In the guise of the first person – the one who tells the joke – the analyst has given back a part of herself to the analysand.

But this alignment of the respective roles in the joke and analytic interpretation ignores the more complex interaction of the latter situation. Indeed, before 'telling' his interpretation, the analyst has first acted as listener, while in recounting her dreams and associations the analysand has acted as teller. It is the combination of the roles as first and third persons which distinguishes the situation of the analyst, for the third person is not a mere passive receiver but one whose response is necessary in order to confirm the success of the witticism and thus its very existence as a joke. What Reik's analogy fails to take account of is the fact that the analysand's laughter marks not only the expected and unexpected character of the supplementation of the repressed but her reaction to being recognized by the analyst's interpretation as a subject in her role as narrator. Surprise or laughter mark the place where something Other produces itself in that divided relation to the signifier which Lacan calls the 'limping', or 'stumbling', of meaning (see our chapter 5). We must become alien to ourselves in order to understand ourselves precisely because the unconscious is the Other within us without which we would not exist as subjects.

If interpretations based on canned theoretical knowledge are doomed to remain ineffective it is because, regardless of the vocabulary in which they are expressed, they inevitably betray to the analysand that she is being considered as a 'case', that is, as simply another member of a preformed class whose essence is its universal definition. The effective interpretation, on the contrary, will be one which gives the analysand the impression that she has been heard as a subject precisely to the extent that as such it escapes from all such categorization; surprise is the mark of that unpredictability which betrays the operation of the subject as a 'cause' opposed to any law.

As mentioned before, this recognition will always have a somewhat illusory aspect, since in fact the only thing that links the analyst to the analysand is the words they use. The existence as subject of the one and the other must remain on the level of a hypothesis, the sup-position of a beyond of language. But that supposition can be reinforced by the precise wording of the interpretation, which, in addition to the lexicon employed, involves its syntactic form. In order to avoid locking the subject into the prefabricated container of a fixed meaning, the analyst must strive to formulate her interpretation in manifestly ambiguous terms.

Only an ambiguous reading can fulfil the two contradictory conditions of simultaneously revealing the signifieds that occupy the numerator and bringing out the irreducible signifier in the denominator around which the subject's desire is organized. The primary historization was itself a reading of the analysand's letters in the sense of a grouping or punctuation, in accordance with his expectation of being, of the chain of signifiers he had received from the Other. Since the symptom is the result of the non-adequation of the subject's earlier attempt to anticipate the reaction of the Other to his desire, the analyst's interpretation must come from the future in order both to supply the missing adequation and point out where that adequation in its turn, like any other, also must fail. And it is that very process of regrouping which institutes the law of the symptom's inexorable repetition.

When Lacan claims in the 'Seminar on "The Purloined Letter"'' that a letter always reaches its destination, the letters he refers to arise as symbols of symbols, through the process of punctuation he calls the signifier's composition with itself. In other words, it is only through rereading that a law of repetition in the temporal sequence of signifiers emerges (see chapter 3). Now, in his analysis of Freud's 'Little Hans' case during his seminar on *La relation d'objet*, Lacan claimed that the coherence of a collection of signifiers like those of Hans's phobic fantasy emerges only if they are regrouped in a second reading. Yet putting them into this sort of series inevitably shows that their order results from the ambiguities inherent in their relations to each other.[80] Moreover, in the 'Introduction' which he appended to the 1966 *Ecrits* version of the 'Seminar on "the Purloined Letter"'', Lacan demonstrated that all such regroupings, and hence any law, must have an ambiguity as its basis, either in the letters so formed or in the places they occupy.[81] Starting from a random sequence of pluses and minuses representing the outcomes that agree or disagree with the subject's expectations, one must define the regrouped segments as including identical, symmetrical or non-symmetrical sequences of signs. But then the first type would include both $+++$ and $---$; the second both $+-+$ and $-+-$; the third both $++-$ and $--+$. If the letters are defined so as to eliminate these ambiguities, one still cannot avoid inserting each original $+$ or $-$ into at least two different letters; e.g. if your letters have only two members and are defined as $++$, $--$, $-+$, and $+-$, the second plus in the sequence $++-+--+$ will belong both to the first letter, $++$, and to the second letter, $+-$. To be sure, it would be possible to eliminate this ambiguity by avoiding all overlap in the choice of letters, e.g. to segment the above series into $++$, $-+$, $--$, and $-+$. But to do so would be to eliminate the emergence of any regularities, of any syntactic rules, in the order of appearance of the letters. Without overlap you have simply replaced one random sequence with another. (See Allouch for a detailed demonstration of these propositions.) In short, ambiguity is absolutely necessary to the establishment of any law.

If psychoanalysis is to open up fresh possibilities of being for the subject, then interpretation of the transference must consist of an ambiguous and retrospective rereading of the analysand's letters in sufferance. Beyond the revelation of the specific impulses that have been after-(re)pressed, the new reading must bring out the ambiguity that formed the basis of the subject's primary historization so as to alter the course of the repetition it instituted. Through progressive randomizations, free association allows the subject's primary historization to appear from within her secondary historization and then breaks the former down in its turn into its constituent elements so that interpretation can effect a new signifying cut which will rearrange everything that previously existed as the structure of the subject's symbolic

---

[80] *La relation d'objet*, pp. 277–9.
[81] *Ecrits*, pp. 44–54.

world. It is this restructuring of the subject's text that constitutes the power of metaphor and of poetry.

In his latest teaching, Lacan proposed that each subject uses her own particular version of deciphering *lalangue*; the unconscious is capable of 'learning to learn'. It thus becomes the individual's style of deciphering his or her *jouissance*.[82] Moreover, starting from *Télévision* (1974), he claims that enjoyment, like meaning, is an effect of the signifier. Speech is not only a means of maintaining a safe distance from *jouissance* but also may be a mode of attaining it. As a result, analysis is capable of affecting the latter by changing the speech of the subject.[83]

From the fifties on, due to its catachretic nature, metaphor exercised two seemingly contradictory functions, fixing meaning and preserving the ambiguity necessary for the existence and recognition, however vanishing and punctual, of the subject. The a-object of the sixties and seventies is a form of metaphor because, as separator, it serves the purpose of 'safeguarding the alterity of the Other',[84] even while it covers over the space left by the lost object. In the seventies, as MacCannell points out, metaphor is associated with the subjugating function of social exchange – the discourse of the master – and thus with the 'ethic' of utility (see chapter 3). But that is because, from the seminar on ethics (1959–60) to that on the 'Signifiant nouveau' (1977), Lacan distinguishes between a 'false', narcissistic, and a 'true', paternal, metaphor. While the former defines beings – the world of attributes, utility and exchange – *l'étant* in the translation of the Heideggerian term Lacan uses – the latter posits (and positions, *la position*) the being (*l'être*) of the subject beyond attribution, in the place of the non-exchangeable, because unique, lost object.[85] The contrast between the narcissistic metaphor of the unitary trait (s1) and the metaphor of love in *Transfert* extends this distinction. By the end of the decade, this opposition is picked up in the contrast between the discourse of the master, whose 'dominant' is the s1, and that of the analyst, which has the a-object in the dominant position. *Encore* continues this trend by contrasting the metaphoric substitution of exchange to the contingent subject of the

[82] Braunstein, *La jouissance*, p. 166.
[83] Miller, 'A Reading of Some Details in *Television*', pp. 28–9.
[84] Weber, *Return to Freud*, p. 159.
[85] *Ethique*, p. 291.

unconscious, whose truth can only be 'half-said', and which escapes universalization. In the terms of 'Signifiant nouveau', poetry fails when it produces only one meaning; it succeeds when it is able to expel meaning and preserve a void of non-meaning. The function of poetry, like that of all art, is to create a form that will both hide and mark the contours of the void of the Thing. In order to make room for the subject-to-subject relation, all analytic interpretation must be poetic.[86]

The relation of poetry to historicity is therefore ambivalent. In a sense, the particularity and alterity aimed at – as we have seen, the two are inseparable for Lacan – lies beyond and in opposition to history understood as including the sum of the subject's physical and psychological characteristics and the vicissitudes of her life. Likewise, there is no 'history of art', if that term is taken to indicate the development of a homogeneous entity; on the contrary, according to Lacan art evolves as a series of discrete and heterogeneous modes. Yet without the signifier there would be neither alterity nor particularity, and the signifier necessarily institutes historization. Thus the work of art can reopen a space for alterity only by reversing the dominant forms and techniques of its times. Similarly, what was once poetic may sooner or later become prosaic. Metaphors fall asleep, as the old rhetoricians put it, losing their metaphorical force unless they are reawakened. Interpretations, theoretical innovations, indeed, whole styles of interpretation are eventually assimilated into the common fund of meanings, thus robbing them of the power of their ambiguity.

The only way to move out of this impasse is to effect new symbolic cuts, taking advantage of the metaphoric capacity of the signifier to act upon itself to form new signifiers as symbols of symbols. It is through this process of composition with itself that mathematical and scientific symbolism and disciplines have evolved, and it is for that reason that they have a 'history'. Each new form is an absolute beginning in that it retrospectively reorganizes the symbolic field of which it has come to be a part, yet it could only have come into existence as a response to a question that could not even have been formulated without the previous layers of symbolization. The invention of industrial, military and other technologies designed to serve the purposes of

---

[86] 'Vers un signifiant nouveau', pp. 16, 21–2.

the good arises from the same historizing structure of self-composition and response, but they aim to suppress rather than nurture the flaws in the system, the non-cognitive, the meaningless and the useless, whether it be the a-object for the masculine, or the signifier of the barred Other for the feminine. The little letters of science are not to be 'read' in the Lacanian sense, for they are under the sway of the universalizing tendency of the signifier, which dictates that they be considered solely on the basis of logic and hence ignores their particularity.

The reading of the letters of the unconscious capable of effecting new symbolic cuts implies a certain limited arbitrariness based on homophonies available in a specific *lalangue*. It is therefore an art that must be learned rather than a science derived from the application of deductive rules. Any actual language is the deposit of the history of the ways a society has metaphorized the lack of a definable sexual relation; that is, it forms a record of the various discrete strata in which are encapsulated the *équivoques*, which means both the reifying lies and the sense-resisting ambiguities – the symptoms – whereby human being has been read and enjoyed.[87] In the seventies, Lacan came to the conclusion that literature contributes to this deposit insofar as it acts as a mode of using the letter to retrieve *jouissance*. In *Le Sinthome*, he argues that in *Finnegan's Wake* Joyce traces the outline of the hole in knowledge, that is, of the space of the subject in the system of signifiers.[88]

The many twists and turns in Lacan's teachings, as well as his repeated creation and dissolution of psychoanalytic organizations, also issued from the historizing effect of the self-composition of the signifier. Each shift resulted from a new metaphoric cut in his own signifiers, the rearticulation of the terms that constituted him as an analyst in a constant dialogue with, and against, himself. Thus, Miller contends that the 'exact theoretical value [of Lacan's formulae] is related to the moment of their enunciation',[89] where the Hegelian notion of the 'moment' indicates the temporal process by virtue of which previous symbolizations form the condition of possibility for the emergence of new

---

[87] 'L'étourdit', p. 46.
[88] Lacan, *Le Sinthome*, esp. 'Séminaire du 11 mai 1976', *Ornicar?* 11 (1976), pp. 3–9. See also Miller, 'Remarques et questions', p. 103.
[89] Cited in Weber, *Return to Freud*, p. 174.

ones. As a function of the moment, each new term or formula responds to an earlier one, which itself has bounced off a series of predecessors. No doubt this repeated self-compounding, with the extreme condensation it produced, is one of the main reasons why Lacan's writings became increasingly difficult to read in proportion to the length of his career.

Given the importance of negation in his thought, it is not surprising that Lacan often contradicted his earlier positions and, as with his analyses of the *fort/da*, reserved his most bitter criticism for positions he himself had formerly held. He began by asserting with Hegel that the individual can reach particularity only by traversing the universal, while he ended by condemning the universal as the mortal enemy of the contingent. Striving at first to eliminate all the 'lies' of the subject's symptoms, he wound up acknowledging that after a certain point the subject refuses to relinquish the basic symptom that alone assures her of her existence. In the early version of his theory, the imaginary was the source of murderous and uncontrollable aggression which could only be mitigated by the symbolic; yet in later variations he promoted the imaginary as a collaborator with the real in the effort to preserve contingency against the encroachments of the universal symbolic concept.

The power of a Lacanian interpretation is to release, for however short a time, the pulsation of the unconscious. As a historization, interpretation ought to strive to preserve a space in which the subject's contingency – the particular history of her desire as the gaps in her historizations – can subsist. The many reversals in Lacan's teachings partake in this process in that they respond to specific historizations, but instead of leading toward an ultimate theoretical synthesis like those of the Hegelian dialectic, they aim to prevent theory from swallowing up the space of subjectivity. This is not the place to examine the various moments in psychoanalysis, culture or society to which those reversals reply, but we can indicate that they obey a kind of general anti-principle: as previously ambiguous interpretations become solidified into universal principles according to prevailing social norms, their weak spots must be uncovered and attacked so that subjectivity may re-emerge as a viable possibility.

This process of reversal resembles the Russian formalists' view of literary history as the constant struggle of a new set of techniques to overturn the dominant conventions of a period. But for them, the literary consists in the conventionality of the convention and thus its strangeness, its difference from an assumed 'nature', or from a convention once experienced as a deviation and then imposed as the norm. Although the Lacanian procedure shares the Sisyphean quality of this never-ending battle, the goal is not the ultimately gratuitous replacement of one king on the mountain of conventionality by another, but the intimation of a plane beyond nature and convention. Interpretation neither supposes that the text can be subsumed under an unknown universal nor exults over the impossibility of so doing, but responds to its desire by recognizing it as a historization and seeking to pinpoint those specific places where it escapes knowability, where the specificity of linguistic ambiguity – the *équivoque* – blocks any universalization. In terms compatible with current debates, the impossible science of the particular known as criticism can fulfil its historizing function neither by claiming that the literary is determined by the discourses of political and economic power nor by asserting its autonomy from those structures. Cultural criticism must remain poetic in the Lacanian sense, ignoring neither history nor textualization; rather it should show how particularity – of the text, of the subject – seeks to escape the structures, 'historical' and 'literary', which nevertheless form the very conditions of their existence.

7

Conclusion: Lacan and Contemporary Criticism

S'y trouvent inscrites [dans 'L'étourdit'], en forme de nécessaire chicane, les deux articulations logiques déterminant cette aspiration du parlant à se trouver compté 'homme' ou 'femme' sans que, de la conjonction des termes, puisse se produire rapport sexuel.

La castration, que la psychanalyse a découverte, peut ici se déprendre des mythes qu'il a fallu à Freud pour l'embaumer, au profit de sa raison; on appréciera comment celle-ci, en retour, peut subvertir, d'une logique, les conséquences totalitaires.   'Liminaire' to 'L'étourdit'

In the seventies and early eighties Lacan was generally inter-preted in the English-speaking world, and especially in American criticism, as a proponent of a formalism, structuralism or post-structuralism which, like the New Criticism, severs the text from the world and proclaims the ethical superiority of the eternal aesthetic over the merely practical, historical or social.[1] He was either praised for exalting the infinite play of the signifier over the imprisoning mastery of establishing meanings, or, on the contrary, chastised for recommending that meaning be fixed in accord with the normative linguistic and social system of a patriarchal order. While these readings are not entirely false, above all they are far from constituting Lacan's truth. Although his thought emerges from the contradictory problematics of romanticism and symbolism, the longing for transcendence in a world without divinity or community and for the valuation of the individual, he begins by demonstrating the impossibility of attaining either one. The thrust of this book has been to show

---

[1] Lacan's distinction between the imaginary and the symbolic was also a fertile source of critical inspiration, both in France and in the United States. Out-standing examples of this tendency are Althusser's 'Freud and Lacan' and 'Ideology and State Apparatuses', *Lenin and Philosophy*, Metz's *Le signifiant imaginaire*, and Kristeva's *Revolution in Poetic Language*, each of which has opened up a rich vein for English-language criticism, but one which has now largely been exhausted.

that, from the time of his theory of metaphor to that of the feminine exception, Lacan's primary concern was to develop a practice and a theory which would foster the formation of a subject, however fleeting and insubstantial, which would not simply resist the pressure of the social but could somehow function within the flaws in universalization.

While the unique being which composes the dignity of the subject can only be postulated as an ever-receding horizon, Lacanian analysis provides specific guidelines for evaluating cultural and literary phenomena in terms of that perspective. From the start, Lacan conceived of the unconscious as that which disrupts the apparently smooth surface of the social code, betraying the subject's resistance to total assimilation to that code. The metaphor whose lightning flash momentarily reveals the subject's being must be based on such a metonymic negation of the pre-existing code; a new signifier must be supplied to substitute for the emptiness – of the subject, but more importantly, of the Other – uncovered by that moment of pure negativity, and the being in question is something that did not exist before but is created by the signifying process. The death drive which manifests itself together with the pleasure principle in the phenomenon of repetition is another mode of avoidance of the normative behaviours considered reasonable and acceptable by one's culture. It betrays the truly Dostoyevskian obstinacy of the subject who rejects the 'Crystal Palace' of utilitarian rationality, and insists on finding her own path to death, to the symbolic suicide which allows one to start life over again from scratch.

For Lacan, the self-referential or autonomous which comes to him from German idealism does not isolate an actual transcendent world of eternal values, but, paradoxically, locates a non-historical vantage point from which the subject can appreciate its own historicity as well as the contingency of social norms. The phenomenon of transference shows, however, that it is not possible to abide in this place; it is only the starting-point for the construction of the subject's desire, whose fulfilment will lead to and depend on the establishment of new forms of social life. Weaning the subject from its narcissistic desire to be loved by the ego ideal which represents standard social values, and from its fear of displeasing same, enables it to separate itself from the conformity and reification inherent in acquiescence to the status quo. But the thirst for being can only be quenched by the metaphor of love and its avatars, all of which entail a relation to the Other.

One form of the Other in Lacan's later teaching is the unconscious as unknown knowledge; that is, the subject's particular way of reading the spoken language he dubs '*lalangue*', a mode which must remain implicit, for if it were spelled out explicitly as a systematic method, the resultant universalization would swallow up its singularity and thus annihilate the subject. In France this concept produced direct and indirect effects on theory and criticism as early as the seventies. One might think here of Foucault's objections to the modern 'science of the individual' which makes each person a 'case' to be studied, classified, tabulated and thereby subjected to forms of power and coercion;[2] or of Lyotard's rejection of the universalizing '*grande histoire*' of the Enlightenment, in favour of particularizing '*petites histoires*' which preserve a space for the individualization of diverse cultures.[3] More directly inspired by Lacanian concepts, Barthes's now classic *S/Z*[4] strives to describe the 'difference' of the text, in contrast both to the universality of schemes of generic classification and to the attempt to specify a pure particularity which would contradict the nature of textuality. He thus maintained the basic insight of structuralism, that language has priority over the individual author or work, yet renounced the global categorizing project of structuralist poetics, or of the classicizing and totalitarian tendency of American New Criticism, to value only the allegedly 'universal human', everything else being considered a deviation from the norm, a 'mere case history'.

Criticism in the English-speaking countries has been slower to exploit the possibilities opened up by Lacan's analysis of the relation of the particular and the universal, especially as a mode of enquiry into questions of desire, power and culture. In the past decade, however, critics in the US and the UK have begun to understand that Lacan's teaching deals with a truth experience which problematizes but does not deny questions of social meaning and reference. Whether it be the historical event or the being of the subject, Lacan's teaching provides a mode of analysis

---

[2] Foucault, *Discipline and Punish*, pp. 182–94.
[3] Lyotard, 'Universal History', pp. 314–23.   [4] Barthes, *S/Z*, p. 3.

that makes it possible to pinpoint the place of uniqueness without actually naming and universalizing it. His claim is that successful 'poetry' can make visible the contours of the hole in the symbolic Other which constitutes the place of the subject. For unlike the individuality posited by the romantics, the particular essence Lacan evokes does not reside in a hidden inner world, but outside both the individual and the Other, and can be preserved only in the latter's lack of knowledge. In a recent series of articles, I have attempted to show how Camus's *The Stranger* is structured around such a resistance to the Other's knowledge (see the bibliography), and I would contend that the history of the modern novel consists of the record of such resistances, just as the history of an actual language is composed of the deposit of equivocations left by the confrontations with the impossible Real.

In *Return to Freud*, Weber emphasizes the ethical implications of reading in Lacanian psychoanalysis.[5] Whereas most modern theories of culture consider the values of individualism to be radically opposed to communal norms, Lacan's theory of the unconscious brings into focus their strange complicity. Although generally presented as antithetical terms – the subjective versus the objective – Lacan lets us understand that both derive from the dream of self-consciousness and self-sufficiency that has haunted modern culture in the west, for both are functions of the ego as the organ of a reifying self-consciousness.[6] Lacan is certainly neither the first nor the only thinker to have highlighted this connection, but he is one of the very small number who at the same time retain the function of the subject. Not only does the Lacanian subject disrupt the standard psychoanalytic and metaphysical notion of the autonomous ego, as we have seen, it also opens up the possibility of preserving a particularity which differs both from the individualism based on self-consciousness and from the collective pressure of patriarchal normalization.

For, although the phallus – castration – is a universal condition of culture, precisely because it has no ultimate content, it opens a space for the endless variety of individual human cultures. Based as it is on non-sense, the writing of the subject must oscillate between two conflicting ethical imperatives – the obligation to meet the need for intelligibility, which requires clear conceptuali-

---

[5] Weber, *Return to Freud*, p. 151.   [6] Cf. ibid., pp. 81–6.

zation, and the duty to recognize the need to resist the petrifying grip of the concept, which requires stylization. As is well known, in his own writing Lacan uses various stylistic ploys to escape theoretical rigidity – constant punning, relative pronouns with multiple or ambiguous antecedents, short, choppy paragraphs, apparent digressions which interrupt the flow of the argument, obscure allusions, frequent redefinitions of technical terms, and many more. He thereby throws into relief what is implicit in any text: since the writing of the subject cannot be formalized, in each case it must be read, differently. Although it is not sufficient in itself, careful reading is therefore necessary to any adequate response to the particularity of the subject, the text or the culture.[7]

Some of the most fruitful contemporary Lacanian studies are those which integrate a concern for the real with attention to the subject's relation to language. Lupton and Reinhard undertake a major re-evaluation of psychoanalytic studies of Shakespeare from this perspective in *After Oedipus: Shakespeare in Psychoanalysis*. In *Testimony*, Felman and Laub re-examine the question of reference through an analysis of fictional and non-fictional accounts of the Nazi attempt to exterminate the Jews. If this event is the quintessential example of the traumatic Real which must ever remain beyond symbolization, especially for those who survived the death camps, narrating one's own experience – witnessing – is nevertheless the only way to counteract the erasure of history, and thus of the subject, proclaimed by those who would deny the event entirely. It is the act of witnessing itself, a narrative repetition of the event Lacan calls 'enunciation', which alone is capable of preserving the content of the singular event and personal experience, without betraying that singularity in the fantasy of the general terms of official history, nor reducing them to a mere instance of the universal 'case'.

Despite the hostility of a large segment of feminist thought to Lacan's emphasis on phallocentrism, many feminist critics have recognized the value of his notions of the body, desire and language to the representation, or lack of representation, of feminine experience in discourse. Kristeva's distinction between the semiotic and the symbolic aspects of language, in which the latter assumes the Lacanian paternal function while the former

---

[7] Ibid., p. 151.

takes on that of the pre-oedipal maternal, allowed her to analyse the role of the feminine in poetic language in *Revolution in Poetic Language*. And in her article 'Women's Time' she assimilates the goals of Lacanian psychoanalysis to those of the feminist movement, proclaiming that:

the struggle is no longer concerned with the quest for equality, but, rather, with difference and specificity ... in order to discover, first, the specificity of the female, and then, in the end, that of each individual woman.[8]

Starting in the eighties, several women have lifted their voices both to defend Lacan against criticism of his phallocentrism and to demonstrate the value of his teachings for feminism. Rose tries to show that those who oppose patriarchy by making femininity depend on an unmediated, pre-oedipal, relation to the maternal language or body thereby renounce all possibility of the unconscious and hence of subjectivity.[9] Ragland-Sullivan objects that the phallus as Lacan defines it is not the male organ but a symbol and is therefore neutral, the mark of pure difference.[10] Rose summarizes this claim in her contention that anatomical difference is not sexual difference but rather figures that difference.[11] Rose's main point is that, precisely because it cannot be represented in the symbolic, feminine sexuation shows up the incompleteness of the social code and the inevitable failure of social norms to capture and fix desire.

Jardine has also underscored Lacan's leading role in what she calls 'gynesis', rethinking the oppositions which have determined western thought and narratives in terms of 'woman' or the 'feminine' as that which has escaped their master categories.[12] As the anti-universal *par excellence*, 'woman' in *Encore* 'designates that which subverts the Subject, Representation, and Truth'.[13] Nevertheless, she takes issue with what she sees as the limitations of Lacanian criticism in regard to the question of subjecthood. Reviewing a series of readings of Marguerite Duras's novel, *The Ravishing of Lol V. Stein*, she points out that for Lacan and his followers the only possible subject is the male narrator

---

[8] Kristeva, 'Women's Time', p. 196.
[9] Rose, *Sexuality in the Field of Vision*, pp. 37–40.
[10] Ragland-Sullivan, 'Gender Identity', p. 10.
[11] Rose, *Sexuality in the Field of Vision*, p. 66.
[12] Alice A. Jardine, *Gynesis*, pp. 24–5.   [13] Ibid., pp. 168–9.

Jacques Hold, Lol, the female protagonist, being only a trope which dissolves subjecthood in the Real; whereas for feminist readings it is Lol herself as woman who represents a new potential subjecthood.[14]

In *What Does a Woman Want?*, Felman

experiment[s] pragmatically with *strategies for reading sexual difference* insofar as it specifically *eludes* codification and resists *any* legitimizing institutionalization. Each chapter explores a different strategy not merely through the use of different tools of theory but through the concrete complexity and the interpretive intensity unpredictably derived, each time, from the *incomparable uniqueness* of a practical textual experience.[15]

Benstock has explored the consequences of this Lacanian notion of exclusion for the relation of women's autobiographical writings to the ambient culture. Whereas men's autobiographies have traditionally participated in the phallic order in the sense that the dream of such efforts has been to assert the coherence of the unified, knowable, subject as a defence against the danger of discordance, women's memoirs have made a place for the unconscious messages which show up the rents in the symbolic order. 'This message is directed at the culture from the position of the Other, by those who occupy positions of internal exclusion within the culture – that is, by women, blacks, Jews, homosexuals, and others who exist on the margins of society.'[16] She is able to conclude that for a Virginia Woolf, ' "Writing the self" is therefore a process of simultaneous sealing and splitting that can only trace fissures of discontinuity.'[17]

More nuanced views of Lacan's value for feminism are found in recent works by Grosz and Butler. Both argue, although in somewhat different ways, that, due to their insistence on the non-biological character of sexual difference and his exposure of the workings of patriarchal culture that lead to women's subjection, his teachings open up the possibility of active, political intervention. Grosz objects, however, to the notion that phallocentrism is a necessary consequence of the fact that people are 'speaking beings'. Both she and Butler see the absence of natural constraints on human sexuation as the opportunity to define it solely in socio-historical terms.[18] And Butler, following Rose on this point,

[14] Ibid., pp. 174, 176.   [15] Felman, *What Does a Woman Want?*, pp. 8–9.
[16] Benstock, 'Authorizing the Autobiographical', p. 1045.   [17] Ibid., p. 1054.
[18] Grosz, *Jacques Lacan: a Feminist Introduction*, pp. 144–6.

views femininity as a pure difference which precludes the fixing of any identity: 'Woman itself is a term in process, a becoming, a constructing that cannot rightfully be said to originate or end.'[19] This, of course, is consistent with Lacan's views. But she takes this to mean that it is therefore 'never possible finally to become a woman',[20] a conclusion in contradiction to Lacan. And in *Bodies That Matter* she goes on to emphasize that difference by claiming that the phallus too is subject to reiteration and hence to the same resignification and plasticity as the feminine.[21]

Responding to the argument in *Gender Trouble*, Copjec points out the distinction Lacan draws between being and meaning and the concept of suture that relates the two, both of which are omitted by Butler as well as by Grosz. Although the concept 'woman', like any other signifier, is subject to the endless play of difference and thus the socio-historical variation that characterizes the symbolic order, being is excluded from the symbolic and thus takes up a position that would be transcendent to that order if it could be positively asserted. Although this real cannot be said to have an actual existence, it does free the subject and sexual difference from the otherwise absolute mastery of social codes. And, due to the two different types of flaw in the symbolic, it does make it both possible and necessary to effect sexuate identifications, as man or as woman.[22]

As Benstock's use of Lacan's 'internal exclusion' (extimity) indicates, that concept has implications for cultural criticism that go beyond the question of feminism to implicate all groups that are marginalized by society. Thus, Bhabha's recent studies of colonial discourse start from the Lacanian premise that it is the loss of meaning which makes culture problematic, a calling into question which comes from the clash of social orders made possible by the position of the subject of enunciation outside the symbolic order.[23] Drawing heavily, although by no means exclusively, on Lacanian concepts, he expands analyses of colonial discourse like those of Fanon and Said by bringing out the desiring function it serves for the colonizer, as well as the effects of this desire on the colonized.

Zizek's rapidly growing list of books on Lacan and popular

---

[19] Butler, *Gender Trouble*, p. 33.   [20] Ibid., p. 33.
[21] Butler, *Bodies That Matter*, p. 90.   [22] Copjec, *Read My Desire*, pp. 201–36.
[23] Bhabha, *The Location of Culture*, pp. 34–5.

film and culture elucidate various aspects of the French psychoanalyst's thought in accessible terms, while bringing out the
crucial effects of the utter senselessness of the real both within the
Other in its role as cultural code, and in its effects on the subject
(see Bibliography).[24] They form a valuable counterpoint to those
studies which emphasize the deleterious effects of the imposition
of meaning, like Said's, as well as to those of thinkers like
Raymond Williams who praise ordinary culture as the creation of
common meanings. If this meaninglessness constitutes the
trauma for the subject, it also holds out the latter's only hope for
even a transitory existence. Thus, as Weber points out, the flaw in
theories like those of Fish (e.g. *Is There a Text in This Class?*),
which make the interpretive community the sole arbiter of sense
and nonsense is that they neglect the place of the Lacanian
subject.[25]

Lacanian analysis of the phallic order has served not only as
the basis for intellectual cultural critique but also as the ground
for programmes of social and political action. Bracher sets forth a
method of cultural analysis which goes beyond standard semiotic
studies of culture in that he isolates the specific points in
discourse which interpellate and thus strive to move the typical
receiver in a discursive community. He organizes his analysis in
terms of the distinctions between narcissistic and anaclitic,
passive and active, desires and in terms of the functions of
identification, fantasy and the real. Reviewing Lacan's four
discourses, Bracher concludes that most cultural critique falls into
the category of the discourse of the hysteric, which privileges the
split subject ($), bringing out the subject's emphatic refusal to
embody 'the master signifiers that constitute the subject positions
that society, through language, makes available to individuals'.[26]
Lacan maintains that this discourse remains tied to the master
signifiers of society nevertheless, in that the person who participates in this discourse demands his or her signifiers from the
Other (society) rather than producing them him- or herself. It is

---

[24] Since the seventies there has, of course, been lively discussion of Lacan in film
studies, both in French, starting with Metz, and in English at first with
contributors to *Screen* such as Heath and Mulvey. The books by Rose and
Copjec cited in this chapter include sections on this topic, about which I do not
feel competent to comment.

[25] Weber, *Return to Freud*, p. 178.

[26] Bracher, *Lacan, Discourse, and Social Change*, p. 66.

only the discourse of the analyst which makes it possible to understand the impetus behind the longing for the master signifiers and thus to displace and redirect them oneself; that is, to assume one's alienation and effect separation (see our chapter 5).[27] By using these concepts to analyse actual discourses of contemporary American society, as he does in the latter part of his book, Bracher aims to trigger the process of liberating analytic discourse in his readers. As a method of writing and of teaching, such analyses attempt to effect social change through individuals but on a larger scale than that of actual psychoanalysis.

Perhaps the grandest political claims for Lacanian analysis are made by Laclau, who sees the overlapping of the two lacks Lacan discusses in *Concepts* – that which the subject covers over by its identity and that of the Other's incompleteness, its lack of universality – as the condition of possibility of radical democratic political action in the contemporary world. He argues that pure particularism of the sort that has characterized recent national-isms and ethnic separatisms is no solution to the problem of asserting the rights of oppressed minorities, because all particular groups construct their identities and make their claims – political, economic, educational, hedonic – in the name of general princi-ples. The only way to refute a separatist system like apartheid is by a process of suture: in order to assert its identity the individual group must invoke a universal that would be outside the play of difference – society as a whole – but then it must show that the latter is empty of any specific content.

This means that the universal is part of my identity insofar as I am penetrated by a constitutive lack – that is, insofar as my differential identity has failed in the process of constitution ... The universal emerges out of the particular not as some principle underlying and explaining it, but as an incomplete horizon suturing a dislocated parti-cular identity.

The universal is the symbol of a missing fullness, and the particular exists only in the contradictory movement of asserting a differential identity and simultaneously canceling it through its subsumption into a nondifferential medium.[28]

Lacking any specific content or preordained representative, this universal acts as a kind of receptacle that attracts the competing

---

[27] Ibid., pp. 65–8.
[28] Laclau, 'Universalism, Particularism, and the Question of Identity', p. 90.

claims of the various groups that constitute the society in question. Thus it is the emptiness of the universal that makes true democracy possible.

In every area of contemporary theory, Lacan's rhetoric of culture implies the ethical and political imperative to map out a place for a new subject. This ethic must begin with close reading in order to locate the flaws in discourse that leave room for the unconscious, the contingent, the feminine exception. It is the impossibility of specifying sexual difference which, in the last analysis, makes it possible to subvert the totalitarian consequences of the logic of the signifier which otherwise rules the life of society. Far from isolating texts from reality, discourse from history or individuals from culture, the metaphorics of the subject and the logic of suture provide the most effective means of discovering the actually effective relations of the subject, the culture and the real, thereby making it possible to develop new signifiers of desire.

Bibliography

Lacan

Works in French

Lacan, Jacques, 'La chose freudienne', in *Ecrits* (Paris: Editions du Seuil, 1966), pp. 401–36.

'Le désir et son interprétation', summary prepared by J.-B. Pontalis, *Bulletin de Psychologie*, 13.5 (1959–60), 263–72, 13.6, 329–35.

'La direction de la cure et les principes de son pouvoir', in *Ecrits* (Paris: Editions du Seuil, 1966), pp. 585–644.

'D'une question préliminaire à tout traitement possible de la psychose', in *Ecrits* (Paris: Editions du Seuil, 1966), pp. 531–84.

Ecrits (Paris: Editions du Seuil, 1966).

Ecrits 1, Points (Paris: Editions du Seuil, 1970), vol. I.

Les écrits techniques de Freud 1953–1954, Jacques-Alain Miller, ed., *Le Séminaire* (Paris: Editions du Seuil, 1975), vol. I.

Encore 1972–1973, Jacques-Alain Miller, ed., *Le Séminaire* (Paris: Editions du Seuil, 1975), vol. XX.

L'envers de la psychanalyse 1969–1970, Jacques-Alain Miller, ed., *Le Séminaire* (Paris: Editions du Seuil, 1991), vol. XVII.

L'éthique de la psychanalyse 1959–1960, Jacques-Alain Miller, ed., *Le Séminaire* (Paris: Editions du Seuil, 1986), vol. VII.

'L'étourdit', *Scilicet*, 4 (1973), 5–52.

'La famille', in *Encyclopédie Française*, 21 vols. (Paris: Société de Gestion de l'Encyclopédie Française, 1935–66), Henri Wallon, ed., vol. VIII, pp. 40.3–16, 42.1–8.

'Fonction et champ de la parole et du langage en psychanalyse', in *Ecrits* (Paris: Editions du Seuil, 1966), pp. 237–322.

'Les formations de l'inconscient', summary prepared by J.-B. Pontalis, *Bulletin de Psychologie*, 11.4–5 (1957–8), 293–6; and 12.2–3 (1958–9), 182–92, 12.4, 250–6.

'Hamlet, par Lacan', *Ornicar?*, 24 (1981), 7–31; 25 (1982), 13–36; 26–7 (1983), 7–44.

'L'instance de la lettre dans l'inconscient ou la raison depuis Freud', in *Ecrits* (Paris: Editions du Seuil, 1966), pp. 493–528.

Bibliography

'Intervention sur le transfert', in *Ecrits* (Paris: Editions du Seuil, 1966), pp. 215–26.

'Introduction' au 'Séminaire de "La lettre volée"', in *Ecrits* (Paris: Editions du Seuil, 1966), pp. 44–61.

'Kant avec Sade', in *Ecrits* (Paris: Editions du Seuil, 1966), pp. 765–90.

'Lituraterre', *Littérature*, 3 (1971), 3–10.

'La métaphore du sujet', in *Ecrits* (Paris: Editions du Seuil, 1966), pp. 889–92.

Le moi dans la théorie de Freud et dans la technique de la psychanalyse 1954–1955, Jacques-Alain Miller, ed., *Le Séminaire* (Paris: Editions du Seuil, 1978), vol. II.

'Parenthèse des parenthèses', in *Ecrits* (Paris: Editions du Seuil, 1966), pp. 54–61.

'Position de l'inconscient', in *Ecrits* (Paris: Editions du Seuil, 1966), pp. 829–50.

'Une pratique de bavardage', *Ornicar?*, 19 (1977), 5–9.

'Propos sur la causalité psychique', in *Ecrits* (Paris: Editions du Seuil, 1966), pp. 151–93.

'Proposition du 9 octobre 1967 (Première Version)', *Analytica*, 8 (1978), 1–26.

Les psychoses 1955–1956, Jacques-Alain Miller, ed., *Le Séminaire* (Paris: Editions du Seuil, 1981), vol. III.

Les quatre concepts fondamentaux de la psychanalyse 1964, Jacques-Alain Miller, ed., *Le Séminaire* (Paris: Editions du Seuil, 1973), vol. XI.

La relation d'objet 1956–1957, Jacques-Alain Miller, ed., *Le Séminaire* (Paris: Editions du Seuil, 1994), vol. IV.

'Remarque sur le rapport de Daniel Lagache', in *Ecrits* (Paris: Edition du Seuil, 1966), pp. 647–84.

'La science et la vérité', in *Ecrits* (Paris: Editions du Seuil, 1966), pp. 855–77.

'Le séminaire sur "La lettre volée"', in *Ecrits* (Paris: Editions du Seuil, 1966), pp. 11–41.

'La signification du phallus', in *Ecrits* (Paris: Editions du Seuil, 1966), pp. 685–96.

Le sinthome 1975–1976, *Ornicar?*, 6,7,8,9,10,11 (1975–6).

'Situation de la psychanalyse et formation du psychanalyste en 1956', in *Ecrits* (Paris: Editions du Seuil, 1966), pp. 459–92.

'Le Stade du miroir comme formateur de la fonction du Je', in *Ecrits* (Paris: Editions du Seuil, 1966), pp. 93–100.

'Subversion du sujet et dialectique du désir dans l'inconscient freudien', in *Ecrits* (Paris: Editions du Seuil, 1966), pp. 793–828.

Télévision (Paris: Editions du Seuil, 1974).

Le transfert 1960–61. Jacques-Alain Miller, ed., *Le Séminaire* (Paris: Editions du Seuil, 1991), vol. VIII.

'Vers un signifiant nouveau', *Ornicar?*, 17/18 (1977), 7–23.

Lacan, Jacques, H. Claude, and P. Migault, 'Folies simultanées', *Annales Médico-psychologiques*, 1 (1931), 483–90.

Works in English translation

Lacan, Jacques, 'The Agency of the Letter in the Unconscious, Or Reason since Freud', in Alan Sheridan, trans., *Ecrits: A Selection* (New York: Norton, 1977), pp. 146–78.

'The Direction of the Treatment and the Principles of Its Power', in Alan Sheridan, trans., *Ecrits: A Selection* (New York: Norton, 1977), pp. 226–80.

Ecrits: A Selection, Alan Sheridan, trans. (New York: Norton, 1977).

The Ego in Freud's Theory and in the Technique of Psychoanalysis, John Forrester, trans., Jacques-Alain Miller, ed., *The Seminar of Jacques Lacan* (New York: Norton, 1988), vol. II.

The Ethics of Psychoanalysis, Dennis Porter, trans., Jacques-Alain Miller, ed., *The Seminar of Jacques Lacan* (New York: Norton, 1992), vol. VII.

The Four Fundamental Concepts of Psychoanalysis, Alan Sheridan, trans., Jacques-Alain Miller, ed. (New York: Norton, 1981).

'The Freudian Thing', in Alan Sheridan, trans., *Ecrits: A Selection* (New York: Norton, 1977), pp. 114–45.

Freud's Papers on Technique 1953–1954, John Forrester, trans., Jacques-Alain Miller, ed., *The Seminar of Jacques Lacan* (New York: Norton, 1988), vol. I.

'The Function and Field of Speech and Language in Psychoanalysis', in Alan Sheridan, trans., *Ecrits: A Selection* (New York: Norton, 1977), pp. 30–113.

'*Hamlet* Seminars', *Yale French Studies*, 55/56 (1977), 11–52.

'Intervention on Transference', in Juliet Mitchell and Jacqueline Rose, eds., Jacqueline Rose, trans., *Feminine Sexuality: Jacques Lacan and the 'Ecole Freudienne'* (New York: Norton, 1982), pp. 61–73.

'Metaphor of the Subject', Bruce Fink, trans., *Newsletter of the Freudian Field* 5.1 & 2 (1991), 10–15.

'The Mirror Stage as Formative of the Function of the I', in Alan Sheridan, trans., *Ecrits: A Selection* (New York: Norton, 1977), pp. 1–7.

The Psychoses, Russell Grigg, trans., Jacques-Alain Miller, ed., *The Seminar of Jacques Lacan* (New York: Norton, 1993), vol. III.

'On a Question Preliminary to Any Possible Treatment of Psychosis', in Alan Sheridan, trans., *Ecrits: A Selection* (New York: Norton, 1977), pp. 179–225.

'Science and Truth', Bruce Fink, trans., *Newsletter of the Freudian Field* 3.1 & 2 (1989), 4–29.

'Seminar on "The Purloined Letter"', in *The Purloined Poe: Lacan, Derrida, and Psychoanalytic Reading*, John P. Muller and William J.

Richardson, eds. (Baltimore: The Johns Hopkins University Press, 1988), pp. 28–54.

'The Signification of the Phallus', in Alan Sheridan, trans., *Ecrits: A Selection* (New York: Norton, 1977), pp. 281–91.

'The Subversion of the Subject and the Dialectic of Desire in the Freudian Unconscious', in Alan Sheridan, trans., *Ecrits: A Selection* (New York: Norton, 1977), pp. 292–325.

Television: A Challenge to the Psychoanalytic Establishment, Joan Copjec, trans. (New York: Norton, 1990).

Lacan, Jacques *et al.*, *Feminine Sexuality: Jacques Lacan and the 'Ecole Freudienne'*, Juliet Mitchell and Jacqueline Rose, eds., Jacqueline Rose, trans. (New York: Norton, 1982).

General

Adorno, Theodor W., 'Freudian Theory and the Pattern of Fascist Propaganda', in Andrew Arato and Eike Gebhardt, eds., *The Essential Frankfurt School Reader* (New York: Urizen Books, 1978), pp. 118–37.

Adorno, Theodor W., and Max Horkheimer, *Dialectic of Enlightenment*, John Cumming, trans. (New York: Continuum-Seabury, n.d).

Allouch, Jean, *Lettre pour lettre: transcrire, traduire, translittérer* (Paris: Editions Erès, 1984).

Althusser, Louis, 'Freud and Lacan', in *Lenin and Philosophy, and Other Essays*, Ben Brewster, trans. (New York: Monthly Review Press, 1972), pp. 189–219.

'Ideology and Ideological State Apparatuses', in *Lenin and Philosophy, and Other Essays*, Ben Brewster, trans. (New York: Monthly Review Press, 1972), pp. 127–86.

Andrès, Mireille, *Lacan et la question du métalangage* (Paris: Point Hors Ligne, 1987).

Aristotle, *The Categories: On Interpretation* (Cambridge MA: Harvard University Press, 1938).

Metaphysics, Richard Hope, trans. (Ann Arbor, MI: University of Michigan Press, 1960).

Poetics, Ingram Bywater, trans. (New York: Modern Library, 1984).

'Topica', in *Posterior Analytics by Hugh Tredenick. Topica by E. S. Forster*, Hugh Tredenick and E. S. Forster, trans. (Cambridge, MA: Harvard University Press, 1960).

Aubenque, Pierre, *Le problème de l'être chez Aristote: essai sur la problématique aristotélicienne* (Paris: Presses Universitaires de France, 1966).

Augustine of Hippo, *On Christian Doctrine*, D. W. Robertson, Jr. trans. (New York: Macmillan Publishing Co., 1985).

The Trinity, vol. XVIII of *Writings of Saint Augustine* (New York: Cima Publishing Co., 1963).

Bibliography

Ayer, Alfred Jules, *Language, Truth and Logic*, first edition 1936 (New York: Dover, n.d.).

Barthes, Roland, *S/Z*, Richard Miller, trans. (New York: Hill and Wang, 1974).

Benstock, Shari, 'Authorizing the Autobiographical', in Robyn R. Warhol and Diane Price Herndl, eds., *Feminisms* (New Brunswick, NJ: Rutgers University Press, 1991), pp. 1040–57.

Bentham, Jeremy, *Bentham's Theory of Fictions*, C. K. Ogden, ed. (New York: Harcourt, Brace and Company, 1932).

An Introduction to the Principles of Morals and Legislation, Laurence Lafleur, introd. (New York: Hafner, 1948).

Benveniste, Emile, *Problèmes de linguistique générale*, 2 vols. (Paris: Gallimard, 1966, 1974).

Benvenuto, Bice, and Roger Kennedy, *The Works of Jacques Lacan: An Introduction* (New York: St. Martin's, 1986).

Bhabha, Homi, *The Location of Culture* (London: Routledge, 1994).

Bloomfield, Leonard, *Language* (London: G. Allen & Unwin, Ltd., 1969).

Bracher, Mark, *Lacan, Discourse, and Social Change: A Psychoanalytic Cultural Criticism* (Ithaca: Cornell University Press, 1993).

Braunstein, Nestor, *La jouissance* (Paris: Point Hors Ligne, 1992).

Bréhier, Emile, *La théorie des incorporels dans l'ancien stoïcisme* (Paris: J. Vrin, 1928).

Breton, André, *Manifestes du surréalisme*, new edition (Paris: Gallimard, 1985).

Butler, Judith P., *Bodies That Matter* (New York: Routledge, 1993).

Gender Trouble: Feminism and the Subversion of Identity (New York: Routledge, 1990).

Subjects of Desire: Hegelian Reflections in Twentieth-century France (New York: Columbia University Press, 1987).

Cantor, Georg, *Contributions to the Founding of the Theory of Transfinite Numbers*, Philip E. B. Jourdain, trans. & introd. (Chicago: The Open Court Publishing Company, 1915).

Grundlagen einer allgemeinen Mannigfaltigkeitslehre: Ein mathematisch-philosophischer Versuch in der Lehre des Unendlichen, (Leipzig: Commissions-Verlag von B. G. Teubner, 1883).

Carnap, Rudolf, *Meaning and Necessity: A Study in Semantics and Modal Logic*, new edition (University of Chicago Press, 1956).

Cassirer, Ernst, *Language and Myth*, Susanne K. Langer, trans. (New York: Dover, 1946).

The Philosophy of Symbolic Forms, 3 vols., Ralph Manheim, trans. (New Haven: Yale University Press, 1953, 1955, 1957).

Sprache und Mythos: Ein Beitrag Zum Problem der Götternamen. Wesen und Wirkung des Symbolbegriffs, new edition (Darmstadt: Wissenschaftliche Buchgesellschaft, 1983).

Bibliography

Chaitin, Gilbert D., 'The Birth of the Subject in Camus's *L'Etranger*', *Romanic Review*, 84.2 (1993), 163–80.

'Confession and Desire in *L'Etranger*', *Symposium*, 46.3 (1992), 163–75.

'Narrative Desire in *L'Etranger*', in Adele King, ed., *Camus's L'Etranger: Fifty Years On* (London: Macmillan, 1992), pp. 125–38.

'Metonymy/metaphor', in Irena R. Makaryk, ed., *Encyclopedia of Contemporary Literary Theory: Approaches, Scholars, Terms* (Toronto University Press, 1993), pp. 589–91.

Chase, Cynthia, 'The Witty Butcher's Wife: Freud, Lacan, and the Conversion of Resistance to Theory', *MLN*, 102.5 (1987), 989–1013.

Copjec, Joan, *Read My Desire: Lacan Against the Historicists* (Cambridge, MA: The MIT Press, 1994).

de Saussure, Ferdinand, *Course in General Linguistics*, Charles Bally and Albert Sechehaye, eds., Wade Baskin, trans. (New York: McGraw-Hill, 1966).

Delacroix, Henri, *Le langage et la pensée* (Paris: Alcan, 1930).

Derrida, Jacques, *Limited Inc*, Samuel Weber, Alan Bass and Jeffrey Mehlman, trans. (Evanston, IL: Northwestern University Press, 1988).

Of Grammatology, Gayatri Chakravorty Spivak, trans. (Baltimore: The Johns Hopkins University Press, 1976).

'The Purveyor of Truth', Willis Domingo *et al.*, trans., *Yale French Studies*, 52 (1975), 31–113.

Speech and Phenomena, and Other Essays on Husserl's Theory of Signs, David B. Allison, trans. (Evanston, IL: Northwestern University Press, 1973).

'Structure, Sign and Play in the Discourse of the Human Sciences', in Alan Bass, ed. & trans., *Writing and Difference* (The University of Chicago Press, 1978), pp. 278–94.

'White Mythology: Metaphor in the Text of Philosophy', in Alan Bass, trans., *Margins of Philosophy* (University of Chicago Press, 1982), pp. 207–72.

Writing and Difference, Alan Bass, trans. (University of Chicago Press, 1978).

Duhem, Pierre, *Etudes sur Léonard de Vinci*, 3 vols. (Paris: A. Hermann et Fils, 1906–1913).

Fanon, Frantz, 'On National Culture', in Jean-Paul Sartre, pref., Constance Farrington, trans., *The Wretched of the Earth* (New York: Grove Press, 1978 [1963]), pp. 206–48.

Felman, Shoshana, 'Turning the Screw of Interpretation', *Yale French Studies*, 55/56 (1977), 94–207.

What Does a Woman Want? Reading and Sexual Difference (Baltimore: The Johns Hopkins University Press, 1993).

Felman, Shoshana and Dori Laub, *Testimony* (New York: Routledge, 1992).

Février, James G., *Histoire de l'Ecriture* (Paris: Editions Payot, 1948).

Fink, Bruce, 'Alienation and Separation: Logical Moments of Lacan's Dialectic of Desire', *Newsletter of the Freudian Field*, 4.1 & 2 (1990), 78–119.

'There's No Such Thing as a Sexual Relationship: Existence and the Formulas of Sexuation', *Newsletter of the Freudian Field*, 5.1 & 2 (1991), 59–85.

Fish, Stanley, *Is There a Text in This Class? The Authority of Interpretative Communities* (Cambridge, MA: Harvard University Press, 1980).

Foucault, Michel, *Discipline and Punish: The Birth of the Prison*, Alan Sheridan, trans. (New York: Pantheon Books, 1977).

Histoire de la folie à l'age classique: folie et déraison (Paris: Plon, 1961).

Frege, Gottlob, *The Foundations of Arithmetic: A Logico-mathematical Enquiry Into the Concept of Number*, J. L. Austin, trans. 2nd edition (Evanston, IL: Northwestern University Press, 1978).

Freud, Sigmund, 'The Aetiology of Hysteria', in James Strachey and Anna Freud, eds., *The Standard Edition of the Complete Psychological Works of Sigmund Freud* (London: Hogarth, 1962), vol. III.

'Beyond the Pleasure Principle', James Strachey, ed. and trans. (New York: Norton, 1961).

'Contributions to the Psychology of Love', in James Strachey and Anna Freud, eds., *The Standard Edition of the Complete Psychological Works of Sigmund Freud* (London: Hogarth, 1956), vol. XI.

'Delusion and Dream', in James Strachey and Anna Freud, eds., *The Standard Edition of the Complete Psychological Works of Sigmund Freud* (London: Hogarth, 1978), vol. IX.

'The Dynamics of Transference', in James Strachey and Anna Freud, eds., *The Standard Edition of the Complete Psychological Works of Sigmund Freud* (London: Hogarth, 1958), vol. XII.

'The Ego and the Id', in James Strachey and Anna Freud, eds., *The Standard Edition of the Complete Psychological Works of Sigmund Freud* (London: Hogarth, 1978), vol. XIX.

'Group Psychology and the Analysis of the Ego', in James Strachey and Anna Freud, eds., *The Standard Edition of the Complete Psychological Works of Sigmund Freud* (London: Hogarth, 1955), vol. XVIII.

'The Interpretation of Dreams', in James Strachey and Anna Freud, eds., *The Standard Edition of the Complete Psychological Works of Sigmund Freud* (London: Hogarth, 1953), vols. IV–V.

Introductory Lectures on Psycho-Analysis, in James Strachey and Anna Freud, eds., *The Standard Edition of the Complete Psychological Works of Sigmund Freud* (London: Hogarth, 1963), vols. XV–XVI.

'Observations on Transference-Love', in James Strachey and Anna Freud, eds., *The Standard Edition of the Complete Psychological Works of Sigmund Freud* (London: Hogarth, 1958), vol. XII.

'On Beginning the Treatment', in James Strachey and Anna Freud, eds., *The Standard Edition of the Complete Psychological Works of Sigmund Freud* (London: Hogarth, 1958), vol. XII.

The Origins of Psycho-analysis: Letters to Wilhelm Fliess, Drafts and Notes: 1887–1902, Marie Bonaparte, Anna Freud and Ernst Kris, eds., Eric Mosbacher and James Strachey, trans. (New York: Basic Books, 1954).

'The Psychopathology of Everyday Life', in James Strachey and Anna Freud, eds., *The Standard Edition of the Complete Psychological Works of Sigmund Freud* (London: Hogarth, 1960), vol. VI.

'Remembering, Repeating, and Working Through', in James Strachey and Anna Freud, eds., *The Standard Edition of the Complete Psychological Works of Sigmund Freud* (London: Hogarth, 1958), vol. XII.

'Studies on Hysteria', in James Strachey and Anna Freud, eds., *The Standard Edition of the Complete Psychological Works of Sigmund Freud* (London: Hogarth, 1955), vol. II.

Gallop, Jane, *Reading Lacan* (Ithaca: Cornell University Press, 1985).

Gernet, Jacques, 'La Chine: aspects et fonctions psychologiques de l'écriture', in Paul Chalus, introd., *L'écriture et la psychologie des peuples* (Paris: Armand Colin, 1963), pp. 29–49.

Gilson, Etienne, *La philosophie au moyen âge* (Paris: Payot, 1944).

Grigg, Russell, 'Metaphor and Metonymy', *Newsletter of the Freudian Field*, 3.1 & 2 (1989), 58–79.

Grosz, Elizabeth, *Jacques Lacan: A Feminist Introduction* (London: Routledge, 1990).

Hartley, David, *Hartley's Theory of the Human Mind: On the Principle of the Association of Ideas*, Joseph Priestley, ed., first edition 1775 (New York: AMS Press, Inc., 1973).

Hegel, Georg Wilhelm Friedrich, *Aesthetics: Lectures on Fine Art*, T. M. Knox, ed., 2 vols. (Oxford: The Clarendon Press, 1975).

Encyclopedia of the Philosophical Sciences, A. V. Miller, trans., 3 vols. (Oxford: The Clarendon Press, 1969–71).

Phenomenology of Spirit, A. V. Miller, trans. (Oxford University Press, 1977).

Heidegger, Martin, *Being and Time*, John Macquarrie and Edward Robinson, trans., first edition 1927 (New York: Harper and Row, 1962).

Early Greek Thinking, David Farrell Krell and Frank A. Capuzzi, trans. (New York: Harper and Row, 1975).

An Introduction to Metaphysics, Ralph Manheim, trans., new edition, (Garden City, NY: Anchor-Doubleday, 1961).

'Logos', in *Early Greek Thinking*, David Farrell Krell and Frank A. Capuzzi, trans. (New York: Harper and Row, 1975), pp. 59–78.

'On the Essence of Truth', in David Farrell Krell, ed., *Basic Writings* (New York: Harper & Row, 1977), pp. 113–42.

The Question Concerning Technology and Other Essays, William Lovitt, trans. (New York: Harper and Row, 1977).

Poetry, Language, Thought, Albert Hofstadter, trans. (New York: Harper & Row, 1971).

'The Thing', in *Poetry, Language, Thought*, Albert Hofstadter, trans. (New York: Harper & Row, 1971), pp. 163–86.

Herder, Johann Gottfried, *Über den Ursprung der Sprache*, Claus Träger, ed. (Berlin: Akademie-Verlag, 1959).

Hintikka, Jaakko, *Time and Necessity: Studies in Aristotle's Theory of Modality* (Oxford: Clarendon Press, 1973).

Horkheimer, Max, 'The End of Reason', in *The Essential Frankfurt School Reader*. Andrew Arato and Eike Gebhardt, eds. (New York: Urizen Books, 1978), pp. 26–48.

Humboldt, Wilhelm von, *Über die Verschiedenheit des Menschlichen Sprachbaues* (Berlin: 1876).

Jakobson, Roman, 'Grammatical Parallelism and Its Russian Facet', in Stephen Rudy, ed., *Selected Writings* (The Hague: Mouton, 1981), vol. III, pp. 98–135.

'Linguistics and Poetics', in Stephen Rudy, ed., *Selected Writings* (The Hague: Mouton, 1981), vol. III, pp. 18–51.

'Two Aspects of Language and Two Types of Aphasic Disturbances', in Roman Jakobson and Morris Halle, *Fundamentals of Language* (The Hague: Mouton, 1956), pp. 55–82.

Jardine, Alice A., *Gynesis: Configurations of Women and Modernity* (Ithaca: Cornell University Press, 1985).

Julien, Philippe, 'Le nom propre et la lettre', *Littoral*, 7–8 (1983), 34–45.

Jung, Carl, 'Psychological Aspects of the Mother Archetype', in *Aspects of the Feminine* (Princeton University Press, 1982).

Kant, Immanuel, *Critique of Judgment*, Werner S. Pluhar, trans. (Indianapolis: Hackett, 1987).

Critique of Pure Reason, Norman Kemp Smith, trans. and ed. (New York: St Martin's, 1964).

Kojève, Alexandre, *Introduction to the Reading of Hegel: Lectures on the 'Phenomenology of Spirit'*, compiled by Raymond Queneau, Allan Bloom, ed., James H. Nicholes, Jr, trans. (Ithaca: Cornell University Press, 1980).

Koyré, Alexandre, 'L'évolution de Heidegger', in *Etudes d'histoire de la pensée philosophique*, first edition 1946 (Paris: Gallimard, 1971), pp. 271–304.

From the Closed World to the Infinite Universe (New York: Harper Torchbooks-Harper and Brothers, 1958).

'Galileo and Plato', *Journal of the History of Ideas*, 4.4 (1943), 400–28.

'Note sur la Langue et la Terminologie Hégéliennes', in *Etudes d'histoire de la pensée philosophique*, first edition 1946 (Paris: Gallimard, 1971), pp. 191–224.

'Le Vide et l'espace infini au XIVe siècle', in *Etudes d'histoire de la pensée philosophique*, first edition 1946 (Paris: Gallimard, 1971), pp. 37–92.

Kristeva, Julia, *Revolution in Poetic Language*, Margaret Waller, trans. (New York: Columbia University Press, 1984).

'Women's Time', in Toril Moi, ed., *The Kristeva Reader* (New York: Columbia University Press, 1986), pp. 187–213.

Laclau, Ernesto, 'Universalism, Particularism, and the Question of Identity', *October*, 61 (1992), 83–90.

Langer, Susanne K., *Philosophy in a New Key: A Study in the Symbolism of Reason, Rite, and Art* (New York: New American Library, 1942).

Lawler, James R., *Lecture de Valéry: une étude de 'Charmes'* (Paris: Presses Universitaires de France, 1963).

Lévi-Strauss, Claude, *The Elementary Structures of Kinship*, Rodney Needham, James Harle Bell and Richard von Sturmer, trans. (Boston: Beacon, 1969).

'Introduction à l'œuvre de Marcel Mauss', in *Anthropologie Structurale* (Paris: Plon, 1958).

Locke, John, *An Essay Concerning Human Understanding*, John W. Yolton, ed. (London: Everyman's Library, 1961).

Lupton, Julia Reinhard, and Kenneth Reinhard, *After Oedipus: Shakespeare in Psychoanalysis* (Ithaca: Cornell University Press, 1993).

Lyotard, Jean-François, 'Universal History and Cultural Differences', in Andrew Benjamin, ed., *The Lyotard Reader* (Cambridge, MA: Basil Blackwell Inc., 1989), pp. 314–23.

MacCannell, Juliet Flower, *Figuring Lacan: Criticism and the Cultural Unconscious* (Lincoln, NB: University of Nebraska Press, 1986).

Mallarmé, Stéphane, *Œuvres complètes*, Henri Mondor and G. Jean-Aubry, eds. (Paris: Gallimard, 1945).

Marie, Gisèle, *Le théâtre symboliste: ses origines, ses sources, pionniers et réalisateurs* (Paris: A.-G. Nizet, 1973).

Marini, Marcelle, *Lacan* (Paris: Belfond, 1986).

Metz, Christian, *Le signifiant imaginaire: psychanalyse et cinéma*, new edition (Paris: C. Bourgois, 1984).

Miller, Jacques-Alain, 'Extimité', in Mark Bracher *et al.*, eds., *Lacanian Theory of Discourse* (New York University Press, 1994), pp. 74–87.

'Préface', in Jacques Aubert, ed., *Joyce avec Lacan* (Paris: Navarin, 1987), pp. 3–15.

'A Reading of Some Details in *Television* in Dialogue with the Audience', *Newsletter of the Freudian Field*, 4.1 & 2 (1990), 4–30.

'Remarques et questions', in *Lacan et la Chose Japonaise, Analytica 55* (Paris: Navarin, 1988), pp. 95–107.

'Réponses du réel', in Markos Zafiropoulos, introd., *Aspects du Malaise dans la Civilisation* (Paris: Navarin, 1987), pp. 9–22.

'Suture', *Screen*, 18.4 (1977/78), 24–34.

'To Interpret the Cause: From Freud to Lacan', *Newsletter of the Freudian Field*, 3.1 & 2 (1989), 30–50.

Müller, F. Max, *Comparative Mythology*, first edition 1856 (New York: Arno, 1977).

'Metaphor', in *Lectures on the Science of Language*, first edition 1864 (New York: Scribner's, n.d.), vol. II.

'The Philosophy of Mythology', in *Chips from a German Workshop*, first edition 1871 (New York: Scribner's, 1881), pp. 53–97.

Nancy, Jean-Luc, and Philippe Lacoue-Labarthe, *Le titre de la lettre: une lecture de Lacan* (Paris: Éditions Galilée, 1973).

Nasio, Juan-David, *Cinq leçons sur la théorie de Jacques Lacan* (Paris: Rivages, 1992).

L'enseignement de sept concepts cruciaux de la psychanalyse (Paris: Rivages, 1988).

Ogden, C. K., and I. A. Richards, *The Meaning of Meaning: A Study of the Influence of Language Upon Thought and of the Science of Symbolism* (New York: Harcourt, Brace and World, 1923).

Perelman, Ch., and L. Olbrechts-Tyteca, *The New Rhetoric: A Treatise on Argumentation*, John Wilkinson and Purcell Weaver, trans. (South Bend, IN: University of Notre Dame Press, 1969).

Pico della Mirandola, Giovanni, 'Oration on the Dignity of Man', Robert A. Caponigri, trans. (New York: Regnery Gateway, Inc., 1956).

Poe, Edgar Allan, 'The Murders in the Rue Morgue', in *The Fall of the House of Usher and Other Writings*, David Galloway, ed. (New York: Penguin Books, 1986), pp. 189–224.

'The Purloined Letter', in *The Fall of the House of Usher and Other Writings*, David Galloway, ed. (New York: Penguin Books, 1986), pp. 330–49.

Pommier, Gérard, *L'exception féminine: essai sur les impasses de la jouissance* (Paris: Point Hors Ligne, 1985).

Porge, Erik, *Se compter trois: le temps logique de Lacan* (Paris: Editions Erès, 1989).

Ragland-Sullivan, Ellie, 'Jacques Lacan: Feminism and the Problem of Gender Identity', *Sub-Stance*, 36 (1982), 6–20.

Reik, Theodor, *Listening with the Third Ear* (New York: Farrar, Straus and Company, 1948).

Richards, I. A., *The Philosophy of Rhetoric* (London: Oxford University Press, 1936).

Rose, Jacqueline, *Sexuality in the Field of Vision* (London: Verso, 1986).

Roudinesco, Elisabeth, *La bataille de cent ans: histoire de la psychanalyse en France, 1885–1939*, 2 vols. (Paris: Editions Ramsay, 1982, 1986).

Jacques Lacan: esquisse d'une vie, histoire d'un système de pensée (Paris: Fayard, 1993).

Rousseau, Jean-Jacques, *The Confessions*, J. M. Cohen, trans. (Harmondsworth, Middlesex: Penguin, 1953).

The Reveries of the Solitary Walker, Charles E. Butterworth, trans. (New York University Press, 1979).

The Social Contract and Discourses, revised edition, G. D. H. Cole, ed., revised by J. H. Brumfitt and John C. Hall (London: J. M. Dent and Sons, 1975).

Russell, Bertrand, *The Analysis of Mind* (London: George Allen & Unwin, 1921).

Introduction to Mathematical Philosophy (London: Macmillan, 1919).

Logic and Knowledge, Robert Charles Marsh, ed. (London: George Allen & Unwin Ltd, 1956).

'Mathematical Logic as Based on a Theory of Types', in *Logic and Knowledge*, Robert Charles Marsh, ed. (London: George Allen & Unwin Ltd, 1956), pp. 59–102.

Mysticism and Logic, and Other Essays (London: Unwin Books, 1963).

Russell, Bertrand, and Alfred North Whitehead, *Principia Mathematica* (Cambridge University Press, 1910).

Ryle, Gilbert, *The Concept of Mind* (New York: Barnes and Noble, 1949).

Said, Edward, *Orientalism* (New York: Random House, 1979).

Sartre, Jean-Paul, *Being and Nothingness*, Hazel E. Barnes, trans. (New York: Philosophical Library, 1956).

Situations (Paris: Gallimard, 1948), vol. I.

Schelling, Friedrich Wilhelm Joseph, 'Einleitung in die Philosophie der Mythologie', in K. F. A. Schelling, ed. *Sämtliche Werke* (Stuttgart: J. G. Cotta, 1856), vol. I.

Philosophie der Kunst (Darmstadt: Wissenschaftliche Buchgesellschaft, 1976).

Schopenhauer, Arthur, *The World as Will and Idea* (London: Routledge & Kegan Paul, 1957), vol. I.

Shelley, Percy Bysshe, *Shelley: Selected Poetry, Prose and Letters*, A. S. B. Glover, ed. (London: Nonesuch, 1951).

Shklovsky, Boris, 'Sterne's *Tristram Shandy*', in Lee T. Lemon and Marion J. Reis, eds. and trans., *Russian Formalist Criticism: Four Essays* (Lincoln, NB: University of Nebraska Press, 1965).

Silverman, Kaja, *The Subject of Semiotics* (New York: Oxford University Press, 1983).

Spitz, René A., *The First Year of Life: A Psychoanalytic Study of Normal and Deviant Development of Object Relations* (New York: International Universities Press, 1965).

Todorov, Tzvetan, *Theories of the Symbol*, Catherine Porter, trans. (Ithaca, NY: Cornell University Press, 1982).

Valéry, Paul, *Poems*, James R. Lawler, ed., David Paul, trans. (Princeton University Press, 1971).

'Poetry and Abstract Thought', in Jackson Mathews, ed., Denise Folliot, trans., *The Collected Works of Paul Valéry* (New York: Pantheon Books, 1958), vol. VII, pp. 52–81.

Weber, Samuel, *Return to Freud: Jacques Lacan's Dislocation of Psychoanalysis*, Michael Levine, trans. (Cambridge University Press, 1991).

Bibliography

Wegener, Philipp, *Untersuchungen über die Grundfragen des Sprachlebens* (Halle: M. Niemeyer, 1885).

Williams, Raymond, 'Culture is Ordinary', first edition 1958, in Ann Gray and Jim McGuigan, eds., *Studying Culture* (London: Edward Arnold, 1993).

Wittgenstein, Ludwig, *Tractatus Logico-philosophicus*, D. F. Pears and McGuiness, trans., introd. by Bertrand Russell, first edition 1922 (London: Routledge and Kegan Paul, 1974).

Zizek, Slavoj, *Enjoy Your Symptom: Jacques Lacan in Hollywood and Out* (New York: Routledge, 1992.)

Everything You Always Wanted to Know about Lacan Without Ever Asking Hitchcock (New York: Routledge, 1992).

Looking Awry: An Introduction to Jacques Lacan Through Popular Culture (Cambridge, MA: The MIT Press, 1991).

The Sublime Object of Ideology (London: Verso, 1989).

Index

Index

Index

Index

phi, 94–5, 110–11, 127, 185, 227, 231
Pico della Mirandola, Giovanni, 196
Plato, 12–13, 15, 65, 67 n37
pleasure, 169
  principle, 174–5, 202, 215–16, 218, 244
Poe, Edgar Allan, 58, 125–6, 149
poetry, 1–3, 8, 12–13, 14–27, 31, 40,
    43–4, 55–6, 62, 65, 67, 70, 102,
    123–5, 135, 178, 194, 238–9, 242,
    245–6, 248
point de capiton, 65–7, 67 n38, 114, 115,
    173, 197
politics, 11, 13, 32, 39, 44, 136, 177, 242,
    249, 251–3
Polynices, 106–7, 127, 132
positivism, 1, 15, 23, 31, 62, 68, 73 n61,
    97–8, 98 n128
poststructuralism *see* deconstruction
preconscious, 117
predication, 3, 7, 46–9, 52–6, 61, 75,
    87–8, 103–5, 107–11, 135, 145 n70,
    148, 183–4, 186, 191 n65
pre-oedipal, 248
primary process, 1, 3, 48, 50, 61, 138,
    143, 159, 196
  see also condensation; displacement
proper name, 105–7, 127, 131, 139, 144,
    146, 186, 199–201, 226
proposition, 47–8, 52, 52–3 n109, 53,
    109–12, 114, 134–5, 145 n70, 149,
    160, 184–7, 219, 220, 223, 230
propositional function, 48, 109–12, 110
    n161, 145, 220, 227–8, 230
psychoanalysis, 1–3, 4–5, 8, 11, 12, 16,
    22, 29, 36, 38, 44, 45, 58–9, 83–4,
    107, 113, 115–16, 130, 150–5, 158,
    168, 173, 175–6, 179–80, 181,
    189–90, 192–4, 195, 198, 200–1, 203,
    206, 208–10, 218, 229, 237, 240–1,
    246, 247, 248, 252
psychosis, 146, 184, 187

Quintilian, 49

Racine, Jean, 65, 114
randomness, 17, 18, 39, 46, 96, 125, 141,
    201, 232, 237
Rat Man, 82
reading, 3, 9, 10, 17, 30, 32–3, 33 n60,
    35, 36, 38, 73, 90 n107, 97, 98 n128,
    113, 116, 123, 132 n45, 139, 167,
    194, 208, 215, 227, 236–7, 240, 243,
    245, 246–7, 248, 253
real, 3, 8–10, 11, 67, 73, 114, 127, 142,
    143, 151, 155, 201, 204, 208, 216–19,

221, 223, 224, 227–8, 230, 241,
    246–7, 249, 250, 251, 253
reality, 26, 41, 51, 67 n37, 73, 77, 81, 86,
    87, 99–100, 112, 129, 141, 143, 151,
    154, 155, 164, 166–7, 171, 179, 181,
    201, 202, 205, 216, 234, 253
recognition, 34, 38, 79, 89, 96, 107,
    160–1, 171, 184, 187, 189, 192,
    233–5, 238
reference *see* referentiality
referentiality, 2, 27, 28, 31, 35 n66, 39
    n78, 52, 54, 57, 105, 109, 110, 117,
    125, 129, 131, 134, 136, 143, 174,
    191, 212, 230, 245, 247
  self-, 31, 42, 61, 66, 83 n86, 90, 132,
    244
reification, 6, 79, 89, 137, 184, 208, 210
    n30, 213, 240, 245, 246
Reik, Theodor, 180 n49, 210–12, 210
    n30, 233–5, 234 n78
rememoration, 166, 202
repetition, 1, 7, 8–9, 75, 118, 152–4, 164,
    166, 181, 190, 194, 198, 201–5,
    208–10, 214–15, 219, 236–7, 244,
    247
representation, 41, 48, 51, 60–1, 62,
    66–7, 73–4, 76–7, 79–81, 84, 88, 95,
    106, 111–13, 114, 119, 127, 129–30,
    133, 137, 144, 146–7, 162, 164–5,
    173, 175, 185–7, 188, 224, 231,
    247–8, 253
repressed, return of, 10, 198, 206–7,
    209, 235
repression, 23, 34, 39, 50, 60, 89–90, 107,
    138, 141–3, 151–2, 156, 158, 160,
    161–2, 164–5, 190, 194, 195–8, 201,
    203, 206–9, 213, 229, 233–5
resemblance *see* similarity
resistance, 8, 11, 21, 34, 41–2, 60, 136,
    143, 150–6, 159, 163–4, 165, 179–80,
    181, 190, 194, 232–3, 240, 244,
    246–7, 249
retrospective interpretation, 10, 42, 67,
    97, 98 n128, 111, 138, 197, 206–7,
    237, 239
rhetoric, 1–4, 7–8, 13, 15, 24, 27, 29–31,
    36–7, 37–8 n75, 41, 43, 44, 49, 61,
    67, 68 n39, 70–1 n54, 73, 89, 101,
    115–16, 126, 129, 159, 161, 174, 239,
    253
  see also metaphor; metonymy
Richards, I. A., 4, 67–75, 68 n39, 68 n40,
    68 n41, 69 n48, 69 n49, 74 n63, 77,
    80–1, 82 n85, 84, 87, 90, 98 n128,
    109, 112–13